*Namkee G. Choi, PhD*
*Editor*

# Social Work Practice with the Asian American Elderly

*Social Work Practice with the Asian American Elderly* has been co-published simultaneously as *Journal of Gerontological Social Work*, Volume 36, Numbers 1/2 2001.

*Pre-publication REVIEWS, COMMENTARIES, EVALUATIONS . . .*

"ENCOMPASSES THE RICHNESS OF DIVERSITY among Asian Americans by including articles on Vietnamese, Japanese, Chinese, Taiwanese, Asian Indian, and Korean Americans. The focus is timely. . . . All the chapters identify social work practice and policy implications."

**Nancy R. Hooyman, PhD, MSW**
*Professor and Dean Emeritus*
*University of Washington*
*School of Social Work*
*Seattle*

*More Pre-publication*
*REVIEWS, COMMENTARIES, EVALUATIONS . . .*

"A VALUABLE ASSORTMENT of research articles . . . includes people who are Chinese, Japanese, Korean, Indian, and Vietnamese. This book, the first of its kind, provides in-depth knowledge based on empirical studies of the true nature of these elders' problems and how best to care for them."

**Martha N. Ozawa, PhD**
*Bettie Bofinger Brown Professor of Social Policy*
*George Warren Brown School of Social Work*
*Washington University*
*St. Louis, Missouri*

"I WAS IMPRESSED. . . . Research on ethnic elders is challenging, and these scholars should be commended for advancing methodological rigor: focusing on subethnic groups, employing ethnic-sensitive measures, mixing quantitative and qualitative methods. The authors have succeeded in drawing important implications for social work practice from their research findings."

**Nancy Morrow-Howell, PhD**
*Associate Professor*
*George Warren Brown School of Social Work*
*Washington University*
*St. Louis, Missouri*

The Haworth Social Work Practice Press
An Imprint of The Haworth Press, Inc.

# Social Work Practice with the Asian American Elderly

*Social Work Practice with the Asian American Elderly* has been co-published simultaneously as *Journal of Gerontological Social Work*, Volume 36, Numbers 1/2 2001.

## The *Journal of Gerontological Social Work* Monographic "Separates"

Below is a list of "separates," which in serials librarianship means a special issue simultaneously published as a special journal issue or double-issue *and* as a "separate" hardbound monograph. (This is a format which we also call a "DocuSerial.")

"Separates" are published because specialized libraries or professionals may wish to purchase a specific thematic issue by itself in a format which can be separately cataloged and shelved, as opposed to purchasing the journal on an on-going basis. Faculty members may also more easily consider a "separate" for classroom adoption.

"Separates" are carefully classified separately with the major book jobbers so that the journal tie-in can be noted on new book order slips to avoid duplicate purchasing.

You may wish to visit Haworth's website at . . .

http://www.HaworthPress.com

. . . to search our online catalog for complete tables of contents of these separates and related publications.

You may also call 1-800-HAWORTH (outside US/Canada: 607-722-5857), or Fax 1-800-895-0582 (outside US/Canada: 607-771-0012), or e-mail at:

getinfo@haworthpressinc.com

---

***Social Work Practice with the Asian American Elderly,*** edited by Namkee G. Choi, PhD (Vol. 36, No. 1/2, 2001). *"Encompasses the richness of diversity among Asian Americans by including articles on Vietnamese, Japanese, Chinese, Taiwanese, Asian Indian, and Korean Americans." (Nancy R. Hooyman, PhD, MSW, Professor and Dean Emeritus, University of Washington School of Social Work, Seattle)*

***Grandparents as Carers of Children with Disabilities: Facing the Challenges,*** edited by Philip McCallion, PhD, ACSW, and Matthew Janicki, PhD (Vol. 33, No. 3, 2000). *Here is the first comprehensive consideration of the unique needs and experiences of grandparents caring for children with developmental disabilities. The vital information found here will assist practitioners, administrators, and policymakers to include the needs of this special population in the planning and delivery of services, and it will help grandparents in this situation to better care for themselves as well as for the children in their charge.*

***Latino Elders and the Twenty-First Century: Issues and Challenges for Culturally Competent Research and Practice,*** edited by Melvin Delgado, PhD (Vol. 30, No. 1/2, 1998). *Explores the challenges that gerontological social work will encounter as it attempts to meet the needs of the growing number of Latino elders utilizing culturally competent principles.*

***Dignity and Old Age,*** edited by Rose Dobrof, DSW, and Harry R. Moody, PhD (Vol. 29, No. 2/3, 1998). *"Challenges us to uphold the right to age with dignity, which is embedded in the heart and soul of every man and woman." (H. James Towey, President, Commission on Aging with Dignity, Tallahassee, FL)*

***Intergenerational Approaches in Aging: Implications for Education, Policy and Practice,*** edited by Kevin Brabazon, MPA, and Robert Disch, MA (Vol. 28, No. 1/2/3, 1997). *"Provides a wealth of concrete examples of areas in which intergenerational perspectives and knowledge are needed." (Robert C. Atchley, PhD, Director, Scribbs Gerontology Center, Miami University)*

***Social Work Response to the White House Conference on Aging: From Issues to Actions,*** edited by Constance Corley Saltz, PhD, LCSW (Vol. 27, No. 3, 1997). *"Provides a framework for the discussion of issues relevant to social work values and practice, including productive aging, quality of life, the psychological needs of older persons, and family issues." (Jordan I. Kosberg, PhD, Professor and PhD Program Coordinator, School of Social Work, Florida International University, North Miami, FL)*

***Special Aging Populations and Systems Linkages,*** edited by M. Joanna Mellor, DSW (Vol. 25, No. 1/2, 1996). *"An invaluable tool for anyone working with older persons with special needs." (Irene Gutheil, DSW, Associate Professor, Graduate School of Social Service, Fordham University)*

***New Developments in Home Care Services for the Elderly: Innovations in Policy, Program, and Practice,*** edited by Lenard W. Kaye, DSW (Vol. 24, No. 3/4, 1995). *"An excellent compilation. . . . Especially pertinent to the functions of administrators, supervisors, and case managers in home care. . . . Highly recommended for every home care agency and a must for administrators and middle managers." (Geriatric Nursing Book Review)*

***Geriatric Social Work Education,*** edited by M. Joanna Mellor, DSW, and Renee Solomon, DSW (Vol. 18, No. 3/4, 1992). *"Serves as a foundation upon which educators and fieldwork instructors can build courses that incorporate more aging content." (SciTech Book News)*

***Vision and Aging: Issues in Social Work Practice,*** edited by Nancy D. Weber, MSW (Vol. 17, No. 3/4, 1992). *"For those involved in vision rehabilitation programs, the book provides practical information and should stimulate readers to revise their present programs of care." (Journal of Vision Rehabilitation)*

***Health Care of the Aged: Needs, Policies, and Services,*** edited by Abraham Monk, PhD (Vol. 15, No. 3/4, 1990). *"The chapters reflect firsthand experience and are competent and informative. Readers . . . will find the book rewarding and useful. The text is timely, appropriate, and well-presented." (Health & Social Work)*

***Twenty-Five Years of the Life Review: Theoretical and Practical Considerations,*** edited by Robert Disch, MA (Vol. 12, No. 3/4, 1989). *This practical and thought-provoking book examines the history and concept of the life review.*

***Gerontological Social Work: International Perspectives,*** edited by Merl C. Hokenstad, Jr., PhD, and Katherine A. Kendall, PhD (Vol. 12, No. 1/2, 1988). *"Makes a very useful contribution in examining the changing role of the social work profession in serving the elderly." (Journal of the International Federation on Ageing)*

***Gerontological Social Work Practice with Families: A Guide to Practice Issues and Service Delivery,*** edited by Rose Dobrof, DSW (Vol. 10, No. 1/2, 1987). *An in-depth examination of the importance of family relationships within the context of social work practice with the elderly.*

***Ethnicity and Gerontological Social Work***, edited by Rose Dobrof, DSW (Vol. 9, No. 4, 1987). *"Addresses the issues of ethnicity with great sensitivity. Most of the topics addressed here are rarely addressed in other literature." (Dr. Milada Disman, Department of Behavioral Science, University of Toronto)*

***Social Work and Alzheimer's Disease,*** edited by Rose Dobrof, DSW (Vol. 9, No. 2, 1986). *"New and innovative social work roles with Alzheimer's victims and their families in both hospital and non-hospital settings." (Continuing Education Update)*

***Gerontological Social Work Practice in the Community,*** edited by George S. Getzel, DSW and M. Joanna Mellor, DSW (Vol. 8, No. 3/4, 1985). *"A wealth of information for all practitioners who deal with the elderly. An excellent reference for faculty, administrators, clinicians, and graduate students in nursing and other service professions who work with the elderly." (American Journal of Care for the Aging)*

***Gerontological Social Work in Home Health Care,*** edited by Rose Dobrof, DSW (Vol. 7, No. 4, 1984). *"A useful window onto the home health care scene in terms of current forms of service provided to the elderly and the direction of social work practice in this field today." (PRIDE Institute Journal)*

***The Uses of Reminiscence: New Ways of Working with Older Adults,*** edited by Marc Kaminsky (Vol. 7, No. 1/2, 1984). *"Rich in ideas for anyone working with life review groups." (Guidepost)*

***A Healthy Old Age: A Sourcebook for Health Promotion with Older Adults,*** edited by Stephanie FallCreek, MSW, and Molly K. Mettler, MSW (Vol. 6, No. 2/3, 1984). *"An outstanding text on the 'how-tos' of health promotion for elderly persons." (Physical Therapy)*

***Gerontological Social Work Practice in Long-Term Care,*** edited by George S. Getzel, DSW, and M. Joanna Mellor, DSW (Vol. 5, No. 1/2, 1983). *"Veteran practitioners and graduate social work students will find the book insightful and a valuable prescriptive guide to the dos and don'ts of practice in their daily work." (The Gerontologist)*

Published by

The Haworth Social Work Practice Press, 10 Alice Street, Binghamton, NY 13904-1580 USA

The Haworth Social Work Practice Press is an imprint of The Haworth Press, Inc., 10 Alice Street, Binghamton, NY 13904-1580 USA.

*Social Work Practice with the Asian American Elderly* has been co-published simultaneously as *Journal of Gerontological Social Work*, Volume 36, Numbers 1/2 2001.



Cover design by Thomas J. Mayshock Jr.

**Library of Congress Cataloging-in-Publication Data**

Social Work Practice with the Asian American Elderly / Namkee G. Choi, editor.
p. cm.
Published also as v. 36, no. 1/2, 2001 of the Journal of gerontological social work.
Includes bibliographical references and index.
ISBN 0-7890-1688-5 (hard: alk. paper) – ISBN 0-7890-1689-3 (pbk: alk. paper)
1. Social work with the aged–United States. 2. Social work with minorities–United States. 3. Asian American aged–Services for–United States. I. Choi, Namkee G., 1955- II. Journal of gerontological social work.

HV1461 .S568 2002
362.6'089'951073–dc21 2002017155

# Social Work Practice with the Asian American Elderly

Namkee G. Choi, PhD
Editor

*Social Work Practice with the Asian American Elderly* has been co-published simultaneously as *Journal of Gerontological Social Work*, Volume 36, Numbers 1/2 2001.

The Haworth Social Work Practice Press
An Imprint of
The Haworth Press, Inc.
New York • London • Oxford

∞ ALL HAWORTH SOCIAL WORK PRACTICE PRESS
BOOKS AND JOURNALS ARE PRINTED ON
CERTIFIED ACID-FREE PAPER

# Indexing, Abstracting & Website/Internet Coverage

This section provides you with a list of major indexing & abstracting services. That is to say, each service began covering this periodical during the year noted in the right column. Most Websites which are listed below have indicated that they will either post, disseminate, compile, archive, cite or alert their own Website users with research-based content from this work. (This list is as current as the copyright date of this publication.)

Abstracting, Website/Indexing Coverage . . . . . . . . . Year When Coverage Began

- *Abstracts in Social Gerontology: Current Literature on Aging* . . . . . . **1989**
- *Academic Abstracts/CD-ROM* . . . . . . . . . . . . . . . . . . . . . . . . . . . . . . **1993**
- *Academic Search: data base of 2,000 selected academic serials, updated monthly: EBSCO Publishing* . . . . . . . . . . . . . . . . . . . . . . **1995**
- *Academic Search Elite (EBSCO)* . . . . . . . . . . . . . . . . . . . . . . . . . . . **1995**
- *AgeInfo CD-Rom* . . . . . . . . . . . . . . . . . . . . . . . . . . . . . . . . . . . . . . . **1995**
- *AgeLine Database* . . . . . . . . . . . . . . . . . . . . . . . . . . . . . . . . . . . . . . **1993**
- *Alzheimer's Disease Education & Referral Center (ADEAR)* . . . . . . . **1994**
- *Applied Social Sciences Index & Abstracts (ASSIA) (Online: ASSI via Data-Star) (CDRom: ASSIA Plus) <www.csa.com>* . . . . . . . . . . . . . . . . . . . . . . . . . . . . . . . . . . . . . . **1987**
- *Behavioral Medicine Abstracts* . . . . . . . . . . . . . . . . . . . . . . . . . . . . **1992**
- *Biosciences Information Service of Biological Abstracts (BIOSIS) a centralized source of life science information. <www.biosis.org>* . . **1993**
- *caredata CD: the social & community care database <www.scie.org.uk>* . . . . . . . . . . . . . . . . . . . . . . . . . . . . . . . . . . . . . **1994**

(continued)

- *CINAHL (Cumulative Index to Nursing & Allied Health Literature), in print, EBSCO, and SilverPlatter, Data-Star, and PaperChase. (Support materials include Subject Heading List, Database Search Guide, and instructional video) <www.cinahl.com>* . . . . . . . . . . . . . . . . . **1994**
- *CNPIEC Reference Guide: Chinese National Directory of Foreign Periodicals* . . . . . . . . . . . . . . . . . . . . . . . . . . . . . **1995**
- *Criminal Justice Abstracts* . . . . . . . . . . . . . . . . . . . . . . . . . . . . . . . . **1993**
- *Current Contents/Social & Behavioral Sciences <www.isinet.com>* . . . . . . . . . . . . . . . . . . . . . . . . . . . . . . . . **1985**
- *e-psyche, LLC <www.e-psyche.net>* . . . . . . . . . . . . . . . . . . . . . . . . . . **2001**
- *Expanded Academic ASAP <www.galegroup.com>* . . . . . . . . . . . . . . **2001**
- *Expanded Academic Index* . . . . . . . . . . . . . . . . . . . . . . . . . . . . . . . . . **1992**
- *Family & Society Studies Worldwide <www.nisc.com>* . . . . . . . . . . . **1996**
- *Family Index Database <www.familyscholar.com>* . . . . . . . . . . . . . . **2001**
- *Family Violence & Sexual Assault Bulletin* . . . . . . . . . . . . . . . . . . . . . **1993**
- *FINDEX <www.publist.com>* . . . . . . . . . . . . . . . . . . . . . . . . . . . . . . **1999**
- *Human Resources Abstracts (HRA)* . . . . . . . . . . . . . . . . . . . . . . . . . . **1982**
- *IBZ International Bibliography of Periodical Literature <www.saur.de>* . . . . . . . . . . . . . . . . . . . . . . . . . . . . . . . . . . . **1996**
- *Index Guide to College Journals (core list compiled by integrating 48 indexes frequently used to support undergraduate programs in small to medium sized libraries)* . . . . . . . **1999**
- *Index to Periodical Articles Related to Law* . . . . . . . . . . . . . . . . . . . . . **1990**
- *InfoTrac Custom <www.galegroup.com>* . . . . . . . . . . . . . . . . . . . . . . . **1996**
- *MasterFILE: updated database from EBSCO Publishing* . . . . . . . . . **1995**
- *National Center for Chronic Disease Prevention & Health Promotion (NCCDPHP)* . . . . . . . . . . . . . . . . . . . . . . . . . . . . . **1998**
- *National Clearinghouse for Primary Care Information (NCPCI)* . . . **1994**
- *New Literature on Old Age* . . . . . . . . . . . . . . . . . . . . . . . . . . . . . . . . . **1995**
- *Periodical Abstracts, Research I (general & basic reference indexing & abstracting data-base from University Microfilms International (UMI))* . . . . . . . . . . . . . . . . . . . . . . . . . . . . . . . . . . **1993**
- *Periodical Abstracts, Research II (broad coverage indexing & abstracting data-base from University Microfilms International (UMI))* . . . . . . . . . . . . . . . . . . . . . . . . . . . . . . . . . . . . . . . . . . . . **1993**
- *Psychological Abstracts (PsycINFO) <www.apa.org>* . . . . . . . . . . . . **1991**
- *RESEARCH ALERT/ISI Alerting Services <www.isinet.com>* . . . . . **1985**

(continued)

- *Social Sciences Citation Index <www.isinet.com>* . . . . . . . . . . . . . . . **1985**
- *Social Sciences Index (from Volume 1 & continuing) <www.hwwilson.com>*. . . . . . . . . . . . . . . . . . . . . . . . . . . . . . . . . . . **1999**
- *Social Science Source: coverage of 400 journals in the social sciences area; updated monthly; EBSCO Publishing* . . . . . . . . . . . **1995**
- *Social SciSearch <www.isinet.com>* . . . . . . . . . . . . . . . . . . . . . . . . . . . **1985**
- *Social Services Abstracts <www.csa.com>*. . . . . . . . . . . . . . . . . . . . . . . . **1989**
- *Social Work Abstracts <www.silverplatter.com/catalog/swab.htm>* . . . **1984**
- *Sociological Abstracts (SA) <www.csa.com>* . . . . . . . . . . . . . . . . . . . **1989**

*Special Bibliographic Notes related to special journal issues (separates) and indexing/abstracting:*

- indexing/abstracting services in this list will also cover material in any "separate" that is co-published simultaneously with Haworth's special thematic journal issue or DocuSerial. Indexing/abstracting usually covers material at the article/chapter level.
- monographic co-editions are intended for either non-subscribers or libraries which intend to purchase a second copy for their circulating collections.
- monographic co-editions are reported to all jobbers/wholesalers/approval plans. The source journal is listed as the "series" to assist the prevention of duplicate purchasing in the same manner utilized for books-in-series.
- to facilitate user/access services all indexing/abstracting services are encouraged to utilize the co-indexing entry note indicated at the bottom of the first page of each article/chapter/contribution.
- this is intended to assist a library user of any reference tool (whether print, electronic, online, or CD-ROM) to locate the monographic version if the library has purchased this version but not a subscription to the source journal.
- individual articles/chapters in any Haworth publication are also available through the Haworth Document Delivery Service (HDDS).

## ABOUT THE EDITOR

**Namkee G. Choi, PhD,** is Professor in the Graduate School of Social Work, Portland State University. She is a gerontological social work researcher with an extensive list of publications in the area of analysis of income-maintenance policies and programs for older persons, retirement and post-retirement work activities, long-term care, intergenerational living arrangements and social support, and minority aging issues. She has served on the editorial board of the *Journal of Gerontological Social Work* for a number of years. She edited *Psychosocial Aspects of the Asian-American Experience* (Haworth, 2001) and co-authored a book, *Long-Term Care and Ethnicity*, with Ada Mui and Abraham Monk.

# Social Work Practice with the Asian American Elderly

## CONTENTS

# Introduction

This special volume on Asian American elders is a product of the time and efforts of many concerned people. Rose Dobrof, Editor of the *Journal of Gerontological Social Work,* called me at the beginning of 2000 and asked me to take charge of this volume. Bill Cohen, publisher of The Haworth Press, enthusiastically supported the idea of the special volume and encouraged me to go ahead with it as soon as possible. Virginia E. Richardson, past president, and Nancy Kropf, current president, of the Association for Gerontology Education in Social Work (AGE-SW) helped by encouraging AGE-SW members to contribute manuscripts. I am also indebted to the Gerontological Society of America and to the Strengthening Aging and Gerontology Education for Social Work (SAGE-SW) group of the Council on Social Work Education for running special ads in their newsletters to solicit manuscripts. I owe a great debt to the illustrious group of reviewers, experts in the subject areas, who generously volunteered their time to anonymously review the submitted manuscripts and offer insightful suggestions for revision. Finally, I thank the contributors who enthusiastically responded to the call for papers and then revised and re-revised their manuscripts in response to the reviewers' comments.

This special collection serves as a timely response to the growing demand for a social work knowledge base on Asian American elders, who constitute a rapidly growing population group. The preliminary release of the 2000 census showed that Asian Americans constituted the second fastest-growing racial/ethnic group in the United States. The Asian American growth rate between 1990 and 2000 was 52.4%, which closely followed the Hispanic growth rate of 57.9% for the same period. When Asian race in combination of other race or races was used, the growth rate was 74.3% (U.S. Bureau of the Census, 2001). Although

[Haworth co-indexing entry note]: "Introduction." Choi, Namkee G. Co-published simultaneously in *Journal of Gerontological Social Work* (The Haworth Social Work Practice Press, an imprint of The Haworth Press, Inc.) Vol. 36, No. 1/2, 2001, pp. 1-3; and: *Social Work Practice with the Asian American Elderly* (ed: Namkee G. Choi) The Haworth Social Work Practice Press, an imprint of The Haworth Press, Inc., 2001, pp. 1-3. Single or multiple copies of this article are available for a fee from The Haworth Document Delivery Service [1-800-HAWORTH, 9:00 a.m. - 5:00 p.m. (EST). E-mail address: getinfo@haworthpressinc.com].

 

Census Bureau projections of future population trends based on the 2000 census data are not yet available, those based on the 1990 census data show that the number and share of Asian Americans age 65 and older will increase at a rate even faster than the Asian American population as a whole (U.S. Bureau of the Census, 1996). According to the projections, by 2050, Asian Americans will make up 6.3% (up from 1.8% in 1995) of the elderly U.S. population, as compared to 9.3% blacks and 17.5% Hispanics (of both white and black races).

Although the census reports tend to lump all Asian Americans into a single racial group, this is, in fact, one of the most internally heterogeneous population groups in the United States with respect to ethnic composition, immigration history, language and religion, and other sociodemographic variables. Of all Asian American age groups, the elderly present the most variations in these characteristics because a large proportion of them are foreign-born, first-generation immigrants and, thus, are more likely to adhere to the culture of their country of origin than are the younger generations, who were born here or, if not, find it easier than their elders to assimilate to the dominant culture.

Despite the dramatically changing demographics, the internal heterogeneity of the Asian American elder population has made it difficult for researchers to conduct large-scale ethnogerontological studies that could be generalized to all Asian American elders. Most existing studies were based on small samples of one or a few ethnic groups in geographically limited areas. For many subethnic groups of Asian American elders, even small-scale, exploratory studies are rare. Lack of an accumulated knowledge base means lack of understanding of this group of elders, with its diverse ethnic/cultural, socioeconomic, and other characteristics, and thus, inadequate and ineffectual provision of services. In these circumstances, both researchers and practitioners face a daunting task of identifying strengths, deficits, needs, and culturally appropriate interventions and service-delivery models for the growing number of Asian American elders and their families.

All the articles in this special volume are also based on small samples of specific subethnic groups from geographically limited areas, and their findings may not be generalizable to other such groups. The articles also cover only five major ethnic groups (Chinese, Japanese, Korean, Indian, and Vietnamese American elders), and deal with a limited number of problem areas. (Two of the ten articles deal with Asian American elders in general, without distinguishing subethnic groups.) Nevertheless, given the paucity of existing studies and the solid empirical methods of inquiry–both quantitative and qualitative–adopted by all the studies, each article in this collection represents an important small step toward building the social work knowledge and skills base needed to work with Asian American elders.

The rapid growth in Asian American elderly population groups, with their diverse economic, health, mental health, and other social service needs, dictates that social workers become culturally competent if they are to work with these elders and their families. I believe all the articles in this volume will enable social workers to increase their cultural competence to allow them to better serve Asian American elders. However, the lack of coverage of other major ethnic groups such as Filipino American elders, Southeast Asian elderly groups other than Vietnamese elders, and Pacific Islander elders, as well as the limited topical areas dealt with in this volume also serve as a reminder of the need to continuously encourage researchers and practitioners to contribute to building the knowledge and skills base.

*Namkee G. Choi, PhD*

## REFERENCES

U.S. Bureau of the Census (1996). *Population projections of the United States by age, sex, race, and Hispanic origin: 1995 to 2050* (Current Population Reports No. P25-1130). Washington, DC: U.S. Government Printing Office.

U.S. Bureau of the Census (2000). *Census 2000 PHC-T-1. Population by race and Hispanic or Latino origin for the United States, 1990-2000.* [On line]. Available: <http://www.census.gov/populations/cen2000>.

# Migratory Grief and Depression Among Elderly Chinese American Immigrants

Banghwa Lee Casado, MSW
Patrick Leung, PhD

**SUMMARY.** This article examines factors that affect psychological distress (depression) among elderly Chinese immigrants. The factors included in the study were their grief experience associated with immigration along with acculturation, length of residence in the U.S. and other demographic factors, such as age, gender, marital status, living arrangement, contact with relatives, relatives in home country, home country visits, and home country identity. A total of 150 Chinese immigrants from a major city in the U.S. aged between 55 and 86 participated in the study. The results of the regression analysis indicated that those respondents who had a higher degree of migratory grief experience and a lower English proficiency score, who visited their home country, and were younger, were more likely to feel depressed. Among these four variables, migratory grief alone contributed to 41.5% of the variance while the remaining three variables

Banghwa Lee Casado and Patrick Leung are affiliated with the Graduate School of Social Work, University of Houston, 4800 Calhoun, Houston, TX 77204-4492 USA.

Address correspondence to: Dr. Patrick Leung, Graduate School of Social Work, University of Houston, 4800 Calhoun, Houston, TX 77204-4492 USA (E-mail: Pleung@uh.edu).

[Haworth co-indexing entry note]: "Migratory Grief and Depression Among Elderly Chinese American Immigrants." Casado, Banghwa Lee, and Patrick Leung. Co-published simultaneously in *Journal of Gerontological Social Work* (The Haworth Social Work Practice Press, an imprint of The Haworth Press, Inc.) Vol. 36, No. 1/2, 2001, pp. 5-26; and: *Social Work Practice with the Asian American Elderly* (ed: Namkee G. Choi) The Haworth Social Work Practice Press, an imprint of The Haworth Press, Inc., 2001, pp. 5-26. Single or multiple copies of this article are available for a fee from The Haworth Document Delivery Service [1-800-HAWORTH, 9:00 a.m. - 5:00 p.m. (EST). E-mail address: getinfo@haworthpressinc.com].

contributed to 12.4% of the variation. Implications for social work practice were discussed. 

**KEYWORDS.** Migratory grief, depression, Chinese elders

According to the U.S. Census report (1996), elderly Asian American was the fastest growing group of elders in the last 20 years. This trend is predicted to continue for the next 10 years. Among them, Chinese American is one of the fastest growing ethnic groups in the United States (U.S. Bureau of the Census, 1991; U.S. Immigration and Naturalization Service, 1997). Immigration and Naturalization Service (INS) reports that between 1994 to1996, approximately 187,000 Chinese immigrants were admitted to the United States. The INS statistical data show that 62,963 Chinese immigrants entered the Unites States in 1996 alone, and that ten percent of these Chinese immigrants were 60 years old and older.

Better understanding of the mental health of elderly Chinese immigrants is in great demand due to the dramatic increase in this population in the last 20 years. A growing number of research studies have found a high prevalence of depressive symptomatology among elderly Chinese Americans, especially among immigrants (Lam, Pacala, & Smith, 1997; Ying, 1988). Yu (1988) found a three times higher rate of suicide among elderly Chinese immigrants than that for U.S.-born Chinese Americans. Miu (1996) further analyzed this alarming rate and highlighted depression as one of the major factors in suicide among Chinese elders. This important finding underscores the urgency for more research on the mental health of elderly Chinese immigrants. Despite the increasing number and high prevalence of mental health problems among this group of immigrants, research on the mental health of elderly Chinese immigrants has been largely neglected (Lam et al., 1997).

Major theories of migration agree that immigration is a process that creates a tremendous amount of stress due to various factors, such as the demand for acculturation, the change in environment, and the social isolation (Kuo, 1976). These theories focus how immigrants are coping with changes incurred during the process of immigration. However, there may be a need for examining the immigration process and its effects on the continuum of life to understand the psychological experience of immigrants. It must look into how immigrants are coping with losses incurred during this process. Immigration is a tremendous change in environment. When people face a change in environment, the experience of loss occurs. As it is well demonstrated in psychology, such experience has considerable effects on the psychological state of all human beings. In such, some researchers have begun to explore the grief experience associated with immigration (Aroian, 1990; Arredondo-Dowd, 1981; Brener, 1991; Detzner, 1996; Disman, 1983; Emmenegger-Hindin, 1993; Lakatos, 1992; Prudent, 1988; Schneller, 1981).

## *PURPOSE OF THE STUDY*

The purpose of this study is to examine factors that affect psychological distress (depression) among elderly Chinese immigrants. While most previous studies (see Bagley, 1993; Cheung & Dobkin de Rios, 1982; Lin, 1986; Mui, 1998; Mui, 1996; Ying, 1988) have focused on stress caused by changes in the process of immigration, this study sought to explore grief caused by the experience of loss in the process of immigration in explaining psychological distress among elderly Chinese immigrants along with other factors such as level of acculturation, length of residence in the U.S., age, gender, marital status, living arrangement, contact with relatives, relatives in their home country, home country visits, and home country identity. Scholars of grief (Bowlby, 1961; Conway, 1988; Lindemann, 1944; Parks, 1965; Rando, 1987; Scrutton, 1995; Worden, 1991) assert that all humans grieve when they experience a loss, whether it is a loved person, object, or abstract thing. The investigators of this study believe that since immigrants experience various kinds of loss in the process of immigration, the experience of grief in immigration needs to be understood thoroughly.

## *LITERATURE REVIEW*

### *The Mental Health of Elderly Chinese Immigrants*

Depression has been widely reported as one of the leading mental disorders among elderly Chinese immigrants. Researchers have reported that elderly Chinese immigrants have a higher risk of depression than their white peers (Ying, 1988; Lam et al., 1997). Higher rates in depression among newly immigrated Chinese elders, compared to long-time residents, have also been reported (Bagley, 1993). It is not surprising to see this result when the demanding task of adjusting to a new environment is considered.

On the other hand, some researchers have found no significant difference in the rate of depression among elderly Chinese immigrants as compared to other groups of elders (Cheung & Dobkin de Rios, 1982; Mui, 1998). However, there may be some cultural factors that affect expressions of mental health problems by Chinese elders. Mui (1996) suggests that some elderly Chinese immigrants tend to show greater moderation and report fewer physical and mental health problems than do white American elders. Sue (1977) points out learned helplessness among Asian Americans that may have influence on their mental health.

Several factors may attribute to the high prevalence of depression among Chinese immigrants: social isolation, lowered social status, grief (Lin, 1986), acculturation stress, financial problems, and other social stressors associated with immigration (Lee, 1996). It is not surprising to see frequent occurrences of depression among elderly immigrants who must deal with two major sources of stress: "aging" and "immigration."

Despite the reports of high prevalence of psychological distress among elderly Chinese immigrants, research on this group of elders has been largely neglected. Several reasons can be suggested, the first being the model minority myth. It is widely believed that Asian immigrants do not have mental health problems (Cheung, 1989; Crystal, 1989; Lam, Pacala, & Smith, 1997). The second is insufficient data. The lack of data on the ethnic groups within Asian immigrants have discouraged investigators from conducting empirical research on this group of people (Mui, 1996). Since people from all Asian and Pacific Island (API) countries or regions are categorized as one group in the U.S. Census data, many researchers experience difficulty in obtaining accurate data on a particular ethnic group within the API group. The third reason is the underutilization of mental health services by Asian immigrants, thereby drawing less attention of mental health professionals and researchers (Crystal, 1989; Loo, Tong & True, 1989; Snowden & Cheung, 1990).

Ryan (1985) suggests Chinese cultural factors of stigmatization of mental and emotional problems and a strong emphasis on privacy and self-control rather than self-disclosure among the reasons that discourage Chinese immigrants from seeking mental health treatment. Because the Chinese culture emphasizes the collective entity of family as the most important institution of society, keeping the family's name is an important duty of the family members. Thus, Chinese immigrants may try to avoid acknowledging mental health problems or seeking professional help in order to protect the family's name from the stigma of mental problems. A preference for relying on traditional sources of help (primarily the family and the extended family) may be another reason for underutilization of mental health services (Ryan, 1985). Traditional Chinese families consider the problem of a family member as the problem of the family. It is the collective responsibility of the family to take care of the disturbed member as long as possible (Lee, 1996). These cultural factors may in turn result in unfamiliarity with mental health treatment among Chinese immigrants that further discourage them from seeking help from mental health professionals.

Insufficient availability and accessibility of mental health services may also be preventing Chinese immigrants from using mental health services. It is often difficult for a Chinese patient to receive culturally sensitive treatment since there is a lack of bilingual and bicultural therapists (Ryan, 1985). They may also experience difficulty in accessing mental health services because of language problems, cost factors, and the lack of transportation (Lee, 1996). A distrust of formal institutions may also contribute to the reluctance of Chinese immigrants to use mental health services (Ryan, 1985).

Finally, the different perspectives or expressions of mental problems may be another cultural factor in addition to stigmatization of mental illness that limits researchers for a fuller investigation of depression among Chinese immigrants. For example, even though Chinese immigrants do display characteristics for a major depressive disorder, many traditional Chinese do not recognize the problem as depression. Instead, they consider what they are experiencing is "neurasthenia," an official diagnosis in China (Lee, 1996). Schwartz (1998) found significant positive relationships between depression and somatic complaints in her study of 125 Chinese immigrants in New York. Depressive symptoms are often expressed with somatic complaints among Chinese people (Chang, 1985; Lee, 1996; Ryan, 1985). This may explain why the mental health problems of Chinese elders are less likely to be identified by mental health professionals (Mui, 1996).

### *The Grief Perspective on the Mental Health of Immigrants*

It is well established in the study of psychology that grief is the normal reaction to loss. Rando (1987) asserts that it is a universal experience. People experience various kinds of loss throughout their lifetime.

Loss is an inevitable part of the existence of all beings. Generally, losses are divided into physical losses and symbolic losses. Physical losses refer to tangible losses, such as loss of loved ones and possessions. Symbolic losses, which are often not recognized as losses, refer to intangible, abstract losses, such as loss of status, social role, and identity.

Both physical and symbolic losses evoke emotional distress and initiate grieving reactions. How an individual experiences grief depends on his/her experience with the lost object; however, a certain response will always follow the experience of a loss. No matter what kind of loss, when an individual experiences a loss, the process of grief will be initiated. Rando asserts that "Grief is the process that allows us to let go of that which was and be ready for that which is to come" (p. 17). Thus, grieving is the necessary process for human beings to accept the loss and move on with their life. In other words, the grieving process is an essential part of living that allows people to grow (Viorst, cited in Conway, 1988). The process of grieving allows people to "move to a new level of functioning that incorporates the loss and grieving experience" (Conway, 1998, p. 544). Grieving is also a psychological defense mechanism against trauma (Scrutton, 1995).

In the study of the mental health of immigrants, grief is a relatively new concept. It has not yet been widely recognized in examining psychological distress among immigrants. Only a small number of researchers have identified the experience of grief as an explanation of immigrants' emotional distress. Arredondo-Dowd (1981) contends that geographical relocation is a life change that creates a sense of loss and the reactions to the loss are very similar to expressions of grief.

Several qualitative researches have been conducted to explore the grief experience of immigrants. Schneller (1981) interviewed thirteen Soviet-Jewish immigrants and identified symptoms of mourning that manifested in phases. Through interviews with twenty-five Polish immigrants, Aroian (1990) also identified several themes that included: loss and disruption, novelty, occupation, language, subordination, feeling at home, grief resolution, and return visits. Emmenegger-Hindin (1993) too found a universal theme of grieving among twelve women from three different cultures (Ecuador, Russia, and Japan) despite their cultural differences. She also identified depressive symptomatology among these twelve women. In an examination of 40 life-histories of elderly Southeast Asian, Detzner (1996) notes that for those elders who came from a culture of filial piety, loss of the honored position in family, society, and culture would be the most difficult as it means an abandonment of their identity.

A few quantitative studies have also reported the grief experience among immigrants. Prudent (1988) found a significant relationship between the symptoms of psychological distress experienced by Haitian immigrants and their grieving experience in her study. She also reported that grief symptoms of Haitian immigrants decreased with time, although time did not seem to reduce psychological distress among the Haitian immigrants. Brener (1991) found that low acculturation correlates with high depression and high perceived losses among the Mexican immigrants in her study. Lakatos (1992) also identified migratory grief to be one of the significant predictors of psychological symptomatology in Hispanic immigrants in her study. In summary, all these researchers argue that immigrants experience various losses (such as loss of language, culture, friends, identity, etc.) in the process of immigration, and the experience of grief due to such losses has significant influences on immigrants' psychological and social status.

## *METHODOLOGY*

### *Sample*

Because of the difficulty in identifying and selecting older Chinese immigrants randomly, a convenience sampling method was used for collecting data. Samples were drawn from two community organizations and a senior housing facility in the Houston Chinese community.

A total of 150 Chinese immigrants aged between 55 and 86 participated in the study (see Table 1). The mean age of the subjects was about 72. The length of residence in the U.S. among the subjects ranged from one half of a year to 40 years with a mean of 10.86 years. Approximately 43% of the respondents were male and 46% were female. Over 62% of them were married. About 85% of them had children in the U.S. The majority of the respondents lived with their family (54%) and over 64% had relatives in the Houston areas. A large percentage of the subjects (39.3%) visited their relatives in the area more than once a week. The majority of them had relatives in their home country (74%) and about 54% visited their home country at least once after their immigration. The most frequently cited reason for coming to the U.S. was "immigration" (40%) followed by "family reunification" (28%). The majority of the respondents identified their home country as Mainland

TABLE 1. Demographic Characteristics of Study Subjects ($N = 150$)

| Variable | N | % |
|---|---|---|
| Age | | |
| 55 to 65 | 28 | 18.7 |
| 66 to 75 | 61 | 40.7 |
| 76 to 85 | 38 | 25.3 |
| 86 and over | 2 | 1.3 |
| Missing | 21 | 14.0 |
| (Range: 55-86; Mean: 71.6; SD: 7.30) | | |
| Gender | | |
| Male | 64 | 42.7 |
| Female | 69 | 46.0 |
| Missing | 17 | 11.3 |
| Marital Status | | |
| Married | 94 | 62.7 |
| Other | 38 | 25.4 |
| Missing | 18 | 12.0 |
| Years in the U.S. | | |
| 5 years and less | 28 | 18.7 |
| 6 to 10 years | 47 | 31.3 |
| 11 to 15 years | 29 | 19.3 |
| 16 to 20 years | 10 | 6.7 |
| 21 to 30 years | 9 | 6.0 |
| 31 years and over | 4 | 2.7 |
| Missing | 23 | 15.3 |
| (Range: .5-40; Mean: 10.86; SD: 7.39) | | |
| Children in the U.S. | | |
| Yes | 127 | 84.7 |
| No | 3 | 2.0 |
| Missing | 20 | 13.3 |
| Live with Family | | |
| Yes | 81 | 54.0 |
| No | 54 | 36.0 |
| Missing | 15 | 10.0 |
| Relatives in the Area | | |
| Yes | 96 | 64.0 |
| No | 32 | 21.3 |
| Missing | 22 | 14.7 |
| Visit Relatives in the Area | | |
| Every day | 9 | 6.0 |
| Once a week | 50 | 33.3 |
| Once a month | 18 | 12.0 |
| Once 1/2 year | 10 | 6.7 |
| Once a year | 12 | 8.0 |
| Never | 0 | 0 |
| Other | 2 | 1.3 |
| Missing | 49 | 32.7 |
| Relatives in Home Country | | |
| Yes | 111 | 74.0 |
| No | 11 | 7.3 |
| Missing | 28 | 18.7 |

| Variable | N | % |
|---|---|---|
| Home Country Visit | | |
| Visited | 81 | 54.0 |
| Never visited | 36 | 24.0 |
| Missing | 33 | 22.0 |
| Reason for Immigration | | |
| Political | 5 | 3.3 |
| Education | 6 | 4.0 |
| Family | 42 | 28.0 |
| Immigration | 60 | 40.0 |
| Economic/Work | 5 | 3.3 |
| Other | 5 | 3.3 |
| Missing | 27 | 18.0 |

China (37%) with significant numbers identifying Taiwan (25%), Hong Kong (25%), and USA (8%) as their home countries.

A self-administered questionnaire was used in the survey. This 60-item questionnaire consisted of four components: the Migratory Grief and Loss Questionnaire, the Acculturation Scale for Southeast Asian (Anderson et al., 1993), the Chinese Depressive Symptom Scale (Lin, 1989), and the Immigration Factors Inventory. The questionnaire was translated in plain Chinese and was pilot tested before data collection. Permissions for conducting the survey were obtained from the local Chinese organizations. Furthermore, consents were obtained from all participants. The survey was conducted anonymously; thus, name of participant would not be identifiable from the collected data. The time needed to complete the questionnaire varied widely depending on individuals, ranging approximately from 10 to 30 minutes.

### *Measures*

*Depression.* Chinese Depressive Symptom Scale-16 (CDS-16) was used to measure depression, the dependent variable of this study. The CDS is a scale designed to measure depressive symptoms among Chinese people in China. This four-point Likert Scale instrument has a score range from 0 to 48 with higher scores indicating greater depressive symptoms. This instrument was developed by Lin (1989) by first translating the Center for Epidemiological Studies-Depression Scale and adding six items to achieve better cultural validity. After a series of psychometric (reliability and validity) analysis, Lin (1989) proposed a 22-item scale (CDS-22) and a subset of 16 items form (CDS-16). Although CDS-22 shows a higher reliability (alpha coefficient of .89), the CDS-16 also has a good internal consistency of alpha .86. Additionally, it has a good criterion validity, showing significant correlations with four quality-of-life factors (social characteristics of work, economic characteristics of work, interpersonal relationships, family relationships, and neighborhood and leisure).

*The Experience of Grief and Loss (Migratory Grief).* Migratory grief is one of the independent variables of this study. It was measured by the total score of the Migratory Grief and Loss Questionnaire (MGLQ). The MGLQ is an instrument developed for this study modeling the symptoms of grief and bereavement identified by Zisook, Devaul, and Click (1982), the Migratory Grief Inventory developed by Lakatos (1993), and the Grief Questionnaire developed by Prudent (1988). This 20-item self-report scale was designed to measure the experience of grief and loss associated with immigration. The MGLQ (see Appendix) was first developed in English and translated in plain Chinese. Back translation and pre-testing were conducted to ensure the accuracy of translation and validity of the instrument before finalizing this instrument.

This instrument uses a four-point Likert Scale and it has possible scores ranging from 0 to 60 with a higher score indicating a more intense level of migratory grief. The MGLQ has a good reliability with an alpha coefficient of .94. All three factors of the MGLQ (searching and yearning, nostalgia, and disorganization) have significant correlations with the total MGLQ, showing content validity of the instrument.

*Acculturation: English Proficiency (EP).* English proficiency is examined as part of acculturation (independent variable). It is measured by the four-item English proficiency subscale of the Acculturation Scale for the Southeast Asian (ASSA), which was originally developed by Anderson and his colleagues (1993) to measure the acculturation level of Southeast Asians (Cambodians, Laotians, and Vietnamese). This study used a Chinese translated version of the Acculturation Scale, which was developed by Lam and his colleagues for their study of depression among elderly Chinese-Americans (1997). It has been reported that the EP has a high internal consistency with an alpha coefficient of .98. The score range for the EP is 4 to 16 with a higher score showing higher English proficiency, thus higher acculturation.

*Acculturation: Language, Social and Food Preference (Cultural Preference).* Cultural preference is also examined as part of acculturation-tion. It is measured by the language, social, and food preference (LSF) subscale of the ASSA, which consists of six items. The total score of the LSF ranges from 6 to 26 with a higher score indicating higher cultural preference for American culture, thus higher acculturation. The LSF has a satisfactory reliability of .79 alpha coefficient.

*Length of Residence in the U.S. (Years in the U.S.).* Length of residence in the U.S. is examined as another independent variable. It is operationalized in years after the arrival in the United States. Several demographic data are also included in this study to examine factors that affect depression among elderly Chinese immigrants. These variables were collected by the Immigration Factors Inventory, which includes: age, gender, marital status, living with family, relatives in the area, visits with relatives in the area, relatives in home country, home country visits, and home country identity.

## *RESULTS*

T-tests and correlation analyses (see Tables 2 and 3) were performed to determine the individual impact of the socio-economic and demographic characteristics, migratory grief total scores, English proficiency scores, and cultural preference scores relative to depression scores. The results from the t-tests suggest that those who had more visits to their relatives (mean = 7.0) had a significantly lower depression score (or less depressed) than those who had less visits (mean = 10.8) ($t = -2.728$, $df = 83$, $p = .008$). The data also suggest that those who had relatives in their home country (mean = 9.0) were more likely to have a higher depression score (or more depressed) than those who did not have relatives in their home country (mean = 3.5) ($t = 2.132$, $df = 97$, $p = .036$). Furthermore, those who had visits to the home country were more depressed (mean = 10.4) than those who did not (mean = 6.9) ($t = 2.467$, $df = 97$, $p = .015$). Interestingly, those who identified Mainland China, Hong Kong and Vietnam as their home country (mean = 10.6) were significantly more depressed than those who identified Taiwan as their home country (mean = 6.7) ($t = 3.019$, $df = 111$, $p = .003$).

The results from the correlation analyses (see Table 3: The sample size was smaller than the original sample size of 150 because the correlation analysis was based on a listwise method; the listwise analysis included only subjects that had no missing values in all variables)

TABLE 2. T-Test For Depression Scores[1]

| Variable | N | M | SD | t |
|---|---|---|---|---|
| Gender | | | | |
| Male | 53 | 8.792 | 7.318 | |
| Female | 56 | 8.982 | 6.845 | −.140 |
| Marital Status | | | | |
| Married | 73 | 8.616 | 6.869 | |
| Other | 40 | 9.375 | 7.206 | −.552 |
| Live with Family | | | | |
| Yes | 66 | 8.773 | 7.569 | |
| No | 44 | 8.932 | 6.256 | −.116 |
| Relatives in the Area | | | | |
| Yes | 82 | 8.854 | 7.184 | |
| No | 27 | 8.734 | 6.855 | .095 |
| Number of Visits to Relatives in the Area | | | | |
| Once a week or more | 52 | 6.962 | 5.325 | |
| Once a month or less | 33 | 10.758 | 7.496 | −2.728** |
| Relatives in Home Country | | | | |
| Yes | 91 | 8.978 | 7.148 | |
| No | 8 | 3.500 | 3.964 | 2.132* |
| Home Country Visit | | | | |
| Visited | 56 | 10.411 | 7.495 | |
| Never visited | 43 | 6.884 | 6.423 | 2.467* |
| Home Country Identity | | | | |
| Mainland China, Hong Kong, & Vietnam | 63 | 10.587 | 7.485 | |
| Taiwan, USA, & other | 50 | 6.740 | 5.627 | 3.019** |

*$p < .05$; **$p < .01$; *** $p < .001$
1. Depression scores range from 0 to 34 with higher scores indicating higher depressive symptomatology.

indicated that those with a higher grief score (r = .645, p < .001), a lower English proficiency (r = −.274, p < .01) and cultural preference score (r = −.261, p < .05), had a higher depression score (or more depressed). Furthermore, the older the respondent (r = −2.700, p < .05) and the longer the length of time in the United States (r = −.234, p < .05), the lower the depression score (or less depressed).

A stepwise regression procedure was performed between the depression score and the variables that demonstrated statistical significance in the t-tests[1] and correlation analyses including the migratory grief, English proficiency and cultural preference score, age, years in the U.S., relatives in the area, relatives in home country, home country visit, and home country identity. Additionally, the regression assumptions were checked, including absence of multicollinearity and singularity, linear-

TABLE 3. Pearson's Correlations with Depression Scores ($N = 74$)[1]

| Variable | Depression |
|---|---|
| Grief Total Score | .645*** |
| English Proficiency Score | −.274** |
| Cultural Preference Score | −.261* |
| Age | −.270* |
| Years in the United States | −.234* |

*$p < .05$; **$p < .01$; ***$p < .001$

1. The sample size was smaller than the original sample size of 150 because the correlation analysis was based on a listwise method. The listwise analysis included only subjects that had no missing values in all variables.

ity, normality, homogeneity, and autocorrelation. Nonetheless, the assumptions were not violated. The results of the regression analysis indicated that four variables contributed significantly ($F (4,69) = 20.144$, $p = .000$) to prediction of total depression score (see Table 4). These four variables accounted for 53.9% of the variance. The analysis suggested that those respondents who had a higher total grief score (or a higher degree of migratory grief experience) and a lower English proficiency score, who visited their home country, and were younger, were more likely to feel depressed. Among these four variables, migratory grief alone contributed to 41.5% of the variance while the remaining three variables contributed to 12.4% of the variation.

## *DISCUSSIONS*

### *Migratory Grief*

This study found those who experience more intense migratory grief had a higher level of depressive symptoms. This result is consistent with the findings from previous studies. There is a significant relationship between migratory grief experience and psychological distress among various immigrant groups. Further, this study concurs with experts and researchers in the grief and bereavement field, who have repeatedly argued that grieving involves psychological distress (Brener, 1991; Lakatos, 1992; Prudent, 1988).

While the focus of most previous studies on the mental health of older immigrants has been on their life after immigration, the finding of migratory grief as a significant contributor to depression provides an

TABLE 4. Multiple Regression of Depression Scores (N = 74)

| Variable | R-square Change | B | Beta | t-test | P |
|---|---|---|---|---|---|
| Grief Total Score[1] | .415 | .350 | .543 | 6.290 | .000 |
| English Proficiency[2] | .458 | −.762 | −.260 | −3.095 | .003 |
| Age | .507 | −.200 | −.197 | −2.358 | .021 |
| Home Country Visit[3] | .539 | 2.861 | .192 | 2.183 | .032 |
| Constant | | 19.662 | | 2.941 | .004 |

$F(4,69) = 20.144$; $p = .000$

1. Grief total scores range from 0 to 52 with higher scores indicating higher degree of migratory grief.
2. English proficiency scores range from 4 to 14 with higher scores indicating higher proficiency in English.
3. Home country visit is categorized into two in this analysis: 1 for "visited" and 0 for "never visited."

important implication to the traditional approach of looking into the psychological well being of immigrants. It suggests that the migratory grief experience, as an important factor, may need to be examined in providing mental health services for older Chinese immigrants. Healthy adaptation to the experience of loss involves the process of resolving grief. In such, identifying the migratory grief experience is critical in providing appropriate services to immigrants who are experiencing psychological distress due to the experience of loss.

### *Age*

The second predictor of depression identified was the age of an individual. The correlation analysis shown in Table 3 indicates a weak inverse relationship between the degree of depression and the age of study subjects. This suggests that younger elderly Chinese immigrants tend to show a higher depression than their older counterparts. The result contrasts with the study by Prudent (1988), indicating that there was no significant relationship between age and psychological distress. However, it is difficult to make any conclusive comparison with the result of her study since the Prudent study used a different instrument in measuring psychological distress of the subjects (measured by the Hopkins Symptoms Checklist).

Interpretation of the result of this study may need to be directed to social factors that affect an immigrant's life. Migration results in more traumatic and disturbing experience among middle-aged and older generations than their younger counterparts due to their tremendous loss of status, both within society and the family (Yee, 1989). However, loss of status may have more impact on the psychological well being among pre-retirement aged elderly, since they often stay active in the outside environment, where loss of status tends to adversely affect their emotional status. On the other hand, as Yee points out, older elderly immigrants are often protected from the outside environment. This may be mainly because they are less likely to be in the work force. Thus, it is understandable to see a higher depression among younger elderly than older elderly. Since previous studies on migratory grief were conducted with various age groups of adult immigrants and found having an effect on their psychological status, it appears that migratory grief is an important factor in determining psychological distress among all immigrants regardless of age. Further investigations are needed to better understand the influence of age on migratory grief and psychological distress among immigrants.

### *English Proficiency*

The third significant predictor of depression found in this study was English proficiency. English proficiency has been often cited by researchers as an integral component of immigrants' adjustment to a new country. Kuo and Tsai (cited in Lam et al., 1997) reported problems with the English language as the most common of all adaptation difficulties among Asian American immigrants. Cheung (1989) also reported language problems as one of the most significant barriers to adjustment, identified by 17 previously conducted studies on elderly Chinese immigrants. Lam et al. (1997) also found a significant inverse relationship between English proficiency and depression among their elderly Chinese American sample. The result of this study is consistent with the findings from previous studies.

Ability of communicating in the English language plays a practical and often critical role for a successful adjustment to a new country: It allows immigrants to find a place in the work force. Successful employment helps immigrants realize not only financial independence, but also self-worth and identity in a new country. Consequently, for new immigrants, fluency in the English language often holds the key to a successful establishment of their new lives both socially and personally. As it has been emphasized by many existing programs, offering English classes may be a valuable part of helping new immigrants' adjustment to this country. However, those who work with older immigrants may need to take additional approaches in helping their clients. Learning a new language is a serious challenge in the later years of life. The process of learning itself may cause psychological distress among older immigrants. Too much emphasis on mastering English may result in negative reactions, such as low self-esteem and feelings of failure when older immigrants experience stagnation in the learning process. Thus, English classes for older immigrants may need to be designed with elements that help them realize their self-integrity and identity. Further, there may be a need to ease the experience of language problems among elderly immigrants by developing services that are provided in both English and their native languages.

### *Home Country Visit*

Home country visit was the fourth predictor of depression in this study. The result may be interpreted with the concept of "attachment." Attachment to home country may affect immigrants' adjustment to a new country. Difficulty in letting go of the things left behind may in turn result in difficulties in adjusting, thus causing psychological distress.

Such analogy may be better understood with cognizance of the nature of grief. It is well established in the field of grief and bereavement that attachment is a common manifestation of grieving. In fact, attachment is a major factor in conceptualizing "grief" in most previous studies on the migratory grief experience, including this study (Prudent, 1988). Prudent reported that the symptoms of psychological distress among Haitian immigrants were inversely related to their feelings of attachment to the homeland and loved ones left behind. As migratory grief was the most significant predictor of depression in this study, thus, the result of this finding again urges mental health professionals to develop a better understanding of the nature of grief in working with older immigrants.

Although other variables, including cultural preference, relatives in home country, years in the U.S., number of visits to relatives in the area and home country identity, were not found to be statistically significant in the regression analysis; however, these variables were significant in the bivariate analyses. Therefore, more research needs to be conducted to assess their impact upon depression among the elderly Chinese in the U.S.

## *IMPLICATIONS FOR SOCIAL WORK PRACTICE*

This study supports the fact that depression among elderly Chinese American immigrants is associated with migratory grief, age, English proficiency and attachment to their home countries. Even though researchers are aware of these four factors that may have contributed to the problem of depression among the Chinese elderly in the United States, practitioners should be aware of the fact that the problem of depression may not be resolved among elderly Chinese immigrants unless these immigrants can actively seek help from the mental health professionals. Nonetheless, practitioners should be aware of six issues in relation to service utilization. First, Chinese seldom pay attention to, or simply do not recognize, mental health problems. Many Chinese Americans who believe in body-mind harmony do not distinguish between mental health and physical health. When they face a mental health problem, they first seek help within their family network. When the problem becomes severe, they then seek help from an herbal doctor, a traditional healer, or a physician. However, they only identify the physical or psychosomatic symptoms such as headache and back pain. Very few would mention their mental health distress because they are supposed to keep quiet in front of authority figures (Chan, 1987; Ho, 1984). Even after the selected helper has identified possible problems associated with depression, the individual or his/her family may refuse to seek help from mental health professionals, either trying to avoid shame or thinking that the problem would naturally heal (Kim, 1995).

A second issue facing elderly Chinese immigrants is that most of them do not seek help at all. One of the main reasons is that they do not want to be stigmatized. Another reason is related to the internal locus-of-control characteristic commonly recognized by Asian cultures (Ho, 1984). When facing a mental health problem, they usually internalize the problem and try to avoid talking about it. Even though some may tell their family about the problem, their family members would also keep it internal and seldom talk to a mental health professional (Sato, 1979).

The perception about western medicine contributes to the third issue. Many elderly Chinese learn the Asian Practice of treatment and think that mental health services are western methods. When a Chinese family uses traditional healing methods or seeks help from a religious leader or a shaman, the family members do not want to disclose to their physician or social work practitioner what they have done. Whether they believe in their traditional methods or not, their intent is to avoid negative comments toward their cultures. Furthermore, they may also believe that these traditional methods cannot be combined with western methods. Many times, clients' hesitation in sharing their personal, familial, or environmental problems can make the social work practitioner's assessment difficult to be reflective of what the actual picture might be. In addition, the basis of western treatment is dependent on an open acknowledgment of the problem and an individual's resolve to seek some form of assistance, which is uncommon to some of these elderly Chinese clients. Some elderly Chinese cannot accept this individualistic concept. Therefore, although they might agree to seek help from a counselor, resistance is often evident.

Language barrier is the fourth issue. When an elderly Chinese is ready to seek help, he/she often faces the problem of service providers who are unable to provide bicultural, bilingual services to accommodate his/her receptive language (Cheung, 1989; Kline & Huff, 1999). Sometimes, a translator is used when services are provided. However, many elderly Chinese feel uncomfortable in the treatment process because they cannot communicate directly and effectively with the counselors (Kaneshige, 1973). In other words, without appropriate language skills, social work practitioners may find rapport building that requires listening skills and cultural sensitivity difficult to achieve (Tsui & Schultz, 1985).

The fifth issue is the cultural competence of the service providers. Even though an elderly Chinese may have a good command of English, some of them may not know how to include his/her cultural heritage to enhance assessment. Similarly, a social work practitioner who speaks the client's language may not fully understand the culture of this client. For example, a Chinese counselor from Hong Kong may not fully understand the culture of an elderly Chinese from Taiwan. Perceptions of needs may vary based on how well the client-worker relationship is established (Hatton, Azmi, Caine & Emerson, 1998).

The final issue is the stereotyping of Chinese Americans as "model minorities." A substantial body of scientific research over the past decade has documented that persons of Asian descent are as equally susceptible to deleterious metal health as non-Asians (Bogart, 1998; Chung & Line, 1994; Dhooper & Tran, 1987; Matsuoka, Breaux, & Ryujin, 1997; Ponipom, 1997; Sue, Nakamura, Chung & Bradbury, 1994). Implicit in the assumption of positive Asian mental health is the popular notion that the close-knit family unit and ethnic communities effectively deal with stressors leading to the development of psychopathology without the assistance of "outside" mainstream intervention (Dhooper & Tran, 1987; Ponpipom, 1997; Sue, 1994; Yee, 1992). Although migratory grief, age, English proficiency and home country visit are important factors contributing to the depression problem among elderly Chinese immigrants in the U.S., a thorough understanding of the above-mentioned six issues will further enhance social work practitioners to work with this population on grief and depression problems more effectively.

## NOTE

1. Home country identities were divided into two categories based on the average total grief score. Mainland China, Hong Kong, and Vietnam respondents were dummy coded as 1 because of their relatively higher total grief score while Taiwan, U.S. and others were dummy coded as 0 because of their relatively lower total grief score.

## REFERENCES

Anderson, J., Moescheberger, M., Chen Jr., M. S., Kynn, P., Wewers, E. E., & Guthrie, R. (1993). An acculturation scale for Southeast Asians. *Social Psychiatry and Psychiatric Epidemiology*, *28*, 134-141.

Aroian, K. L. (1990). A model of psychological adaptation to migration and resettlement. *Nursing Research*, *39*(1), 5-10.

Arredondo-Dowd, P. M. (1981). Personal loss and grief as a result of immigration. *Personnel and Guidance Journal*, *59*(6), 376-378.

Bagley, C. R. (1993). Mental health and social adjustment of elderly Chinese immigrants in Canada. *Canada's Mental Health*, *41*(3), 6-10.

Bogart, L. M. (1998). The relationship of stereotypes about helpers to help-seeking judgments, preferences, and behaviors. *Personality and Social Psychology Bulletin*, *24*(12), 1264-1275.

Bowlby, J. (1961). Process of mourning. *International Journal of Psychoanalysis*, *42*, 317-340.

Brener, E. (1991). Losses, acculturation and depression in Mexican immigrants (Doctoral dissertation, California School of Professional Psychology: San Diego). *Dissertation Abstracts International*, *51*(12-B), 6148.

Brown, C., Fong, R., & Mokuau, N. (1994). The mental health of Asian and Pacific Island elders: Implication for research and mental health administration. *Journal of Mental Health Administration*, *21*(1), 52-59.

Chan, C. S. (1987). Asian-American women: Psychological responses to sexual exploitation and cultural stereotypes. *Asian American Psychological Association Journal*, *12*(1), 11-15.

Cheung, F. & Dobkin de Rios, M. (1982). Recent trends in the study of the mental health of Chinese immigrants to the United States. *Research in Race and Ethnic Relations*, *3*, 145-163.

Cheung, M. (1989). Elderly Chinese living in the United States: Assimilation or adjustment? *Social Work*, *34*(5), 457-461.

Chung, R. & Lin, K. (1994). Help-seeking behavior among Southeast Asian refugees. *Journal of Community Psychology, 22*(2), 109-120.

Conway, P. (1988). Losses and grief in old age. *Social Casework: The Journal of Contemporary Social Work, 69*(9), 541-549.

Crystal, D. (1989). Asian Americans and the myth of the model minority. *The Journal of Contemporary Social Work, 70*(7), 405-413.

Detzner, D. F. (1996). No place without a home: Southeast Asian grandparents in refugee families. *Generations, 21*(1), 45-48.

Dhooper, S. & Tran, T. (1987). Social work with Asian Americans. *Journal of Independent Social Work, 1*(4), 51-62.

Disman, M. (1983). Immigrant and other grieving people: Insights for counseling practices and policy issues. *Canadian Ethnic Studies, 15*(3), 106-118.

Emmenegger-Hindu, I. (1993). The experience of culture loss, grieving/mourning, and acculturative stress associated with depressive symptomatology among adults in cultural transition (Doctoral dissertation: Massachusetts School of Professional Psychology, 1993). *Dissertation Abstracts International, 54*(4-B), 2195.

Hatton, C., Azmi, S., Caine, A., & Emerson, E. (1998). Informal carers of adolescents and adults with learning difficulties from the South Asian communities: Family circumstances, service supports and carer stress. *British Journal of Social Work, 28*(6), 821-837.

Ho, M. K. (1984). Social group work with Asian/Pacific-Americans. *Social Work with Groups, 7*(3), 49-61.

Kaneshige, E. (1973). Cultural factors in group counseling and interaction. *Personnel and Guidance Journal, 51*(6), 407-412.

Kim, Y. O. (1995). Cultural pluralism and Asian Americans: Culturally sensitive social work practice. *International Social Work, 38*(1), 69-78.

Kline, M. V., & Huff, R. M. (1999). Tips for working with Asian American populations. In R. M. Huff & M. V. Kline (Eds.), *Promoting health in multicultural populations: A handbook for practitioners* (pp. 383-394). Thousand Oaks, CA: Sage.

Kuo, W. (1976). Theories of migration and mental health: An empirical testing on Chinese-Americans. *Social Science and Medicine, 10*(6), 297-306.

Lakatos, P. (1992). The effects of migratory grief on the adjustment of the adult Hispanic immigrant (Doctoral dissertation: California School of Professional Psychology: Los Angeles, 1992). *Dissertation Abstracts International, 53*(8-B), 4367-4377.

Lam, R. D., Pacala, J. T., & Smith, S. L. (1997). Factors related to depressive symptoms in an elderly Chinese American sample. *Clinical Gerontologist, 17*(4), 57-70.

Lee, E. (1996). Chinese families. In M. McGoldrick, J. Giordano, & J. K. Pearce (Eds.), *Ethnicity and family therapy (2nd Ed.)* (pp. 249-267). New York: The Guilford Press.

Lin, K. M. (1986). Psychopathology and social disruption in refugees. In C. William & J. Westermeyer (Eds.), *Refugee mental health in resettlement countries* (pp. 61-73). Washington, DC: Hemisphere.

Lin, N. (1989). Measuring depressive symptomatology in China. *Journal of Nervous and Mental Disease, 177*, 121-131.

Lindemann, E. (1994). Social isolation and mental illness in old age. *American Sociological Review, 29*, 54-70.

Loo, C., Tong, B., & True, R. (1989). A bitter bean: Mental health status and attitudes in Chinatown. *Journal of Community Psychology, 17*, 283-296.

Matsuoka, J., Breaux, C. & Ryujin, D. (1997). National utilization of mental health services by Asian Americans/Pacific Islanders. *Journal of Community Psychology, 25*(2), 141-145.

Mui, A. C. (1996). Depression among elderly Chinese immigrants: An exploratory study. *Social Work, 41*(6), 633-645.

Mui, A. C. (1998). Living alone and depression among older Chinese immigrants. *Journal of Gerontological Social Work, 30*(3-4), 147-66.

Parkes, C. M. (1965). Bereavement and mental illness (Part 2): A classification of bereavement reactions. *British Journal of Medical Psychology, 33*, 13.

Ponpipom, A. (1997). Asian-American ethnic identify development: Contributing factors, assessment, and implications for psychotherapy. *Dissertation Abstracts International, Section B, The Sciences and Engineering, 58*(1-B), 0425.

Prudent, S. (1988). The grief associated with immigration: An examination of Haitian immigrants' psychological adjustment to the United States (Doctoral dissertation, Pennsylvania State University, 1988). *Dissertation Abstracts International, 49*(10-B), 4555-4556.

Rando, T. A. (1984). *Grief, dying, and death: Clinical interventions for caregivers.* Champaign, IL: Research Press Company.

Ryan, A. S. (1985). Cultural factors in casework with Chinese-Americans. *Social Casework: The Journal of Contemporary Social Work, 66* (6), 333-340.

Sato, M. (1979). He shame factor: Counseling Asian Americans. *Journal of the Asian American Psychological Association, 5*(1), 20-24.

Schneller, D. (1981). The immigrant's challenge: Mourning the loss of homeland and adapting to the new world. *Smith College Studies in Social Work, 51*(2), 95-125.

Schwartz, P. Y. (1998). Depressive symptomatology and somatic complaints in the acculturation of Chinese immigrants (Doctoral dissertation. New York University, 1998). *Dissertation Abstracts International, 59*(5-B), 2434.

Scrutton, S. (1995). *Bereavement and grief: Supporting older people through loss.* London: Edward Arnold.

Snowden, L. R. & Cheung, F. K. (1990). Use of impatient mental health services by members of ethnic minority groups. *American Psychologist, 45*, 347-355.

Sue, S., Nakamura, C., Chung, R., Yee-Bradbury, C. (1994). Mental health research on Asian Americans. *Journal of Community Psychology, 22*(22), 61-67.

Tsui, P., & Schultz, G. L. (1985). Failure of rapport: Why psychotherapeutic engagement fails in the treatment of Asian clients. *American Journal of Orthopsychiatry, 55*(4), 561-569.

U.S. Bureau of the Census (1996). Population projections of the United States by age, sex, race, and Hispanic origin: 1995 to 2050. *Current Population Reports*, P25-1130. Washington, DC: U.S. Government Printing Office.

U.S. Bureau of the Census (1991). *Census and you* (Press release no. CB91-100). Washington, DC: U.S. Government Printing Office.

U.S. Immigration and Naturalization Service (1997). *Statistical yearbook of the Immigration and Naturalization Service 1996.* Washington, DC: U.S. Government Printing Office.

Worden, J. M. (1991). *Grief counseling and grief therapy: A handbook for the mental health practitioner, 2nd Ed.* New York: Springier Publishing Company.

Yee, B. W. K. (1989). Loss of one's homeland and culture during the middle years. In R. Kalish (Ed.), *Midlife loss: Coping strategies* (pp. 281-300). Newbury Park, CA: Sage Publications, Inc.

Ying, Y. W. (1988). Depressive symptomatology among Chinese-Americans as measured by the CES-D. *Journal of Clinical Psychology, 44*, 739-746.

Yu, E. S. H. (1986). Health of the Chinese elderly in America. *Research on Aging, 8*(1), 84-109.

Zisook, S., Dvaul, R. A., & Click, Jr., M. A. (1982). Measuring symptoms of grief and bereavement. *American Journal of Psychiatry, 139*, 1590-1593.

## APPENDIX. Migratory Grief and Loss Questionnaire

We are interested in what you think and feel about your homeland. For each statement, please circle the number that most accurately describes how often you have felt this way during the PAST 30 DAYS.

| | Never | Occasionally | Often | Always |
|---|---|---|---|---|
| 1. I miss my homeland. | 0 | 1 | 2 | 3 |
| 2. I feel things were nicer in my homeland. | 0 | 1 | 2 | 3 |
| 3. I dream about going back to my homeland. | 0 | 1 | 2 | 3 |
| 4. Since I left my country, I feel that I have more strongly adopted the customs of my homeland. | 0 | 1 | 2 | 3 |
| 5. I think and worry about my homeland and its people. | 0 | 1 | 2 | 3 |
| 6. I feel there is no better place than my homeland. | 0 | 1 | 2 | 3 |
| 7. I feel my thoughts are drawn to things associated with my homeland. | 0 | 1 | 2 | 3 |
| 8. I think of pleasant things about my homeland. | 0 | 1 | 2 | 3 |
| 9. I feel I did things better in my homeland. | 0 | 1 | 2 | 3 |
| 10. I feel leaving my homeland was like having a part of me cut off. | 0 | 1 | 2 | 3 |
| 11. I feel like a stranger in this country. | 0 | 1 | 2 | 3 |
| 12. I find myself thinking about my homeland. | 0 | 1 | 2 | 3 |
| 13. I only have pleasant memories of my homeland. | 0 | 1 | 2 | 3 |
| 14. I feel like crying when I recall memories of my homeland. | 0 | 1 | 2 | 3 |
| 15. It upsets me to think about being far away from my homeland. | 0 | 1 | 2 | 3 |
| 16. I feel I am not sure of who I am since I moved to this country. | 0 | 1 | 2 | 3 |
| 17. No matter where I am, I feel my homeland will always be my home. | 0 | 1 | 2 | 3 |
| 18. I feel I am different since I moved to this country. | 0 | 1 | 2 | 3 |
| 19. I feel lost in this country. | 0 | 1 | 2 | 3 |
| 20. I feel a need to have something that reminds me of my homeland. | 0 | 1 | 2 | 3 |

# Screening for Depression in Immigrant Chinese-American Elders: Results of a Pilot Study

Sandy Chen Stokes, RN, MSN
Larry W. Thompson, PhD
Susan Murphy, RN, DNS
Dolores Gallagher-Thompson, PhD

**SUMMARY.** *Background*: Depression is a common mental health problem among Chinese elderly, but it often goes undiagnosed and untreated. Despite an increase in the population of elderly Chinese immigrants in the US, there have been few published studies on this topic.

*Objective*: Our purpose was to determine the extent of depression in the participant population, using an updated Chinese translation of the original 30-item Geriatric Depression Scale (GDS; Yesavage et al., 1983).

*Study Design*: A convenience sample of 102 Mandarin speaking Chinese elderly participants in two senior centers in Santa Clara County, CA was recruited.

---

Sandy Chen Stokes is Geriatric Nurse Specialist, Older Adult Transitions Program, El Camino Hospital, Mountain View, CA and is Asian Elder Program Manager, John XXIII Multi-Service Center, Catholic Charities, San Jose, CA. Larry W. Thompson is Professor, Pacific Graduate School of Psychology, Palo Alto, CA. Susan Murphy is Professor, School of Nursing, San Jose State University, San Jose, CA. Dolores Gallagher-Thompson is affiliated with VA Palo Alto Health Care System and Stanford University School of Medicine.

Address correspondence to: Sandy Chen Stokes, RN, MSN, 4070 Cactus Road, Shingle Springs, CA 95682 (E-mail: eslhotel@yahoo.com *or* dolorest@stanford.edu).

[Haworth co-indexing entry note]: "Screening for Depression in Immigrant Chinese-American Elders: Results of a Pilot Study." Stokes et al. Co-published simultaneously in *Journal of Gerontological Social Work* (The Haworth Social Work Practice Press, an imprint of The Haworth Press, Inc.) Vol. 36, No. 1/2, 2001, pp. 27-44; and: *Social Work Practice with the Asian American Elderly* (ed: Namkee G. Choi) The Haworth Social Work Practice Press, an imprint of The Haworth Press, Inc., 2001, pp. 27-44. Single or multiple copies of this article are available for a fee from The Haworth Document Delivery Service [1-800-HAWORTH, 9:00 a.m. - 5:00 p.m. (EST). E-mail address: getinfo@haworthpressinc.com].

 

*Results*: A total of 29.4% of participants showed symptoms of depression, higher than the range found in the older adult American population (13-20%). Those most likely to be depressed ranged in age from 60 to 69 years (32%), lived with their children (37%), rated their financial and health status as below average, had less than a high school education, and lived in the US for less than 5 years.

*Conclusion*: This updated Chinese translation of the GDS is a promising screening measure to detect depressive symptoms in elderly Chinese.


**KEYWORDS.** Depression, Chinese elder, Geriatric Depression Scale, immigrant

## *BACKGROUND*

### *The Growth of the Elderly Population*

Siegel's (1999) review of population statistics points out that the expected rate of population growth will be more rapid for minority elders than for non-Hispanic Whites. In fact, the proportion of elderly persons that is made up of non-Whites and Hispanics is expected to increase from 14.6% in 1995 to 25.4% in 2030 and to 34.0% in 2050 (Siegel, 1999, p. 2). Elderly Asian/Pacific Islanders will increase from about 7% of the total population of minority elders to about 13% in 2020 and 15% in 2050; 1990 census data indicated that Chinese elders were the largest subgroup, comprising 29.5% of the total, followed by Japanese (23.3%), Filipino (22.9%), Korean (7.8%), Asian Indian (5.1%), Vietnamese (4.0%) and others (the remaining indicated Pacific Islander or other Asian) (Siegel, 1999, p. 7). Thus, Chinese elderly are one of the most rapidly growing minorities in the United States today. In 1980, the U.S. Census bureau reported that 812,000 Chinese persons were living in the United States. That number grew to 1.65 million by 1993 and is expected to reach over 3 million by the year 2030. The Census also reported that over 85% of Chinese elders in the United States were foreign born (U.S. Bureau of the Census, 1991).

### *Depression Among the Elderly*

Depression has been reported by many to be the most prevalent mental health problem among the elderly (Blazer & Koenig, 1996). Prevalence studies report significant rates of depression, both major and minor, in various populations of older adults: community dwelling (13-20%), medical outpatients (12%-36%), acute care (30%) and nursing homes (43%) (Blazer, 1993; Blixen & Wilkinson, 1994; Steiner & Marcopulos, 1991). Major depression is known to be one of the primary contributing causes of suicide in the elderly (U.S. Surgeon General, 1999). However, only 25 to 30 percent of depressed patients actually seek help for their depression from their physicians or have their disorder diagnosed (U.S. Surgeon General, 1999) and only one in 50 is hospitalized for this potentially life-threatening disorder (Sainsbury, 1986). One out of every four suicides is committed by a person 65 years of age or older, and depression underlies two thirds of these suicides (Blazer, 1993; McDougall, Blixen, & Suen, 1997).

### *Depression Among Chinese Elders*

Chinese-American elderly are no exception to this trend: According to Yu (1986), Chinese Americans have a higher rate of suicide than white Americans. Furthermore, the suicide rate for elderly Chinese immigrants is almost three times higher than the rate for U.S. born older Chinese Americans (Yu, 1986).

Studies suggest that older Chinese immigrants are at a higher risk of depression than the older white population (Ying, 1988). They are also less likely to be identified as having depression by service providers, and less likely to seek out and utilize mental health services (Snowden & Cheung, 1990; Loo, Tong, & True, 1989), in spite of indications that they are likely to be in great need of assistance (Tsai, Teng & Sue, 1981; Wong, 1982). A recent report of the prevalence of depression among elderly Chinese immigrants in Canada (Lai, 2000) found that, overall, 20.9% of those assessed verbally (mainly in Cantonese) using the short form of the Geriatric Depression Scale (GDS-SF; Sheikh & Yesavage, 1986) indicated depressive symptoms. Of these, about 12% were moderately to severely depressed (attaining a score between 10 and 15, with 15 being the maximum).

Most prior research on depression among elderly Chinese has been done in China and its territories: In Hong Kong, 29% of elderly men and 41% of elderly women surveyed were found to be moderately to severely depressed (Woo, Ho, Lau et al., 1994). In Taiwan, a prevalence rate of 35% has been reported (Lu, Liu & Yu, 1998), while in Singapore, only about 5% of those evaluated were classified as depressed (Kua, 1989). In studies conducted in the US, one report found that about 20% of elderly Chinese in a mid-western city were moderately depressed, and 11% were severely depressed (Lam, Pacala & Smith, 1997); another found that about 16% of elderly Chinese in New York City were mildly depressed, with only about 2% reporting moderate to severe symptoms (Mui, 1996a).

### *Factors Associated with Depression Among Chinese Elderly Immigrants*

A number of sociodemographic factors seem to be associated with the development of depression in Chinese elderly immigrants. For example, the dual stress of immigration and loss of family support systems may increase levels of depression for U.S. Chinese (Rankin, Gailbraith & Johnson, 1993). Poor communication skills in spoken and written English contribute to unfamiliarity with services offered in the health care system and difficulties in communication with health providers, thereby preventing Chinese elders from using health services effectively (Chang, 1991; Rankin et al., 1993).

Another barrier to health care stems from the philosophical perspective derived from Confucianism that emphasizes a loyalty to family and devotion to tradition and which downplays the expression of individual feelings. According to Confucius, avoidance of emotional expression is necessary to maintain harmony in the family and in social relationships (Lee, 1986). Wong (1982) has pointed out that immigrants are least likely to utilize such services because they do not share the values of western health providers, nor believe that help-seeking for depression is an appropriate action to take.

### *Treating Depression Among Chinese Elders*

Depression in later life is a most treatable mental disorder. Many kinds of antidepressant medications and various forms of psychotherapy have been shown to be effective with a broad range of depressive disorders in older adults, as reviewed in Gallagher-Thompson and Thompson (1996), Gatz, Fiske, Fox et al. (1998), and Powers, Thompson, Gallagher-Thompson and Futterman (in press). However, most of these authors note that the overwhelming amount of existing treatment outcome research has been done with elderly Whites, and not with persons of color. Thus, at present, we do not have an empirical basis upon which to decide which treatments would be most effective with elderly Chinese who are depressed. Hopefully this situation will be remedied in the not-too-distant future, as service needs increase and more appropriately trained professionals are available to conduct the needed research, and translate results into practice settings. In the interim elderly Chinese will no doubt continue to consult herbalists and use other traditional approaches, consistent with cultural beliefs about health and illness, to treat their depression, as described in detail by Matocha (1998).

### *Measuring Depression in the Chinese Elder Population*

Although depression is a common problem among the Chinese elderly, few researchers have focused on ways to measure depression in Chinese elders. Exceptions to this are the research of Chiu, Lee, Wing et al. (1994), Lee, Chiu, Kwok et al. (1993), Mui (1996b), and Rankin et al. (1993). Chiu and colleagues established the reliability and validity of the original 30-item Geriatric Depression Scale (GDS; Brink, Yesavage, Lum et al., 1982; Yesavage, Brink, Rose et al., 1983), while Lee and colleagues validated the short form GDS, among both normal and depressed Chinese elderly in Hong Kong. The GDS-SF was later used to assess the prevalence of depressive symptoms among Chinese elders over age 70 in a citywide random sample survey conducted in Hong Kong by Woo et al. (1994) and, as noted above, high prevalence was found for both men and women in that study.

The studies of Mui (1996b) and Rankin et al. (1993) were conducted in the U.S. Rankin's group focused on a different measure of depression than the one of interest here, so it will not be discussed further. Mui investigated psychometric properties of both the short and long form versions of the GDS with a sample of 50 elderly Chinese in New York City, and found that the Chinese language version of the long form GDS that she used evidenced high internal consistency, but the short form did not. Factor analysis was then used to develop a new version of the GDS-SF with better internal consistency than the original. In this new version, 10 of the original 15 items of the GDS-SF were the same, but five were different. They were changed to reflect greater cultural sensitivity; for example, "prefer to stay at home" is almost a virtue in Chinese culture, according to Mui (1996b), and older people stay at home to take care of grandchildren; therefore, endorsement of this item should not be considered indicative of depression. Thus, it was deleted from her new version. Her study found that about one-third of the sample were moderately to severely depressed, using a cut-off score of five or greater with this new version of the GDS-SF. When the data from the original GDS-SF were compared to these results (using the same cut-off score), only 26% of the sample was considered to be depressed. However, no independent validation of presence or extent of depression was used in that study, and no subsequent studies could be found that actually used Mui's new version of the short form GDS. Given that a third of the items were actually replaced (from the original scale), it is difficult to compare Mui's results with other studies in the literature that used the GDS-SF–either with Chinese or with non-Chinese elderly.

### *Purpose of the Present Study*

Since depressive disorders may often go unrecognized and untreated in the Chinese-American elderly population, and treatment for depression can dramatically improve the quality of these later years, correct assessment may contribute to a higher quality of life for this population. A practical screening instrument for use in the health care professions might facilitate detection of depression and increased utilization of treatment resources in this population.

Accordingly, the primary goals of this study were: (1) to redesign the Chinese long form of the GDS using an updated translation (based on Mui's work) that would be more appropriate for the predominately Mandarin-speaking population in Santa Clara County, CA and in other regions of the U.S. with large numbers of Mandarin-speaking Chinese; and (2) to use this version of the GDS to detect depressive symptoms among community-residing Chinese elderly.

## *METHODOLOGY*

### *Sample and Setting*

A convenience sample of 113 (72 female and 41 male) community-residing Chinese elderly was recruited from two senior centers in Santa Clara County (in northern California) to participate in this study. The primary author explained the nature of the project to attendees on different occasions and anyone who volunteered was then asked to respond to several brief screening questions, as follows: Participants (a) must be at least 60 years of age, (b) must have emigrated from

China, Hong Kong, Taiwan, or other Asian countries, (c) must be speakers of the Mandarin dialect of the Chinese language, (d) must neither be diagnosed as terminally ill nor suffer from any diagnosed form of senile dementia, and (e) must have lived in the United States for a minimum of three months. Eleven of those who volunteered were screened out because they were under age, leaving a sample of 102 elders. Data were collected on-site at the senior centers, in small groups. The primary author, who is fluent in Mandarin, was present at these centers weekly over a three-month period to clarify instructions and respond to procedural questions. Since most elderly Chinese have had little or no experience as participants in research, she had to explain the consent form and reassure them about the confidential nature of their responses. All the questionnaires were completed individually and turned in to a specially labeled box at the center upon completion. The primary author reviewed all of the data and contacted participants to try and fill in any missing data, although she was not always able to reach them or get data for every missing item.

The instruments used were: (a) a demographic questionnaire (translated into Chinese), and (b) a new translation of the long form of the GDS, called in this paper the C-GDS. In addition, an open-ended interview was conducted with those who scored between 21 and 30 on the GDS, to clarify some of their depressive responses and to inquire about various barriers that may have been deterring them from seeking help. Results of these interviews will be discussed in a separate paper that is in preparation.

*Demographic Questionnaire.* Information was obtained about gender, age, living situation, country of origin, medical insurance, number of years in the U.S., education, religious preference, marital status, financial status, and perception of current health.

*The Geriatric Depression Scale.* The GDS long form of 30 items (Brink et al., 1982; Yesavage et al., 1983) was used in the study because the original English form was specifically designed to serve as a screening tool for depressive symptoms in older adults. Yesavage and colleagues thought that most depression rating scales in existence at that time were not sensitive to the needs of the elderly, so they created a new scale that addressed the following issues. First, depression in the elderly is often accompanied by subjective experiences of memory loss and cognitive impairment (Kahn, Zarit, Hilbert, & Niederehe, 1975). It is, therefore, easy to confuse depression with dementia in this group. Second, somatic symptoms such as sleep disturbances, decline of sexual function, constipation, and pain–usually key to a diagnosis of depression in the young–are less useful as indicators with elderly populations because such disturbances are also common in non-depressed elderly (Coleman, Miles, Guilleminault et al., 1981; Thompson et al., 1988). Third, elderly are typically more resistant to psychiatric evaluation than young patients (Salzman & Shader, 1978; Wells, 1979) and questions related to mental health often make them defensive. It is also common for the elderly to interpret such questions differently and to respond in a socially desirable manner, which often leads to an under-reporting of problems (Salzman & Shader, 1978).

The 30 items on the original long form of the GDS tap into the more psychological aspects of depression, such as feelings of low self-esteem, whether or not a person is satisfied with his/her life, and whether or not they look forward to the future. There are no somatic items, and the response choice is a simple 'yes' or 'no' for how the person felt about that item in the past week. In numerous studies of the GDS with older Caucasian adults, it was found to have excellent reliability (test-retest correlation coefficients averaging .85 with internal consistency, as measured by Cronbach's alpha, averaging .94). Validity has been established by the high degree of congruence between the use of certain cut-off scores (from the self-administered GDS) and results of a clinical interview from which Research Diagnostic Criteria (Spitzer, Endicott & Robins, 1978) for establishing diagnoses of depressive disorders were used. It was found that a total score of 10 or below is within the normal range and is indicative of no depression; a score between 11 and 20 indicates mild depression, and scores of 21 to 30 indicate moderate to severe depression (Yesavage et al., 1983). Finally, the GDS long form has been widely and successfully used as a screening tool with both non- and institutionalized elderly (Thompson, Futterman, & Gallagher, 1988; Olin, Schneider, Eaton et al., 1992). For all of these reasons, it was selected as our measure of choice for the present study.

*Development of the Current C-GDS*. We obtained copies of the different versions and translations of the GDS used in the earlier studies cited mostly with Cantonese speakers, and then had a panel of four bilingual experts intensively review the translations to determine both if vocabulary and syntax were appropriate for Mandarin speakers, and if the language matched the intent of the original English instrument. Mui's (1996b) version of the long form GDS was selected for more intense study because it was used with Chinese immigrants in this country. It was back-translated into English by a psychiatric nursing professor, a Chinese studies major, and an English major who spoke both English and Mandarin Chinese. The back-translation was then translated into Chinese a second time and carefully compared to Mui's original work. It was noted that the wording of some of her items did not seem to reflect the original intent of those same items on the English language version of the original GDS and were confusing. Further consultation with a small panel of elder Mandarin speaking volunteers confirmed the confusion; these items were revised until a consensus was achieved that their intent matched the original English language meaning. Thus, the present study used most of Mui's (1996) translation of the long form GDS, but with certain items modified as described above. Copies of this version can be obtained from the first author upon request.

### *Research Procedures*

Volunteers who met the entry criteria (N = 102) were given a research packet which contained (a) the Chinese version of the written informed consent document, which included the purpose and voluntary nature of the study and assurances of confidentiality; (b) the demographic questionnaire; and (c) the C-GDS. Completion time for the packet ranged from 30 to 50 minutes. Participants were identified by code number only on all measures and only the immediate research team had access to this information. Data were double-entered into a computerized data base management file for analyses.

## *RESULTS*

### *Depressive Symptomatology*

Descriptive statistical procedures were used to compute frequencies, percentages, and ranges for demographic and C-GDS variables. The overall mean on the C-GDS for the 102 respondents was 4.49 (SD = 4.41). We found that 70.6% scored in the non-depressed range (that is, a total score of 10 or below; N = 71) while 25.5% scored between 11 and 20 (N = 27) and 3.9% scored between 21 and 30, in the moderate to severe range (N = 4). In Mui's (1996) research with elderly Chinese immigrants, only 18% were depressed using her translation of the long form GDS, a rate that is well below the results found in this study. Table 1 shows the percentage of respondents who endorsed each item in a depressed versus nondepressed direction for the full 30 item long form GDS. The Table is presented in English for the reader's understanding. Inspection of these items reveals that there are nine that were endorsed

TABLE 1. Percent of Subjects Endorsing Each Item of the Chinese Geriatric Depression Scale (C-GDS) as Depressed or Non-Depressed (N = 102)

| C-GDS Item | Percent of subjects endorsing as | |
|---|---|---|
| | Depressed | Non-depressed |
| 1. Satisfied with life | 5.0 | 95.0 |
| 2. Dropped activities and interests | 36.0 | 64.0 |
| 3. Life is empty | 14.7 | 85.3 |
| 4. Often get bored | 21.2 | 78.8 |
| 5. Hopeful about the future | 22.9 | 77.1 |
| 6. Obsessive thoughts | 33.7 | 66.3 |
| 7. In good spirits | 25.8 | 74.2 |
| 8. Afraid bad things might happen | 33.7 | 66.3 |
| 9. Happy most of the time | 21.0 | 79.0 |
| 10. Often feel helpless | 30.3 | 69.7 |
| 11. Restless and fidgety | 17.8 | 82.2 |
| 12. Prefer to stay home | 17.8 | 82.2 |
| 13. Worry about the future | 34.7 | 65.3 |
| 14. Problems with memory | 39.4 | 60.6 |
| 15. Wonderful to be alive | 9.8 | 90.2 |
| 16. Feel downhearted and blue | 17.2 | 82.8 |
| 17. Feel worthless | 27.0 | 73.0 |
| 18. Worry about the past | 10.0 | 90.0 |
| 19. Life is exciting | 14.7 | 85.3 |
| 20. Hard to start new projects | 53.5 | 46.5 |
| 21. Full of energy | 39.2 | 60.8 |
| 22. Situation appears hopeless | 25.7 | 74.3 |
| 23. Other people are better off | 25.3 | 74.7 |
| 24. Get upset over little things | 22.0 | 78.0 |
| 25. Feel like crying | 18.6 | 81.4 |
| 26. Have trouble concentrating | 36.0 | 64.0 |
| 27. Enjoy getting up in the morning | 5.9 | 94.1 |
| 28. Avoid social gatherings | 29.3 | 70.7 |
| 29. Easy to make decisions | 21.2 | 78.8 |
| 30. Mind as clear as before | 41.0 | 59.0 |

| Proportion of subjects classified as depressed using original cut-off scores for the GDS | | | |
|---|---|---|---|
| Normal (0-10) | 70.6% | Total Mean | SD |
| Mild Depression (11-20) | 25.5% | | |
| Moderate to Severe Depression (21-30) | 3.9% | 4.49 | 4.41 |

in the depressive direction by at least one-third of the sample. They are: (1) #20: hard to start new projects (53.5%); (2) #30: mind is as clear as it used to be (41%); (3) #14: problem with memory (39.4%); (4) #21: full of energy (39.2%); (5) #26: trouble with concentration (36%); (6) #2: dropped activities and interests (36%); (7) #13: worry about the future (34.7%); (8) #6: obsessive thoughts (33.7%) and (9) #8: afraid bad things will happen (33.7%). Items reflecting negative feelings, such as feeling like crying or feeling downhearted and blue were endorsed in the depressed direction by less than 20% of this sample.

### *Relationship Between Depressive Symptoms and Sociodemographic Factors*

A total of 11 independent variables were examined to begin to evaluate their relationship to depression in this group: gender, age, living situation, marital status, religious identification, education completed, country of origin, years in the US, self-rated health, medical insurance, and self-rated financial status. For each item, in addition to the total *N* and percent endorsing it, we also provide information on the percent of those depressed who endorse it, compared to the percent who are not depressed who endorse it. In this way, a pattern can begin to emerge as to possible risk factors associated with higher levels of depression among Chinese elderly immigrants in the US (see Table 2).

*Gender*: There were 64 women and 34 men in the sample (four persons declined to indicate their gender); 18 of the women were depressed, as were 10 of the men, which is close to 30% for each gender. The common expectation that elderly females are more depressed than males (Aneshensel, Frerichs & Clark, 1981) is not borne out by the data.

*Age*: The mean age of respondents was 71.85 years (SD = 5.51) with a range from 60 to 87 years. Of those between 60 and 69 years of age, 32% had C-GDS scores of 11 or above, suggesting at least mild depression. Of those between 70 and 79 years of age, 25% were at least mildly depressed. Of those aged 80 and above, only 11% were depressed. Thus, the common assumption in the literature that depression increases with age does not appear to be borne out in these data, although it is possible that the results are due in part to a higher (and thus earlier) mortality for depressed people.

*Living Situation*: Only about 22% lived alone; the remainder lived with either spouse, children, or both, with five participants declining to answer the question. Among those living with spouses or children, 30% and 37%, respectively, were depressed. Only four respondents who lived alone were at least mildly depressed. Contrary to prior findings, living alone did not appear to be a risk factor for depression in this sample.

*Marital Status*: The majority (about 72%) of respondents were married, with about 17.5% being widowed and the remainder, about 10%, being single. For persons who were married, 26% (n = 18) were at least mildly depressed, which is similar to the rate found among those widowed (29%) or single (30%). Thus, marital status does not appear to be associated with depression in this sample.

TABLE 2. Proportion of Individuals Scoring Above 10 on the Chinese Geriatric Depression Scale (C-GDS) for Specific Sociodemographic Factors

| Sociodemographic Variable | Percent in Depressed Range |
|---|---|
| Sex | |
| Male | 29 |
| Female | 28 |
| Age Range | |
| 60-69 years | 32 |
| 70-79 years | 25 |
| 80 and above | 11 |
| Living Arrangement | |
| Living with spouse | 30 |
| Living with children | 37 |
| Living alone | 25 |
| Marital Status | |
| Married | 26 |
| Widowed | 29 |
| Single | 30 |
| Religious Preference | |
| Buddhist or Catholic | 30 |
| No religious preference | 15 |
| Education | |
| High school graduate or less | 50 |
| Some college or advanced degree | 25 |
| Years in the United States | |
| One year or less | 100 |
| 2-5 years | 42 |
| 5 years or more | 22 |
| Self-Rated Financial Status | |
| Average | 20 |
| Below average | 35 |
| Poor | 46 |

*Religious Preference*: About 37% were Buddhist (n = 35) and 37% were Christian, with an additional 10% being Catholic and the reminder being "other" or expressing no religious preference. Of those who were Buddhist, Christian, or Catholic, about 30% (n = 24) were depressed, while only about 15% of those who had no religious preference were. Thus, religion does not appear to be a protective factor for Chinese elderly.

*Education*: About half of the total sample indicated that they had completed high school or vocational school, with about 17% having lower educational attainment, and about 33% having a college or advanced degree. Among those with high school or less education, over 50% were at least mildly depressed, in contrast to those with a college degree or higher, where only about 25% reported depression. This is consistent with other findings conducted with Caucasian samples, that lower educational levels are associated with greater likelihood of depression.

*Country of Origin*: All respondents were originally from China (78%) or Taiwan (20%) with the exception of one couple who were Chinese but came from Vietnam. About 30% of those from either China or Taiwan were at least mildly depressed. All preferred to speak in Mandarin and most were monolingual Chinese, with very little English language speaking ability.

*Years in the US*: The amount of time respondents lived in the US ranged from six months to 24 years, with a mean of 8.55 years (SD = 6.33). All of those who had lived in the US for one year or less were depressed and 42% of those who lived in the US between two and five years were depressed. In comparison, only 22% of those who had lived in the US for longer than five years were depressed, and only one in ten of those who had lived here for over 15 years were depressed. Thus, recency of immigration appears to be a strong contributing factor to depressive symptoms.

*Self-Rated Health*: About 87% of the overall sample considered their health to be "fair" but of these, only about 8% were depressed. One woman who rated her health as "poor" was highly depressed on the C-GDS.

*Medical Insurance*: About 83% of the overall sample have Medicare and/or Medical/Medicaid, with about 8% having no medical insurance, and 8% having private insurance. Of those with Medicare or Medicaid, about 25% were depressed in contrast to about 50% depression found in those with no insurance. Thus absence of health insurance appears to be a risk factor for depression among Chinese elders.

*Self-Rated Financial Status*: About 46% considered themselves "average" with about 38% reporting their finances to be "below average" and another 13% indicating that they were "poor." Twenty percent of those who considered themselves average were depressed, as were 35% of those who considered themselves below average and 46% of those who considered themselves poor, suggesting that poor financial status is a risk factor for depression in Chinese elders.

## DISCUSSION AND IMPLICATIONS FOR FUTURE RESEARCH

It is notable that 102 active Chinese elders were able to be recruited for this study, and that most were able to complete the measures on their own, without much assistance, despite their lack of familiarity or prior participation in research. This suggests that Chinese elderly are interested in being informed about research and being given the opportunity to participate, and that they will do so when there are few barriers, such as having to get somewhere to be interviewed, or having long and complex questionnaires to complete. Given the difficulty that other researchers have reported in getting Chinese elderly to participate in research (cf. Guo, Levy, Hinton et al., 2000), this seems like an accomplishment in itself. Second, the study confirms some earlier findings about higher rates of depression likely among elderly Chinese immigrants compared to their Caucasian counterparts. It is noteworthy that close to 30% of this sample of relatively advantaged Chinese elders self-reported mild to moderate/severe depressive symptoms. This study also underscores the role of factors such as poor health, poverty, length of time living in the US, and low educational attainment as risk factors likely to be associated with depression. Third, the study suggests a profile which, of course, needs to be replicated in future research, but which can alert practitioners in the community to conduct a more thorough assessment for depression. In this study, participants most likely to be depressed were both men and women between the ages of 60 and 69 who were living with their spouses or children, rated their financial status below average or poor, had not completed high school, had lived in the US for less than five years, and rated their health status as poor. Those least likely to be depressed were over the age of 80 and living alone, but were active in senior center activities, rated their financial and health status as good or excellent, had completed high school or college and lived in the US for more than five years. Gender, religious preference, and country of origin were not associated risk factors in this sample.

A limitation of the present study relates to the convenience sampling: All participants were actively involved in senior center activities specifically for Chinese elders, and therefore may not be representative of older Chinese who are less involved in community organizations. Chinese elderly who are relatively isolated from a social network may be at greater risk for depression, but that will need to be studied in future research. A further limitation is the lack of validation of the self-report cut-off scores against clinical diagnoses; again, this is a fruitful topic for future research. Additional work is needed with the authors' translation of the GDS to determine its usefulness in other parts of the US with large Mandarin speaking populations, and to help refine it if necessary.

This study suggests that depression can be detected using a carefully translated questionnaire that is relatively easy for the elder to complete on his or her own. Since few immigrants are likely to seek mental health services, we believe agencies that serve Chinese elderly, such as culture-specific senior centers (which provide language assistance and other services to immigrants and follow them over the long term) need to initiate their own screening for depression. Offering C-GDS at culturally acceptable sites is not only convenient and appealing to the client, but also minimizes the potential sense of shame that seeking assessment and service for mental health problems generally entails (Hsu, 1985; Matocha, 1998). Offering this preventive service in agencies that assist immigrants with other survival needs normalizes options for dealing with the sadness and frustration one inevitably encounters when relocating in a foreign country (Ying, 1990). Taking advantage of these services (e.g., psychological counseling or drug therapy) then becomes part of the senior center culture and again, stigma is minimized.

Finally, we recommend that health care professionals consider including screening tests for depression in their routine geriatric assessments (Beers, Fink & Beck, 1991). For those who do not participate in senior center activities, family physicians may be more acceptable for administering the C-GDS than mental health professionals because of the stigma attached to seeking psychiatric help. Mental health personnel can participate in training primary care physicians on the use of the C-GDS, as well as educating them about referrals, so that follow-through with a treatment plan is more likely. It goes without saying that Chinese elders will seek care more often when it is provided in the Chinese elders' preferred language. Given the complex issues that arise with translation (and then validation) of existing screens for depression, it is hoped that the slowly accumulating body of knowledge about the GDS with Chinese elders will encourage future researchers to study this measure more carefully, and to continue to add to knowledge about its effectiveness with this and other populations.

## REFERENCES

Aneshensel, C., Frerichs, R. R. & Clark, V. A. (1981). Family roles and sex differences in depression. *Journal of Health and Social Behavior, 22*, 379-393.

Beer, M. H., Fink, A. & Beck, J. C. (1991). Screening recommendations for the elderly. *American Journal of Public Health, 81*, 1131-1140.

Blazer, D. G. (1993). *Depression in late life*, 2nd ed. St. Louis: Mosby.

Blazer, D. G. & Koenig, H. G. (1996). Mood disorders. In E. W. Busse & D. G. Blazer (Eds.), *Textbook of geriatric psychiatry*, 2nd ed. (pp. 235-263). Washington, D.C.: American Psychiatric Press.

Blixen, C. E. & Wilkinson, L. K. (1994). Assessing and managing depression in the older adult: Implications for advanced practice nurses. *Nurse Practictioner, 19*(7), 66-69.

Braun, K. L. & Browne, C. V. (1998). Perceptions of dementia, caregiving, and help-seeking among Asian and Pacific Islander Americans. *Health and Social Work, 23*, 262-273.

Brink, T. L., Yesavage, J., Lum, O., Heersma, P., Adey, M. & Rose, T. A. (1982). Screening tests for geriatric depression. *Clinical Gerontologist, 1*, 37-44.

Chang, K. (1991). Chinese Americans. In J. N. Giger & R. E. Davidhizar (Eds.), *Transcultural Nursing* (pp. 359-377). St. Louis: Mosby.

Chiu, H. F., Lee, H. C., Wing, Y. K., Kwong, P. K., Leung, C. M. & Chung, D. W. (1994). Reliability, validity and structure of the Chinese Geriatric Depression Scale in a Hong Kong context: A preliminary report. *Singapore Medical Journal, 35*(5), 477-480.

Coleman, R. M., Miles, L. E., Guilleminault, C., Zarcone, V. P., van der Hoed, L. & Dement, W. C. (1981). Sleep-wake disorders in the elderly: A polysomnographic analysis. *Journal of the American Geriatrics Society, 29*, 289-296.

Gallagher-Thompson, D. & Thompson, L. W. (1996). Applying cognitive therapy to the common psychological problems of later life. In S. Zarit & B. Knight (Eds.), *Psychotherapy and aging: Effective interventions with older adults* (pp. 61-82). Washington, D. C.: American Psychological Association Press.

Gatz, M., Fiske, A., Fox, L. S., Kaskie, B., Kasl-Godley, J. E., McCallum, T. J., & Wetherell, J. L. (1998). Empirically validated psychological treatments for older adults. *Journal of Mental Health and Aging, 4*(1), 9-46.

Guo, Z., Levy, B. R., Hinton, W. L., Weitzman, P. F. & Levkoff, S. E. (2000). The power of labels: Recruiting dementia-affected Chinese American elders and their caregivers. *Journal of Mental Health and Aging, 6*(1), 103-112.

Hsu, F. (1985). The self in cross-cultural perspective. In M. J. Marsella, G. DeVos & F. Hsu (Eds.), *Culture and self* (pp. 45-55). London: Tavistock.

Kahn, R. L., Zarit, S. H., Hilbert, N. M. & Niederehe, G. (1975). Memory complaint and impairment in the aged: The effect of depression and altered brain function. *Archives of General Psychiatry*, *32*, 1569-1573.

Kua, E. H. (1989). Depressive disorders in elderly Chinese people. *Acta Psychiatrica Scandinavia*, *81*, 386-388.

Lam, R. E., Pacala, J. T. & Smith, S. L. (1997). Factors related to depressive symptoms in an elderly Chinese American sample. *Clinical Gerontologist*, *17*(4), 57-70.

Lai, D. W. L. (2000). Prevalence of depression among the elderly Chinese in Canada. *Canadian Journal of Public Health*, *91*(1), 64-66.

Lee, R. N. (1986). The Chinese perception of mental illness in the Canadian mosaic. *Canada's Mental Health*, *34*(4), 2-4.

Lee, H. C. B., Chui, H. F. K., Kwok, W. Y., Leung, C. M., & Kwomg, P. K. (1993). Chinese elderly and the GDS short form: A preliminary study. *Clinical Gerontologist*, *14*, 37-42.

Loo, C., Tong, B. & True, R. (1989). A bitter bean: Mental health status and attitudes in Chinatown. *Journal of Community Psychology*, *17*, 283-296.

Lu, C. H., Liu, C. Y. & Yu, S. (1998). Depressive disorders among the Chinese elderly in a suburban community. *Public Health Nursing*, *15*(3), 196-200.

Matocha, L. K. (1998). Chinese-Americans. In L. D. Purnell & B. J. Pulanka (Eds.), *Transcultural health care: A culturally competent approach* (pp. 163-188). Philadelphia, PA: F. A. Davis Company.

McDougall, G. J., Blixen, C. L. & Suen, L. J. The process and outcome of life review psychotherapy with depressed homebound older adults. *Nursing Research*, *46*(5), 277-283.

Mui, A. C. (1996a). Depression among elderly Chinese immigrants: An exploratory study. *Social Work*, *41*, 633-645.

Mui, A. C. (1996b). Geriatric Depression Scale as a community screening instrument for elderly Chinese immigrants. *International Psychogeriatrics*, *8*, 445-458.

Olin, J., Schneider, L. S., Eaton, E. M., Zemansky, M. F. & Pollack, V. E. (1992). The Geriatric Depression Scale and Beck Depression Inventory as screening instruments in an older adult outpatient population. *Psychological Assessment*, *42*, 190-192.

Powers, D. V., Thompson, L. W., Gallagher-Thompson, D. & Futterman, A. (in press). Depression in later life: Epidemiology, assessment, impact and treatment. In L. Gotlib & C. Hammen (Eds.), *The handbook of depression*, 3rd ed. NY: Guilford Press.

Rankin, S. H., Galbraith, M. E. & Johnson, S. (1993). Reliability and validity data for a Chinese translation of the Center for Epidemiological Studies-Depression Scale. *Psychological Reports*, *73*, 1291-1298.

Sainsbury, P. (1986). Depression, suicide, and suicide prevention. In A. Roy (Ed.), *Suicide* (pp. 73-88). Baltimore, MD: Williams & Wilkins.

Salzman, C. & Shader, R. I. (1978). Depression in the elderly: Relationship between depression, psychological defense mechanisms and physical illness. *Journal of the American Geriatrics Society*, *26*, 253-259.

Sheikh, J. I. & Yesavage, J. A. (1986). Geriatric Depression Scale (GDS): Recent evidence and development of a shorter version. *Clinical Gerontologist, 5*, 165-173.

Siegel, J. S. (1999). Demographic introduction to racial/Hispanic elderly populations. In T. P. Miles (Ed.), *Full-color aging: Facts, goals, and recommendations for America's diverse elders* (pp. 1-19). Washington, D.C.: Gerontological Society of America.

Snowden, L. R. & Cheung, F. K. (1990). Use of inpatient mental health services by members of ethnic minority groups. *American Psychologist, 45*, 347-355.

Steiner, D. & Marcopoulos, B. (1991). Depression in the elderly: Characteristics and clinical management. *Nursing Clinics of North America, 26*, 585-600.

Spitzer, R. L., Endicott, J. & Robins, L. N. (1978). Research diagnostic criteria: Rationale and reliability. *Archives of General Psychiatry, 35*, 773-782.

Thompson, L. W., Futterman, A. & Gallagher, D. (1988). Assessment of late life depression. *Psychopharmacology Bulletin, 24*, 577-586.

Tsai, T., Teng, L. N. & Sue, S. (1981). Mental health status of the Chinese in the United States. In A. Kleinman & T. Y. Lin (Eds.), *Normal and abnormal behaviors in Chinese culture* (pp. 291-310). Dordrecht: Reidel.

U.S. Bureau of the Census (1991). *Census and you* (Press Release No. CB91-100). Washington, D.C.: US Government Printing Office.

U.S. Surgeon General (1999). Mental health and aging (chapter 5) in *Mental health: A report of the Surgeon General*. Rockville, MD: U.S. Dept. of Health and Human Services, National Institutes of Health, National Institute of Mental Health.

Wells, C. E. (1979). Pseudodementia. *American Journal of Psychiatry, 136*, 895-900.

Wong, H. (1982). Asian and Pacific Americans. In L. Snowden (Ed.), *Reaching the underserved: Mental health needs of neglected populations* (pp. 185-200). Beverly Hills, CA: Sage.

Woo, J., Ho, S. C., Lau, J. et al. (1994). The prevalence of depressive symptoms and predisposing factors in an elderly Chinese population. *Acta Psychiatrica Scandinavia, 89*, 8-13.

Yesavage, J. A., Brink, T. L., Rose, T. A., Lum, O., Huang, V., Adey, M. B., & Leirer, V. O. (1983). Development and validation of a geriatric depression screening scale: A preliminary report. *Journal of Psychiatric Research, 17*, 37-49.

Ying, Y. W. (1988). Depressive symptomatology among Chinese Americans as measured by the CES-D. *Journal of Clinical Psychology, 44*, 739-746.

Ying, Y. W. (1990). Explanatory models of major depression and implications for help-seeking among immigrant Chinese American women. *Culture, Medicine and Psychiatry, 14*, 393-408.

Yu, E. S. H. (1986). Health of the Chinese elderly in America. *Research on Aging, 8*(1), 84-109.

# Social Integration and Health Among Asian Indian Immigrants in the United States

Sadhna Diwan, PhD
Satya S. Jonnalagadda, PhD

**SUMMARY.** This research examines the relationship between social integration and health status (i.e., prevalence of chronic health conditions) among older first generation Asian Indian (AI) immigrants in the U.S. Data were collected through a telephone survey from 226 respondents (50 years and over) in the Southeastern U.S. The correlates of health status were determined using a Poisson regression analysis. The prevalence of major chronic conditions such as heart disease, diabetes and hypertension in this sample was similar to those found in other studies of AI immigrants. Better health was associated with greater perceived

---

Sadhna Diwan is Associate Professor, School of Social Work, Georgia State University, Atlanta, GA. Satya S. Jonnalagadda is Associate Professor, School of Social Work, Georgia State University, Atlanta, GA.

Address correspondence to: Dr. Sadhna Diwan, School of Social Work, Georgia State University, 140 Decatur Street, 1027 ULB, Atlanta, GA 30303 (E-mail: sdiwan@gsu.edu).

This study was funded in part by a Research Initiation Grant from Georgia State University and grants from the National Institute on Aging (T32-AG0017 and RO3AG19049).

The authors thank Huggy Rao for statistical assistance, and the research assistants as well as the participants in this study.

[Haworth co-indexing entry note]: "Social Integration and Health Among Asian Indian Immigrants in the United States." Diwan, Sadhna, and Satya S. Jonnalagadda. Co-published simultaneously in *Journal of Gerontological Social Work* (The Haworth Social Work Practice Press, an imprint of The Haworth Press, Inc.) Vol. 36, No. 1/2, 2001, pp. 45-62; and: *Social Work Practice with the Asian American Elderly* (ed: Namkee G. Choi) The Haworth Social Work Practice Press, an imprint of The Haworth Press, Inc., 2001, pp. 45-62. Single or multiple copies of this article are available for a fee from The Haworth Document Delivery Service [1-800-HAWORTH, 9:00 a.m. - 5:00 p.m. (EST). E-mail address: getinfo@haworthpressinc.com].

support and having relatives nearby, whereas poorer health was associated with higher body mass index, longer residence in the U.S., being older, and being female. Implications for interventions designed to address the diversity within this immigrant community are discussed. 

**KEYWORDS.** Social support, social ties, ethnicity, Asian and Pacific Islanders, minorities

## *INTRODUCTION*

The API population, which numbered approximately 10.9 million in 1999, comprised 4% of the total U.S. population (Humes & McKinnon, 2000). It is anticipated that APIs will have one of the largest growth rates in the U.S. within the next 20 years and are expected to number 34 million (9% of the population) by the year 2050 (U.S. Census Bureau, 1998). Within the API population, there is considerable diversity in terms of language, culture, socioeconomic status (SES), and recency of immigration given that APIs encompass among others, Japanese, Chinese, Filipinos, Asian Indians, Koreans, Vietnamese, Cambodians, and Pakistanis (Yu & Liu, 1992). Asian Indian immigrants are the fourth largest group among APIs, with their numbers having grown from 15,000 in 1965 to around one million in 1992 (Gibson, 1988; Enas, Yusuf, & Mehta, 1992).

A study of this immigrant group in the U.S. is merited as Asian Indian immigrants in several Western countries have been found to be at greater risk for morbidity and mortality as compared to the native and other immigrant populations. For example, evidence from the United Kingdom (U.K.) suggests that AI immigrants suffer from higher rates of mortality and morbidity due to coronary heart disease and diabetes as compared to the native population (McKeigue, Miller & Marmot, 1989; McKeigue, Shah & Marmot, 1991). Similar trends have been noted among AI immigrants in Singapore (Gupta, de Belder & Hughes, 1995), and Canada (Sheth, Nair, Nargundkar, Anand & Yusuf, 1999), and preliminary work confirms this trend among Asian Indian physicians in the U.S. (Enas, Davidson, Garg, Nair & Yusuf, 1991). Whereas researchers have focused on physiological variables that may account for these differences in health status, to date no data are available on the impact of psychosocial variables on the health of this immigrant group. This paper helps address this void by examining the relationship between social integration and health in a sample of AI immigrants in the U.S. The paper reviews the available literature on the health status of this group and uses a theory of social integration to examine the relationship between social relations and health.

## *ASIAN INDIAN IMMIGRANTS*

Data from the U.S. Census Bureau (based on the 1990 census) indicate that in general, AI immigrants are highly educated with the average educational attainment being a Bachelor's degree, and are economically well off with a median income higher than that of non-Hispanic whites (Bennett & Martin, 1997). Nonetheless, there is significant diversity in educational level, socioeconomic status and within-group differences in language and diet within this AI immigrant community. The level of education ranges from highly educated professionals with post-graduate degrees to working class individuals with a high school education. Those who immigrate under the family preference provisions of the immigration law tend to have lesser skills, lesser fluency in English, and lower SES.

Among the various chronic diseases prevalent in the Western world, cardiovascular disease (CVD) is the leading cause of death among older people. In the U.K., deaths due to CVD represented an excess mortality of 36% in Asian Indian men and 46% in Asian Indian women as compared to the overall mortality rates in that country (Balarajan, 1991). Furthermore, myocardial infarction (MI) was observed to occur at an earlier age among AIs (50 years) as compared to their white counterparts (55 years). Similarly, in the U.S., limited data from seven states with the highest API population indicates that heart disease is the leading cause of death in both genders of this Asian Indian population although the risk factors that predispose this population to the disease are unclear (Hoyert & Kung, 1997). Of the known risk factors of CVD, diabetes mellitus is the only identifiable risk factor in this Asian Indian immigrant population that might predispose them to premature CVD (Seely, 1996), and studies have shown Asian Indians to be more insulin resistant than African Americans and Caucasians (Banerji, Faridi, Atluri, Chaike & Lebovitz, 1999; Laws et al., 1994). Asian Indian women living in the U.S. were found to have greater risk of developing breast cancer as compared to their counterparts in India (incidence rate of 93 vs. 28 per 100,000), but lower than that of Caucasian females (153 per 100,000). A similar trend was observed for colon cancer, suggesting that immigration may have an adverse effect on the cancer risk of this population (Blesch, Davis & Kamath, 1999).

In the literature on the health of older individuals in general, researchers (see van den Akker, Buntinx, Metsemakers & Knottnerus, 2000) have noted a remarkable similarity in the risk factors related to diverse diseases indicating that factor specific research may make a useful contribution to understanding general disease susceptibility and co-morbidity. It has been suggested that psychosocial factors such as life changes associated with social and cultural mobility, lack of social support and coping resources may cause increased disease susceptibility with a wide range of disease outcomes (van den Akker et al., 2000). Hao and Johnson (2000) note that for immigrants who face the added stresses of adaptation to a new country, social resources may be particularly important to their well-being.

As this minority group continues to grow older and more numerous, there is a need to better understand the prevalence of chronic diseases and the multiplicity of factors contributing to these disease conditions. Such an understanding will support the development of interventions that will target the specific health care needs of this ethnic population and facilitate better training of health and social service agencies to provide appropriate care.

## *SOCIAL INTEGRATION AND HEALTH*

Durkheim's theory on social integration (1951) has been used by researchers to understand the relationship between health and social relations (see Su & Ferraro, 1997). This theory asserts that social integration creates cohesion and provides individuals meaning and purpose in life, and promotes a sense of well-being. The concept of social integration according to Seeman (1996) is broadly conceived as the opposite of social isolation, i.e., disengagement from social ties, institutional connections, or participation in community-based social, cultural, and religious activities. Social integration thus refers to the existence of social ties or network of relationships that individuals maintain with family, friends, and other groups such as social, cultural and religious organizations. It is through these ties that individuals are socially integrated into the larger society in which they live (Seeman, 1996), and these ties may control or regulate an individual's behaviors and thoughts that could influence health and well-being. Social integration often leads to the receipt of social support, thereby protecting the individual from isolation (Su & Ferraro, 1997).

The concept of social integration thus includes social ties, social support, and affiliation and participation in social, cultural, and religious activities. Social ties are typically a measure of the number of social relationships, marital status, and amount or frequency of social contact. Research among minorities and immigrants has shown geographic propinquity and strong kinship ties among family members to be important factors contributing to well-being (Kim & McHenry, 1998). Social support is measured by instrumental and emotional support received from others, and perceived support, i.e., the perception that support is available when needed. Research indicates that perceived support is associated with better physical and mental health in that it acts as a buffer against the impact of stressful life events (Thoits, 1995). Participation in social, cultural, and religious institutions are assessed by frequency of participation in these activities (Unger, McAvay, Bruce, Berkman & Seeman, 1999; Seeman, 1996). Religious involvement such as church attendance has been shown to have a salutary effect on health (Ellison & Levin, 1998; Seeman, 1996).

The voluminous literature on social integration indicates that this variable is a key determinant of well-being. Among older individuals, social integration is associated with health outcomes such as a lower risk of mortality, CVD, cancer mortality, and functional decline (see Unger et al., 1999). Although social integration varies by gender and ethnicity, the extent to which the effects of social integration on health vary across population subgroups is not known.

## *OTHER PREDICTORS OF HEALTH STATUS*

Although social integration is the variable of interest in this study, it is necessary to examine other known correlates of health and account for their impact on the health status of older immigrants. In the general population, the excess morbidity and mortality associated with chronic diseases have been attributed to greater prevalence of a number of risk factors such as obesity, physical inactivity, poor nutrition, and other factors such as lower SES (Morbidity and Mortality Weekly Report, 2000). Body mass index (BMI), which is a measure used to determine obesity, is recognized as an independent risk factor for CVD, elevated blood lipids, cancer, and chronic conditions such as hypertension, arthritis, and a decrease in functional capacity of individuals. Ferraro, Farmer and Wybraniec (1997) noted that obese individuals tended to report more negative health ratings, higher morbidity, increased disability, and increased restriction in activities. Thus, the impact of BMI needs to be accounted for when examining other predictors of health.

Increasing age and lower socioeconomic status have been found to be strongly associated with poorer health status (van den Akker et al., 2000). Other studies have found gender and race (being female and white) to be associated with increased risk for individual chronic conditions such as heart disease, with a decline in these differences as age increases (Fillenbaum, Pieper, Cohen, Cornoni-Huntley & Guralnik, 2000).

Acculturation is another factor that can influence the health outcomes of first generation immigrants. Acculturation refers to the cultural change that occurs as a result of continued contact between two distinct cultures. Greater length of residence in the U.S. has been associated with dietary changes in a sample of Asian Indians where consumption of non-ethnic foods and alcohol increased with longer residence (Raj, Ganganna & Bowering, 1999; Yagalla, Hoerr, Song, Enas & Garg, 1999). Length of residence in the U.S. could have an impact on an individual's health status not only through the changes that occur in diet and lifestyle, but also through changes in social integration. Therefore, length of residence in the U.S. is used as a proxy variable for acculturative changes.

Thus, despite the growing numbers of older, first-generation immigrant Asian Indians who appear to be at greater risk for morbidity and mortality, relatively few studies have examined the psychosocial factors that may be associated with the overall health of this group. This exploratory study therefore seeks to understand the relationship between poor health (defined as the presence of one or more chronic health conditions) and the social integration of older Asian Indian immigrants. The hypothesis is that greater social integration will be associated with better health after controlling for the impact of BMI, length of residence in the U.S., and demographic characteristics in a sample of older, first generation Asian Indian immigrants to the U.S.

## *METHODS*

### *Sample*

Asian Indian men and women over 50 years of age residing in the metropolitan Atlanta area and who have lived in the U.S. for a minimum of five years were the target population for this study. Estimates of the total AI population in the metropolitan Atlanta area in 1999 ranged from approximately 30,000 to 50,000 individuals. Access to this ethnic population was obtained by getting membership information from various Asian Indian community organizations that cover a wide variety of religious, cultural, professional, and linguistic affiliations. Several participants also referred us to their friends and acquaintances for inclusion in the sample. The sampling strategy used for this study was purposive and non-random. The sampling frame consisted of members of ten Asian Indian community organizations representing the various linguistic groups in India. Many older, first generation AI immigrants belong to one or more of these ethnic community organizations given the significance of these organizations in maintaining social, cultural, and religious traditions. As Kim and McHenry (1998) note, Asian Americans have a greater likelihood of participating in nationality groups as compared to other minorities. This sampling approach was necessary as existing data sets on aging populations in the U.S. rarely include sufficient numbers of APIs to enable an examination of the health of various subgroups within this minority classification (LaViest, 1995).

Using the techniques recommended by Dillman (1978), potential participants (i.e., those around age 50 or more) from the various databases provided by the organizations were sent an initial recruitment letter, which explained the purpose of the study. Subsequently a trained interviewer contacted the participants via telephone to conduct the survey. Participants were given the option not to answer any of the survey questions and their willingness to complete the survey was taken as an indicator of consent to participate in the study. Letters were sent to a total of 542 individuals of which 6% were unreachable due to the lack of correct phone numbers, and 26% were unreachable after numerous attempts on evenings, weekends, and additional efforts to locate them at varying times over several months. As suggested by Dillman (1978), the response rate was calculated on the basis of the number of individuals with whom an actual phone contact was made. Thus, of the 365 individuals successfully contacted by telephone 237 (65%) completed the survey, 75 (20%) refused, 40 (11%) were under 40 years of age, and 13 (4%) were unable to communicate in English. After a preliminary analysis we found eleven respondents to be under 50 years of age, and we excluded them from further analysis in this study.

### Measures

*Health status* was measured by an index of seven self-reported health conditions, i.e., heart disease, stroke, high blood pressure, diabetes, cancer, arthritis, and weakness in the arms or legs. These conditions are among the most commonly reported problems in older populations. The use of self-reported data to determine health status has been discussed extensively in the literature and findings indicate this method to yield valid results (Ferraro & Farmer, 1999).

The social integration variables were based on several items used in large-scale surveys of older Americans such as the Health and Retirement Survey (HRS). Three aspects of social integration were assessed: perceived availability of support, social ties, and social contact and participation in community-based activities. *Perceived social support* was measured by an index of two questions that assessed the perceived availability of persons to depend on for everyday matters and for emergencies. Higher scores on perceived support indicated perception of greater support. Social ties were assessed through marital status, and presence of family and friends nearby. *Marital status* was measured dichotomously as married (1) or not married (0). *Family nearby* was a dichotomous variable that asked whether the individual had any relatives living nearby within an hour's drive (1 = yes, 0 = no). *Friends nearby* was also a dichotomous variable that asked whether the individual had any good friends in the neighborhood (1 = yes, 0 = no). Social contact and participation were assessed through two variables: frequency of *social activity with friends* which had the following response categories: more than once a week, once a week, every 2-3 weeks, every month or two, 1-5 times a year, less than once a year, never; and frequency of *Visits to place of worship* which was coded as: more than once a week, once a week, once in 2-3 weeks, once a month, less than once a month. Higher scores on both the social contact variables indicated greater contact.

*Body Mass Index* (BMI) was calculated as the ratio of weight (kg) to height squared ($m^2$). Height and weight measures were self-reported. Acculturation was assessed by *length of residence in the U.S.* measured in number of years. *Demographic characteristics* included age, gender, and income. *Income* was assessed by a scale measuring income in intervals of $15,000 ranging from below $10,000 to $100,000 or more.

### Data Analysis

Descriptive data (mean, SD, and frequencies) were used to provide a profile of the sample. Pearson correlation coefficients were calculated for all the study variables to examine their bivariate relationships. Because the dependent variable (health status) is based on a count of the number of chronic health conditions in an individual, Poisson regression was used (see McCullagh & Nelder, 1989). Count outcomes are characterized by the fact that most individuals have a score of zero and the proportion of individuals with a specific positive value decreases as the value of the count increases (Frone, 1997). The assumption in Poisson regression is that the variance of the count variable (number of chronic conditions) is equal to its mean. Counts in which the variance is greater than the mean are said to be overdispersed, and a commonly used alternative for model estimation in the presence of overdispersion is to fit a negative binomial model to the data (Zorn, 1998; Frone 1997).

Using STATA (Statacorp, 1997, version 6), a Poisson regression analysis of the predictors of health status was done with a robust variance estimator for data clustered by couples. This method is appropriate because of the presence of several married couples (n = 40) in the sample where some correlation is likely between the responses of husbands and wives on variables such as income. The robust variance estimator developed by White (1980) (also called the Huber or sandwich estimator) was used to yield consistent standard errors for clustered data.

## *RESULTS*

### *Characteristics of the Sample*

Table 1 presents the characteristics of the sample. Seventy-two percent of the respondents were males and 93% were married. The ages of the respondents ranged from 50 to 78 years, with the mean age being 57.6 years (s.d. = 5.8). The average length of residence in the U.S. was 24.8 years (s.d. = 8.7). Fifty-eight percent of the sample had post-graduate and professional degrees, 68% were employed fulltime, and 79% were employed in executive and professional jobs. Participants hailed from all parts of India, representing at least 15 different states or linguistic groups. Data on the current annual household income indicates that the study participants were a diverse group with respect to SES. The mean BMI of 24.9 (s.d.= 3.2) was indicative of an overweight sample in general.

The median score on health status was 1 (mean = 0.95; s.d. = 1.01) with a range of 0 to 4 health conditions. Hypertension was the most common self-reported morbid condition followed by diabetes, weak-

TABLE 1. Sample Characteristics (n = 226)

| | N | % |
|---|---|---|
| Females | 64 | 28 |
| Married | 211 | 93 |
| **Education*** | | |
| High school or less | 16 | 7 |
| Some college | 13 | 5 |
| College graduate | 65 | 29 |
| Post graduate/professional degree | 130 | 58 |
| **Employment Status** | | |
| Employed full-time | 154 | 68 |
| Retired | 38 | 17 |
| Other | 34 | 16 |
| **Occupation*** | | |
| Executive/administrative/managerial | 75 | 34 |
| Professional/technical | 99 | 45 |
| Other | 44 | 21 |
| **Current Annual Household Income*** | | |
| < $ 10,000 | 3 | 1.4 |
| $10,000-$40,000 | 28 | 13 |
| $40,000-$70,000 | 39 | 19 |
| $70,000-$100,000 | 36 | 17 |
| > $100,000 | 103 | 49 |
| | **Mean SD** | |
| Age (years) | 57.6 (5.8) | |
| Length of residence in the U.S. (years) | 24.8 (8.7) | |
| BMI (kg/m2) | 24.9 (3.2) | |

*Numbers do not add up to 226 due to missing data

ness in arms and legs, and arthritis (see Table 2). The prevalence of hypertension (31.2%), diabetes (18%), and heart disease (7.1%) observed in this sample is similar to studies of AI immigrants in other countries as reported by Sheth et al. (1999), Sherwin and Sengupta (1996), Bhatnagar et al. (1995), Chaturvedi and Fuller (1996) and the U.K. Prospective Diabetes Study Group (1998).

A majority of the study participants perceived having some form of social support for both daily and emergency needs. The mean score on the perceived support index was 2.55 (s.d. = 0.62) and the range was from 1 to 3, with higher scores indicating greater perceived support. The mean scores on frequency of socializing and going to places of worship were 3.4 (s.d. = 1.19) and 2.62 (s.d. = 1.42) respectively, with

TABLE 2. Presence of Chronic Health Conditions in the Sample

| | N | % reporting presence of condition |
|---|---|---|
| High blood pressure | 70 | 31.2 |
| Diabetes | 40 | 18 |
| Weakness in arms and legs | 38 | 17 |
| Arthritis | 37 | 17 |
| Heart disease | 16 | 7.1 |
| Cancer | 9 | 4 |
| Stroke | 6 | 2.7 |

higher scores indicating greater frequency. Sixty-six percent reported having a good friend in the neighborhood, and 52 percent reported having a relative living nearby.

Table 3 presents the Pearson correlation coefficients between the study variables. Health status was associated with age, gender, BMI and having family nearby. None of the other variables had significant independent associations with health status.

### *Predictors of Health Status*

A Poisson regression analysis was done with health status as the dependent variable. The independent variables were perceived support, marital status, frequency of socializing, frequency of visiting places of worship, presence of relatives and friends nearby, BMI, length of residence in the U.S., age, gender, and income. Poorer health status was associated with not having family nearby, perceiving less availability of social support, older age, female gender, higher BMI scores, and longer length of residence in the U.S. (see Table 4). The full model was significant (chi sq = 91.06, $p < 0.0000$). To test whether the results would change after explicitly controlling for over-dispersion, the model was also estimated using a negative binomial specification that yielded results identical to the Poisson regression with no change in the log-likelihood. Table 4 indicates that the risk of poorer health status increased by 6% for every unit increase in BMI, by 7% for each year increase in age, by 2% for each additional year of residence in the U.S., and by 57% for not having family nearby. The risk of poorer health status decreased by 26% with a one-unit increase in perceived support. Women had a 83% greater risk of reporting poorer health status.

TABLE 3. Pearson Correlation Coefficients Between Study Variables

| | HLT | AGE | GEN | INC | BMI | USY | WOR | SOC | SUPP | FAM | FRI | MARS |
|---|---|---|---|---|---|---|---|---|---|---|---|---|
| HLT | **1.00** | | | | | | | | | | | |
| AGE | 0.40* | **1.00** | | | | | | | | | | |
| GEN | 0.18* | −0.12 | **1.00** | | | | | | | | | |
| INC | −0.12 | −0.12 | −0.06 | **1.00** | | | | | | | | |
| BMI | 0.16* | −0.02 | −0.01 | 0.06 | **1.00** | | | | | | | |
| USY | 0.11 | 0.20* | −0.01 | 0.34* | −0.09 | **1.00** | | | | | | |
| WOR | −0.02 | 0.03 | 0.06 | −0.08 | −0.01 | −0.08 | **1.00** | | | | | |
| SOC | −0.11 | −0.19* | −0.05 | 0.13 | 0.04 | −0.04 | 0.21* | **1.00** | | | | |
| SUPP | −0.07 | −0.07 | 0.06 | 0.08 | 0.07 | 0.07 | 0.01 | 0.20* | **1.00** | | | |
| FAM | 0.16* | −0.02 | −0.02 | −0.05 | 0.05 | 0.01 | 0.01 | 0.13* | 0.10 | **1.00** | | |
| FRI | −0.01 | −0.14* | −0.13 | −0.05 | 0.11 | 0.03 | 0.10 | 0.01 | 0.14* | 0.10 | **1.00** | |
| MARS | −0.06 | −0.06 | −0.11 | 0.01 | 0.07 | −0.13* | 0.04 | 0.15* | 0.02 | 0.02 | 0.10 | **1.00** |

HLT = health status, GEN = gender, INC = income, BMI = body mass index, USY = length of residence in U.S., WOR = go to place of worship, SOC = socialize with friends, SUPP = perceived support, FAM = relatives nearby, FRI = friends nearby, MARS = marital status
* $p < 0.05$

## *IMPLICATIONS FOR SOCIAL WORK*

This study expands previous research on the health of AI immigrants by examining the impact of social integration on health. The results indicate that greater perceived support and having relatives nearby had a significant impact on health status after controlling for the influence of several covariates. Other factors significantly associated with health were BMI, longer length of residence in the U.S., being older, and being female.

The findings of this study are consistent with those found in the literature on social integration and well-being. Although this study is cross-sectional and cannot make claims regarding direction and causality, one can expect these results to be similar to those found in longitudinal studies on social integration and health among Caucasian and other minority populations. Thus, among older Asian Indian immigrants, we are likely to find social integration to be protective of health and emotional well-being. Undoubtedly, panel data on this population is needed to verify this assumption.

As with other minority groups (Kim & McHenry, 1998) family contact plays a vital role in the well-being of this immigrant community. However, about half of the respondents did not have any family members living nearby. This may partly be explained by the greater geographic mobility among this highly educated and professionally trained group of immigrants. It may therefore be important for this group of first-generation immigrants to develop closer ties with individuals and groups outside the family.

The findings suggest that interventions to increase social integration may enhance the health of this immigrant group. These interventions should include increasing opportunities for social contact and for involvement in social networks geared to meet a variety of needs. Such interventions are likely to be accepted in this community, as they would address a need expressed by the respondents themselves. For instance, at the end of the survey, respondents were asked by an open-ended question to describe any services, programs, etc., that they would like to see provided by ethnic community organizations. Many respondents remarked on the need for a place for older people to meet and socialize, and for social activities to be organized. These interventions can be implemented both by mainstream as well as ethnic community organizations.

The literature on the impact of social integration on nutrition and health behaviors suggests that individuals who are more isolated, or

TABLE 4. Predictors of Health Status

| | Odds Ratio | Confidence Interval (95%) | Z values | Probability |
|---|---|---|---|---|
| Perceived support availability | 0.74 | 0.60-0.90 | −2.94 | 0.003 |
| Family nearby (0 = No) | 1.57 | 1.15-2.15 | 2.89 | 0.004 |
| Friends nearby (0 = No) | 1.05 | 0.75-1.49 | 0.32 | 0.74 |
| Visit place of worship | 0.90 | 0.83-1.02 | −1.42 | 0.15 |
| Socialize | 1.01 | 0.88-1.15 | 0.17 | 0.86 |
| Marital Status (0 = Unmarried) | 1.01 | 0.46-2.20 | 0.04 | 0.96 |
| Body Mass Index | 1.06 | 1.01-1.10 | 2.86 | 0.004 |
| Age | 1.07 | 1.04-1.09 | 5.90 | 0.0005 |
| Gender (0 = Male) | 1.83 | 1.35-2.47 | 3.95 | 0.0005 |
| Income | 0.93 | 0.86-1.01 | −1.56 | 0.11 |
| Length of residence in U.S. | 1.02 | 1.00-1.05 | 2.26 | 0.02 |

have fewer social supports, tend to have poorer diets and fewer health-promoting behaviors (Rosenbloom & Whittington, 1993). Thus, interventions to promote socialization should also include education and awareness of issues related to health promotion and disease prevention. For example, individuals need to become aware of the impact on health of body mass index and acculturative stress, and be educated in ways to alter or lessen the impact of these conditions.

Consistent with the literature (Fillenbaum et al., 2000) increasing age and female gender were associated with poorer health status in this sample. The research on other minority populations (mostly African American and Hispanic) shows women to have higher BMIs than men. We examined the interaction between gender and BMI to assess whether it influenced health status and found it not to be significant. Due to the relatively smaller number of women in this sample it was not feasible to do separate analyses by gender. There is, however, a need to further investigate the relationship between gender and health status among AI immigrants.

In this ethnic community, the role of temples and other places of worship need to be considered in developing social and health interventions. Frequency of visiting places of worship approached significance as a variable influencing health status. The bivariate correlations indicate that this variable was significantly related to frequency of socialization. Places of worship play a significant role in the life of community members and can be assets or resources in reaching out to large numbers of individuals in the community, especially for whom religious activity is the primary source of social contact.

By examining a cross-section of older Asian Indian immigrants, this research highlights the needs of more vulnerable individuals within this community. Anecdotal evidence suggests that many members of this community buy into the idea of being a model minority, thus ignoring the needs of individuals who are less well off within the community. This results not only in this at-risk group being ignored by mainstream researchers and service providers, but also by members of the ethnic community themselves. Future research will need to examine predictors of social isolation (for example, personality factors and feelings of being marginal within the mainstream and the ethnic community) to guide interventions and services specifically targeted to such individuals.

One of the limitations of this study is the non-random nature of the sample. It is possible that these findings may be attributable to sample selection issues. Thus, generalizability of the findings is limited to the groups represented in the sample (members of various organizations) but not to other individuals, for example, those who could not speak English fluently. Despite the non-random nature of the sample, its strength is that it does represent various segments of the immigrant AI community with respect to diversity in income and linguistic affiliation. Although it is not possible to establish cause and effect with a cross sectional sample, the findings of this research are consistent with previous studies on social integration and health status among other populations.

Despite these limitations this study has some important findings. Considerable diversity exists within this Asian Indian immigrant community in the US, and this research provides a glimpse of the impact of this diversity on the health status of the community. The prevalence of morbidity observed in this sample is similar to that found in studies of AI immigrants in other countries. This study highlights the usefulness of examining psychosocial correlates of morbidity, as differences in health status within this immigrant group can be attributed to many variables beyond the physiological characteristics currently examined in the literature.

Future research will need to encompass greater numbers of women, older individuals who have immigrated later in life, and those who are unable to communicate in English to better understand variations in the health and well-being members of this immigrant group.

## REFERENCES

Balarajan, R. (1991). Ethnic differences in mortality from ischemic heart disease and cerebrovascular disease in England and Wales. *British Medical Journal*, 302, 560-564.

Banerji, M.A., Faridi, N., Atluri, R., Chaiken, R.L., & Lebovitz, H.E. (1999). Body composition, visceral fat, leptin, and insulin resistance in Asian Indian men. *Journal of Clinical Endocrinology and Metabolism*, 84, 137-144.

Bennett, C.E. & Martin, B. (1997). The Asian and Pacific Islander population. *Asian and Pacific Islanders in the United States. 1990 CP-3-5, 1990 Census Report*, U.S. Census Bureau.

Bhatnagar, D., Anand, I.S., Durrington, P.N., Patel, D.J., Wander, G.S., & Mackness, M.I. (1995). Coronary risk factors in people from the Indian subcontinent living in West London and their siblings in India. *Lancet*, 345, 405-409.

Blesch, K.S., Davis, F., & Kamath, S.K. (1999). A comparison of breast and colon cancer incidence rate among Native Asian Indians, US immigrant Asian Indians, and whites. *Journal of the American Dietetic Association*, 99, 1275-1277.

Chaturvedi, N., & Fuller, J.H. (1996). Ethnic differences in mortality from cardiovascular disease in the UK: Do they persist in people with diabetes? *Journal of Epidemiology and Community Health*, 50, 137-139.

Dillman, D.A. (1978). *Mail and telephone surveys: The total design method.* New York, NY: Wiley-Interscience Publication.

Durkheim, E. (1951). *Suicide*. Original publication 1897. New York, NY: Free Press.

Ellison, C.G., & Levin, J.S. (1998). The religion-health connection: Evidence, theory, and future directions. *Health Education and Behavior*, 25(6), 700-720.

Enas, F.A., Davidson, M.A., Garg, A., Nair, V.M, & Yusuf, S. (1991). Prevalence of coronary heart disease and its risk factors in Asian Indian migrants to the United States. *Proceedings International Symposium, Atherosclerosis*, Rosemont, IL.

Enas, E.A., Yusuf, S., & Mehta, J.L. (1992). Prevalence of coronary artery disease in Asian Indians. *American Journal Cardiology*, 70, 945-949.

Ferraro, K.F., & Farmer, M.M. (1999). Utility of health data from social surveys: Is there a gold standard for measuring morbidity? *American Sociological Review*, 64, 303-315.

Ferraro, K.F., Farmer, M.M., & Wybraniec, J.A. (1997). Health trajectories: Long-term dynamics among Black and White adults. *Journal of Health and Social Behavior*, 38, 38-54.

Fillenbaum, G.G., Pieper, C.F., Cohen, H.J., Cornoni-Huntley, J.C., & Guralnik, J.M. (2000). Comorbidity of five chronic health conditions in elderly community residents: Determinants and impact on mortality. *Journal of Gerontology: Medical Sciences*, 55A(2), M84-M89.

Frone, M.R. (1997). *Regression models for discrete and limited dependent variables*, Research Methods Division, Academy of Management. <www.aom.pace.edu/rmd/1997_forum_regression_models.html>. Accessed 9/1/2000.

Gibson, M.A. (1988). *Accommodation without assimilation: Sikh immigrants in an American high school*. Ithaca, NY: Cornell University Press.

Gupta, S., deBelder, A., & Hughes, L.O. (1995). Avoiding premature coronary deaths in Asians in Britain. *British Medical Journal (International)*, 311, 1035-1036.

Hao, L., & Johnson, R.W. (2000). Economic, cultural, and social origins of emotional well-being: Comparisons of immigrants and natives at midlife. *Research on Aging*, 22(6), 599-629.

Hoyert, D.L., & Kung, H.C. (1997). Asian or Pacific Islander mortality, selected states, 1992. *Monthly Vital Statistics Report*, 46 (suppl 1), 1-64.

Humes, K. & Mckinnon, J. (2000). *The Asian and Pacific Islander population in the United States: March 1999*. U.S. Census Bureau, Current Population Reports, Series P20-529, Washington, D.C., U.S. Government Printing Office.

Kim, H.K., & McKenry, P.C. (1998). Social networks and support: A comparison of African Americans, Asian Americans, Caucasians, and Hispanics. *Journal of Comparative Family Studies*, 29(2), 313-334.

LaViest, T.A. (1995). Data sources for aging research on racial and ethnic groups. *The Gerontologist*, 35(3), 328-339.

Laws, A., Jeppesen, J.L., Maheux, P.C., Schaaf, P., Chen, Y.D., Reaven, G.M. (1994). Resistance to insulin-stimulated glucose uptake and dyslipidemia in Asian Indians. *Arteriosclerosis Thrombosis*, 14, 917-922.

McCullagh, P., & Nelder, J.A. (1989).*Generalized Linear Models*, London, England: Chapman & Hall Ltd.

McKeigue, P.M., Miller, G.J., & Marmot, M.G. (1989). Coronary heart disease in South Asians overseas: A review. *Journal of Clinical Epidemiology*, 42, 597-609.

McKeigue, P.M., Shah, G., & Marmot, M.G. (1991). Relation of central obesity and insulin resistance with high diabetes prevalence and cardiovascular risk in South Asians. *Lancet*, 337, 382-386.

Morbidity and Mortality Weekly Reports. (2000). Age-specific excess deaths associated with stroke among racial/ethnic minority populations-United States, 1997. *Morbidity and Mortality Weekly Reports*, 49(5), 94-97.

Raj, S., Ganganna, P., & Bowering, J. (1999). Dietary habits of Asian Indians in relation to length of residence in the United States. *Journal of the American Dietetic Association*, 99, 1106-1108.

Rosenbloom, C.A., & Whittington, F.J. (1993). The effects of bereavement on eating behaviors and nutrient intakes in elderly widowed persons. *Journal of Gerontology: Social Sciences*, 48, S223-S229.

Seely, S. (1996). The Indian puzzle. *International Journal of Cardiology*, 56, 299-300.

Seeman, T. (1996). Social ties and health: The benefits of social integration. *Annals of Epidemiology*, 6(5), 442-451.

Sherwin, R., & Sengupta, A. (1996). Blood pressure in minorities screened for the multiple risk factor intervention trial (MRFIT). *Public Health Reports*, 111 (Suppl), 68-70.

Sheth, T., Nair, C., Nargundkar, M., Anand, S., & Yusuf, S. (1999). Cardiovascular and cancer mortality among Canadians of European, South Asian and Chinese origin from 1979 to 1993: An analysis of 1.2 million deaths. *Canadian Medical Association Journal*, 161, 132-138.

StataCorp. (1997). *Stata Statistical Software: Release 6.0*, College Station, TX: Stata Corporation.

Su, Y., & Ferraro, K.F. (1997). Social relations and health assessments among older people: Do the effects of integration and social contributions vary cross-culturally? *The Journals of Gerontology: Social Sciences*, 52B(1), S27-S36.

Thoits, P.A. (1995). Stress, coping, and social support processes: Where are we? What next? *Journal of Health and Social Behavior*, Extra issue, 53-79.

U.K. Prospective Diabetes Study Group. (1998). Ethnicity and cardiovascular disease. The incidence of myocardial infarction in white, South Asian, and Afro-Caribbean patients with type 2 diabetes (U.K. Prospective Diabetes Study 32). *Diabetes Care*, 21, 1271-1277.

Unger, J.B., McAvay, G., Bruce, M.L., Berkman, L., & Seeman, T. (1999). Variation in the impact of social network characteristics on physical functioning in elderly persons: MacArthur studies of successful aging. *Journals of Gerontology*, 54B, S245-S251.

U.S. Census Bureau. (1998). Census Bureau facts for features: Asian and Pacific Islander heritage month. CB98-FF.05. <www.census.gov/Press-Release/ff98-05.html>. April 27, 1998.

van den Akker, M., Buntinx, F., Metsemakers, J.F.M., & Knottnerus, J.M. (2000). Marginal impact of psychosocial factors on multimorbidity: Results of an explorative nested case-control study. *Social Sciences & Medicine*, 50, 1679-1693.

White, H. (1980). A heteroskedasticity-consistent covariance matrix estimator and a direct test for heteroskedasticity. *Econometrica*, 48, 817-830.

Yagalla, M.V., Hoerr, S.L., Song, W.O., Enas, E. & Garg, A. (1996). Relationship of diet, abdominal obesity, and physical activity to plasma lipoprotein levels in Asian Indian physicians in the United States. *Journal of the American Dietetic Association*, 96, 257-261.

Yu, E.S., & Liu, W.T. (1992). U.S. National health data on Asian Americans and Pacific Islanders: A research agenda for 1990s. *American Journal Public Health*, 82, 1645-1652.

Zorn, C.J. (1998). An analytic and empirical examination of zero-inflated and hurdle Poisson specifications. *Sociological Methods & Research*, 26, 368-401.

# Stress, Coping, and Depression Among Japanese American Elders

Tazuko Shibusawa, PhD
Ada C. Mui, PhD

**SUMMARY.** This study examines the correlates of depression among Japanese American elders among 131 community-dwelling Japanese American elders aged 60 years or older. Predictors of depression were examined from a stress and coping framework. Depression was measured using the Geriatric Depression Scale (GDS). Close to 20% of the respondents were mildly depressed. Multiple regression analyses revealed that health, fear of dependency on family, number of close friends, and availability of emotional support were associated with depression. Previous studies indicate that traditional Japanese values of interdependence facilitate dependency on family among Japanese American elders. The findings of this study, however, suggest that the prospect of becoming dependent on family is a source of distress in this population. Culturally appropriate ways for social

---

Tazuko Shibusawa and Ada C. Mui are affiliated with Columbia University School of Social Work.

Address correspondence to: Tazuko Shibusawa, PhD, MSW, Assistant Professor, Columbia University School of Social Work, 622 West 113th Street, New York, NY 10025-4600 (E-mail: ts250@columbia.edu).

This research was supported by the Center for the Study of Social Work Practice, a joint program of the Columbia University School of Social Work and the Jewish Board of Family and Children's Services.

[Haworth co-indexing entry note]: "Stress, Coping, and Depression Among Japanese American Elders." Shibusawa, Tazuko, and Ada C. Mui. Co-published simultaneously in *Journal of Gerontological Social Work* (The Haworth Social Work Practice Press, an imprint of The Haworth Press, Inc.) Vol. 36, No. 1/2, 2001, pp. 63-81; and: *Social Work Practice with the Asian American Elderly* (ed: Namkee G. Choi) The Haworth Social Work Practice Press, an imprint of The Haworth Press, Inc., 2001, pp. 63-81. Single or multiple copies of this article are available for a fee from The Haworth Document Delivery Service [1-800-HAWORTH, 9:00 a.m. - 5:00 p.m. (EST). E-mail address: getinfo@haworthpressinc.com].

 

workers to address fear of dependency among Japanese American elders are presented. 

**KEYWORDS.** Japanese American, dependency, stress and coping, depression, social support

In recent years, Asian American and Pacific Islander (API) elders had the largest increase among all ethnic elderly populations in the United States. The population of older APIs increased by 115% between 1980 and 1990. Although data from the 2000 Census were not available at the time of this writing, there is no reason to think that this trend has not continued. It is estimated that in the next 50 years, the number of older APIs will increase by 1000% (U.S. Bureau of the Census, 1993, as cited by Tanjasiri et al., 1997).

The older API population is diverse, comprising of at least 60 different nationalities (Kagawa-Singer, Hikoyeda, & Tanjasiri, 1997). Their immigration history also varies. The Pacific Islanders in Hawaii are native to the United States, while the Chinese and Japanese first immigrated to the United States in the late 1800s. However, the Southeast Asians such as the Vietnamese, Cambodian, Laotian, and Hmong immigrated during the 1970s and 1980s.

Despite the increase in this population, substantial knowledge gaps exist regarding their physical and mental health status. This is, in part, because Asian Americans were not included as an ethnic category in the national health statistics until 1979 and, were not disaggregated by subethnic groups until 1992 (Elo, 1997). Furthermore, methodological difficulties in sampling due to small population size and misperceptions regarding the existence of health and mental health problems have resulted in the lack of epidemiological studies.

## *MENTAL HEALTH STATUS OF ASIAN AMERICAN ELDERS*

Most studies examining the mental health status of Asian American elders have relied on relatively small, nonrandom samples. In recent years, however, studies utilizing validated measurements have become more available. Table 1 presents research using validated instruments among community-dwelling Asian American elders. Although not all the instruments have been validated for use with Asian Americans, the studies represent an emerging field of empirically based research among this population. For example, Kuo's (1984) study using the Center of Epidemiological Studies of Depression Scale (CES-D) to examine the mental health status of Asian American elders indicates higher rates of depression among Chinese, Filipino, Japanese, and Korean elders than among white elders. Gender differences were also found in which Chinese and Filipino women, and Japanese and Korean men had the highest rates of depression. In general, poor health status, lack of social support, and low acculturation have been reported as the main predictors of depression among Asian American elders (Lam, 1999; Lee et al., 1996; Moon & Pearl, 1991). Mui (1996b) reported that poor self-rated health status, living alone, and dissatisfaction with family support were predictors of depression among Chinese elders in New York.

Only two studies using validated measurements have been conducted to specifically examine mental health among Japanese American elders (Iwamasa, 1998). Yamamoto et al. (1985) identified 27% with symptoms of dysthymia and 3% with symptoms of major depression in a nonclinic sample of 78 respondents. Iwamasa (1998), using the Geriatric Depression Scale (GDS) among 86 community-dwelling elders, did not find any respondents with depressive symptoms. In the present study, a stress and coping framework (Lazarus & Folkman, 1984) is used to conceptualize and examine the relationship among stresses, coping resources, and depression in Japanese American elders.

## *STRESS AND COPING AMONG OLDER ASIAN PACIFIC ISLANDERS*

According to the stress and coping framework, stress is conceptualized as events and conditions that are perceived by the individual as a potentially difficult situation (Lazarus & Folkman, 1984). Stressors have been linked with negative mental health outcomes such as depression and anxiety (Lazarus & Folkman, 1984). Sources of stress include major life events, enduring problems, and daily hassles (Pearlin & Schooler, 1978). Responses to stress are associated with an individual's ability to cope and the resources that enable him or her to do so, including physical, psychological, spiritual, and social skills, as well as social support, which are seen as mitigating stress (Pearlin & Schooler, 1978). Sources of stress among older adults often include multiple losses such

TABLE 1. Depression Studies Among Community-Dwelling Asian American Elders Using Measurements

| Authors | Ethnicity/setting sample size | Measurement | Major findings |
|---|---|---|---|
| Iwamasa et al., (1998) | Japanese American Los Angeles (n = 86) | GDS[a] | Respondents were not depressed Mean score: males, 4.44; females, 4.36 |
| Kuo (1984) | Chinese, Filipinos, Japanese, Koreans Seattle | CES-D[b] | All four groups had higher CES-D scores than did Caucasians |
| Lam et al. (1997) | Chinese (n = 45) | GDS[a] | 30% were mildly to severely depressed; depression was associated with life satisfaction, satisfaction, health, years in the United States, acculturation, and language skills |
| Lee et al. (1996) | Elderly Korean immigrants (n = 200) | CES-D[b] | Depression was associated with having less friends and less social contacts. |
| Mui (1996) | Elderly Chinese (n = 50) New York | GDS[a] | Mean: 7.2, with 18% mildly to severely depressed; depression was associated with poor self-rated health, living alone, and dissatisfaction with family help |
| Pang (1995) | Elderly Korean immigrants (n = 69) | DIS-III[c] | Lifetime prevalence rate for the Korean immigrants, 7.1%. |
| Wong et al. (1999) | Asian elders (n = 77) Caucasians (n = 128) | BDI[d] | Self-reinforcement predicted depression for both groups while perceived control predicted only depression for the Caucasian group |
| Yamamoto et al. (1985) | Japanese American elders (n = 78) Los Angeles | DIS-III[c] | 27% dysthymia, 3% major depression |
| Yamamoto et al. (1994) | Elderly Korean immigrants (n = 100) Los Angeles | DIS-III[c] | Prevalence of generalized anxiety disorder, affective disorder and phobia among females and alcohol abuse and dependence among men. |

[a]GDS: Geriatric Depression Scale
[b]CES-D: Center for Epidemiological Studies of Depression Scale
[c]DIS-III: Diagnostic Interview Schedule
[d]BDI: Beck Depression Inventory

as the death of family and close friends and the decline of physical, social, and financial status.

Older APIs experience fear of racial discrimination and lack of culturally appropriate services in addition to the stressors just mentioned (Damon-Rodriguez, Wallace, & Kington, 1994). Furthermore, recently arrived older API immigrants experience loss of familiar environment, support systems, identity, and status as well as language barriers, altered social resources, changes in family relationships, and feelings of helplessness (Cheung, 1989; Kao & Lam, 1997; Le, 1997; Tsai & Lopez, 1997). Wong and Ujimoto (1998) point to the "the dual challenge of aging and acculturation" in which immigrant elders have to contend with their aging process and acculturation at the same time.

A major stressor among elders is the need to seek and depend on family members for care. Close to 40% of community-dwelling older adults in the United States are dependent on others for basic health and social support (Brody, 1985). Yet studies indicate negative associations between dependency and psychological well-being. In fact, the most important variable in low self-esteem among older adults is not the care they receive from their families, but the lack of physical, financial, and emotional independence (Clark, 1972; Stoller, 1985). In a society that values independence and self-reliance, elders who are unable to cope on their own suffer from embarrassment, shame, and a sense of failure (Johnson, 1990).

A number of studies examine dependency and psychological well-being among community-dwelling elders from the perspective of reciprocity. Elders are defined as being dependent if they receive more care or support than they give. The studies are based on the premise that elders have better psychological well-being if there is reciprocity. Attempts to link reciprocity and psychological well-being, however, show nondefinitive results. Some studies indicate positive associations between reciprocity and well-being (Antonucci & Akiyama, 1987), while others show negative (Lee & Ellithorpe, 1982) or inconclusive (Lee, Netzer, & Coward, 1995) associations.

Older immigrants tend to be more dependent on their families because they lack language skills and access to resources (Lubben & Becerra, 1983). This dependency, however, can threaten intergenerational solidarity and negatively impact older immigrants if families are not able or willing to provide assistance. Adult offspring may not be able to assist their parents because of their own struggles in adjusting to a new country (Yu & Wu, 1985). Other offspring may prefer to live in nonethnic neighborhoods and chose not live with their parents (Ishii-Kuntz, 1997). Isolation and lack of respect and caring from adult offspring have been identified as sources of stress among older Chinese immigrants (Cheung, 1989).

A study of Hispanic elders, using data from the 1988 National Survey of Hispanic Elderly People, found fear of overdependence on families to be a strong predictor of psychological distress among Cuban American and Puerto Rican elders (Mui, 1996c). As in Asian cultures, family bonding and reciprocity between generations is expected in Hispanic cultures (Mui, 1996c). The findings suggest that dependence on family can be a source of psychological distress especially among elders in family-centered cultures.

The present study examines stress and coping factors associated with depressive symptoms among older Japanese Americans. Among API elders, Japanese Americans have the largest proportion of elders 60 and over; 84% of Chinese and 92% of Korean elders are foreign born compared with only 32.4% of Japanese elders (U.S. Bureau of the Census, 1993). This is because the major wave of immigration from Japan took place between the late 1800s and early 1900s. Elders constitute 12% of the Japanese American population, an age structure similar to that of the white population (Lee, 1998). Currently, the largest elderly grouping in the Japanese American community comprises the second-generation men and women known as *Nisei,* who were born to first-generation immigrants, known as *Issei.* There are two groups of *Nisei*: those who grew up in the U.S., and those known as *Kibei Nisei,* who were born in the United States and then sent to Japan during their childhood to be educated in their parents' homeland. The latter are less acculturated than the former, preferring to speak Japanese, and sharing similarities with later-arriving immigrants from Japan known as *Shin Issei,* the "new first generation."

Research indicates that the first-generation Japanese American elders (*Issei*) adapted well to old age, and expressed less conflict over becoming dependent on their families than did their white counterparts (Kendis, 1989; Kiefer, 1974; Osako, 1979). Keifer (1974) attributes this to traditional Japanese culture, which views dependency as a normal part of the aging process. Elders in traditional Japanese society are expected to become dependent on their adult children when they become frail. This expectation is reinforced by Confucian norms of filial obligation (Keifer, 1974). Research among the second-generation *Nisei,* who embrace the Western values of independence and autonomy, on the other hand, indicate reluctance to become dependent on their children (Tomita, 1998). The norm of filial piety is declining among later-generation Japanese Americans, and thus the *Nisei* may not expect their children to care for them in old age (Ishii-Kuntz, 1997).

## METHOD

### Sample and Data Collection

The sample consists of 131 elderly Japanese Americans (53 male, 78 female), living in a major U.S. metropolitan area, who volunteered to participate in the study. Respondents were recruited through senior citizen centers and community service centers in the Japanese American community. They were included in the study when a social worker judged them to be mentally competent to participate. The response rate was 97%. Social workers and trained graduate students conducted face-to-face structured interviews at the senior centers or in the respondents' homes. Respondents were given the option of being interviewed in English or in Japanese. Each interview lasted between an hour and an hour and a half. Data were collected on sociodemographic characteristics, monthly income, social support, health and mental health status, life stressors, help-seeking attitudes, and knowledge and utilization of formal services.

### *Measurement*

#### *Dependent Variable*

The GDS was used to measure depression (Brink et al., 1982). It is a 30-item inventory with scores ranging from 0 to 30 representing the total number of depressive symptoms. Used widely in measuring depression among older adults, the GDS has excellent reliability and validity (test-retest reliability = .85; internal consistency = .94). The GDS correlates highly with other depression measures, and the authors reported an alpha reliability coefficient of .94 and a split-half reliability of .94 (Yesavage et al., 1983). A Japanese version of the GDS, which has been used widely in Japan (Matsubayashi et al., 1994) was used with the Japanese-speaking respondents.

#### *Independent Variables*

Stress factors included the total number of stressful life events, fear of dependency, and self-rated health. Stressful life events were measured by asking respondents if they had experienced the following 11 events in the preceding three years: (1) children moving out, (2) serious illness or injury, (3) being robbed or burglarized, (4) addition of new family members, (5) death of spouse, (6) death of other family member or good friend, (7) divorce or separation, (8) illness or injury of a family member, (9) change in residence, (10) family discord, and (11) change in financial status. These stressful life events were selected because they were used in previous research with Chinese elders (Chi & Boey, 1993) and found to have significant impact on depressive symptoms. Fear of dependency was measured by asking if the respondents worried about becoming too dependent on their family members (1 = yes, 0 =

no). Self-rated health was measured using a five-point scale with five being the highest. Acculturation, emotional support from family and friends, and number of close friends were conceptualized as coping resources. Acculturation was measured by language preference (Japanese or English), which is a commonly used method to assess acculturation among Asian elders (Burr & Mutcher, 1993). Social support was measured by the number of close family and friends, frequency of contact with other people, and the amount of emotional support from family or friends. A four-point Likert-like scale was used, with higher scores indicating more support (0-3).

## *RESULTS*

### *Sample Characteristics*

The sociodemographic characteristics of the respondents are presented by grouping them according to whether or not they fear dependency (Table 2). The respondents ranged from 63 to 97 years of age, with a mean age of 77 years; 60% were female while 40% were male; 35% were married, 45% widowed, and 19% divorced, separated, or never married. Close to 60% lived alone. The majority were either second generation born and raised in the United States (*Nisei*, 33.6%), second generation born in the United States and raised in Japan (*Kibei Nisei*, 29.8%), or new immigrants who had immigrated after the 1965 revision of the Immigration Act (*Shin Issei*, 32.8%). Of the respondents, 37% preferred to speak English while 63% preferred to speak Japanese. Close to one third of the respondents (31%) feared becoming dependent on their family, while two thirds (66%) did not fear dependency. Several significant differences were found between the two groups. Those who were female, less educated, unemployed, with lower levels of income, and and/or who were less acculturated tended to fear dependency.

### *Stresses, Coping Resources, and Depression*

As seen in Table 3, close to 30% of the respondents had experienced the death of a family member or friend, and had also experienced illness or injury in the preceding three years. Those who had suffered injury or illness were less likely to fear dependency on family. Over 16% had encountered illness or injury among family member(s). Most of the re-

TABLE 2. Demographic Characteristics of Sample by Attitudes Toward Dependency

| Characteristic | Total (n = 128) | No fear (n = 41) | Fear (n = 87) |
|---|---|---|---|
| **Age** | | | |
| 60-69 | 12.2 | 9.8 | 13.8 |
| 70-79 | 55.0 | 51.2 | 56.3 |
| 80-89 | 29.8 | 34.1 | 27.6 |
| 90+ | 3.1 | 4.9 | 2.3 |
| Mean age (*SD*) | 77.1 (6.50) | 78.5 (6.60) | 76.3 (6.48) |
| **Sex**** (female) | 59.5 | 39.0 | 67.8 |
| **Marital status** | | | |
| Married | 34.5 | 34.1 | 35.6 |
| Widowed | 45.8 | 43.9 | 47.1 |
| Separated/divorced | 11.5 | 14.6 | 9.2 |
| Never married | 8.4 | 7.3 | 8.0 |
| **Living arrangement** | | | |
| Alone | 58.0 | 61.0 | 55.2 |
| With spouse only | 29.0 | 24.4 | 32.3 |
| With spouse/child/grandchild | 5.3 | 7.3 | 4.6 |
| With child/grandchild | 4.6 | 7.3 | 3.4 |
| With other relatives | 0.8 | 0.0 | 1.1 |
| Other | 2.3 | 0.0 | 3.4 |
| **Education**** | | | |
| Less than high school | 13.0 | 14.6 | 11.5 |
| Some high school | 11.5 | 4.9 | 14.9 |
| High school graduate | 48.9 | 39.0 | 54.0 |
| Some technical training | 12.2 | 24.4 | 8.0 |
| Other | 0.8 | 2.4 | 0.0 |
| **Place of birth** | | | |
| United States | 64.9 | 75.6 | 59.8 |
| Japan | 32.8 | 22.0 | 37.9 |
| Other | 0.2 | 2.4 | 2.3 |
| **Language preference***** | | | |
| English | 37.4 | 61.0 | 26.4 |
| Japanese | 62.6 | 39.0 | 73.6 |
| **Generation** | | | |
| Issei | 3.1 | 4.9 | 2.3 |
| Shin Issei | 32.8 | 19.5 | 39.1 |
| Nisei | 33.6 | 48.8 | 25.3 |
| Kibei Nisei | 29.8 | 26.8 | 32.2 |
| Sansei | 0.8 | 0.0 | 1.1 |

TABLE 2 (continued)

| Characteristic | Total (n = 128) | No fear (n = 41) | Fear (n = 87) |
|---|---|---|---|
| **Employment*** | | | |
| Not employed | 87.8 | 77.4 | 94.9 |
| Employed | 12.2 | 22.6 | 5.1 |
| **Monthly income**** | | | |
| Less than $500 | 4.6 | 4.9 | 4.6 |
| $501-$1,000 | 49.6 | 34.1 | 57.5 |
| $1,001-$1,500 | 19.8 | 22.0 | 19.5 |
| $1,501-$2,000 | 10.7 | 17.1 | 6.9 |
| $2,001-$2,500 | 6.9 | 12.2 | 4.6 |
| $2,501 or more | 8.4 | 9.8 | 6.9 |
| **Self-rated health** | | | |
| Excellent | 6.9 | 7.3 | 6.9 |
| Very good | 14.5 | 7.3 | 18.4 |
| Good | 37.4 | 43.9 | 34.5 |
| Fair | 24.4 | 26.8 | 21.8 |
| Poor | 16.8 | 14.6 | 18.4 |

*$p < .05$, **$p < .01$, *** $p < .0001$

spondents considered themselves to be in good health, and thus health was not a stress factor in this population. In terms of coping resources, the two groups did not differ significantly in the number of close family and friends, the frequency of contact with other people, and the amount of emotional support from family or friends.

Responses to the GDS items and the mean scores are presented in Table 4. Respondents who expressed fear of dependency were more likely to feel helpless (item 10), worry about the future (item 13), and worry about the past (item 18) than those who did not. The overall mean for this group was 7.3 (*SD* = 5.7), which is significantly higher that the group that did not express fear of dependency (mean = 4.6, *SD* = 3.8). The alpha coefficient of GDS in this sample was .87, which indicates good reliability. Brink and colleagues (1982) consider a score of 10 on the GDS as the cutoff point for depression. Those who score between 11 to 20 are considered to be mildly depressed, and those who score 21 or above are considered to be moderately to severely depressed. According to the original cutoff points, 22.4% the respondents who expressed fear of dependency were mildly depressed compared to 10.3% of those who did not. Although the results of this study are not intended for population estimates, the rate of mild depression in this community sample was 18%, which is slightly higher than that of an elderly Chinese Amer-

TABLE 3. Stressful Life Events and Social Support by Attitudes Toward Dependency

| | Total (n =128) | No fear (n = 41) | Fear (n = 87) |
|---|---|---|---|
| **Stressful life events** | | | |
| Children move out | 3.1 | 4.9 | 2.3 |
| Robbed/burglarized | 9.2 | 12.2 | 8.0 |
| New family member | 9.2 | 9.8 | 9.2 |
| Death of spouse | 2.3 | 4.9 | 1.1 |
| Death of family/friend | 28.2 | 29.3 | 26.4 |
| Illness/injury (self)* | 29.0 | 41.5 | 23.0 |
| Illness/injury (family) | 16.8 | 17.1 | 16.1 |
| Change in residence | 6.9 | 12.2 | 4.6 |
| Family discord | 1.5 | 0.0 | 2.3 |
| Change in financial status | 3.8 | 7.3 | 2.3 |
| Mean | 1.10 (1.12) | 1.39 (1.38) | .95 (.99) |
| **Family satisfaction** | | | |
| Very satisfied | 76.4 | 82.5 | 72.9 |
| Somewhat satisfied | 16.5 | 10.0 | 20.0 |
| Somewhat dissatisfied | 4.7 | 5.0 | 4.7 |
| Very dissatisfied | 2.4 | 2.5 | 2.4 |
| **Social support mean (0-3)** | | | |
| Comfort | 1.68 (1.31) | 1.68 (1.37) | 1.70 (1.28) |
| Financial | .19 (.62) | .09 (.43) | .24 (.70) |
| Advice | 1.39 (1.27) | 1.24 (1.22) | 1.47 (1.28) |
| ADL | .27 (.82) | .31 (.84) | .26 (.81) |
| When ill | 1.59 (1.35) | 1.56 (1.38) | 1.62 (1.34) |
| Escort | .29 (.77) | .31 (.75) | .28 (.79) |
| **Has close friends (%)** | 80.9 | 87.8 | 77.0 |
| No. of close family | 2.81 (2.35) | 3.12 (2.41) | 2.53 (2.16) |
| No. of close friends | 2.57 (2.90) | 2.71 (2.34) | 2.65 (2.97) |

*$p < .05$, **$p < .01$, ***$p < .0001$

ican community sample as well as other community samples of elderly persons (Mui, 1996b; Rankin, Galbraith, & Johnson, 1993).

## *Correlates of Depression*

Depression was regressed with sociodemographic variables, fear of dependency, stress, and coping resource variables. Sociodemographic variables included age, gender, living arrangement, and income. Living arrangement was recoded into whether or not the respondents lived alone. Stress included self-rated health, and a sum of stressful events that the respondents had encountered during the preceding three years. Coping resources included the amount of emotional support received from others and the number of close friends.

TABLE 4. Percentage of Respondents Agreeing with Geriatric Depression Scale (GDS) Items

| Scale Item | Total ($n$ = 128) | No fear ($n$ = 41) | Fear ($n$ = 87) |
|---|---|---|---|
| 1. Satisfied with life | 93.1 | 92.7 | 93.1 |
| 2. Dropped activities and interest | 14.5 | 12.2 | 16.1 |
| 3. Life is empty | 25.0 | 23.1 | 25.6 |
| 4. Often got bored | 19.1 | 19.5 | 18.4 |
| 5. Hopeful about future | 52.7 | 74.4 | 43.7 |
| 6. Obsessive thoughts | 13.8 | 10.0 | 14.9 |
| 7. In good spirits | 94.6 | 97.6 | 93.0 |
| 8. Fear bad things | 13.0 | 14.6 | 12.6 |
| 9. Happy most of the time | 88.3 | 92.7 | 85.9 |
| 10. Often feel helpless* | 17.7 | 7.3 | 22.1 |
| 11. Often get restless | 15.3 | 12.2 | 16.1 |
| 12. Prefer to stay home | 44.5 | 33.3 | 50.0 |
| 13. Worry about the future* | 16.2 | 7.3 | 19.8 |
| 14. Problem with memory | 34.4 | 24.4 | 40.2 |
| 15. Wonderful to be alive* | 85.5 | 95.1 | 82.4 |
| 16. Feel downhearted and blue | 16.6 | 12.2 | 17.2 |
| 17. Feel worthless | 18.3 | 12.2 | 20.7 |
| 18. Worry about the past* | 9.2 | 2.4 | 11.5 |
| 19. Life is exciting | 72.3 | 80.5 | 69.0 |
| 20. Hard to start new projects | 38.5 | 40.0 | 37.9 |
| 21. Full of energy | 75.6 | 78.0 | 73.6 |
| 22. Situation hopeless | 20.0 | 14.6 | 20.9 |
| 23. Others are better off | 27.7 | 24.4 | 30.2 |
| 24. Upset over little things | 27.5 | 19.5 | 31.0 |
| 25. Feel like crying | 13.0 | 9.8 | 14.9 |
| 26. Trouble concentrating* | 19.2 | 9.8 | 24.4 |
| 27. Enjoy getting up in the morning* | 80.8 | 92.5 | 74.7 |
| 28. Avoid social gatherings | 32.8 | 24.4 | 36.8 |
| 29. Easy to make decisions | 74.6 | 82.5 | 70.1 |
| 30. Mind as clear as used to be | 68.5 | 78.0 | 62.8 |
| Mean** | 6.44 (5.29) | 4.63 (3.84) | 7.30 (5.70) |
| Diagnosis | | | |
| Normal (1-10) | 80.2 | 89.7 | 75.3 |
| Mildly depressed (11-20) | 18.3 | 10.3 | 22.4 |
| Moderately to severely depressed (21-30) | 1.5 | 0 | 2.4 |

*$p < .05$, ** $p < .001$, *** $p < .0001$

Table 5 shows the results of the hierarchical regression models. Depression was first regressed with sociodemographic variables and fear of dependency (Model 1). While none of the sociodemographic variables predicted depressive symptoms, fear of dependency (beta = .26) was a significant predictor of GDS scores. This model accounted for 7% of the variance. Stress and coping resource variables were then added to this model (Model 2). The most important predictive stressor was self-rated health (beta = −.45). The coping resource factors, which were significant in predicting depressive symptoms, were the number of close friends (beta = −.18) and the amount of emotional support (beta = −.16). This model explains 35% of the variance in GDS scores. The results suggest that respondents with poorer self-rated health, fear of dependency on family, fewer close friends and lack of emotional support reported more depressive symptoms.

TABLE 5. Predictors of Depressive Symptoms Among Japanese American Elders

| Predictors | Model 1<br>Betas | Model 2<br>Betas |
|---|---|---|
| Age | .066 | .053 |
| Gender | .123 | .020 |
| Income | −.155 | −.076 |
| Living alone | −.148 | −.025 |
| Fear of dependency | .256** | .236** |
| | | |
| Stressful events | | .051 |
| Self-rated health | | −.447*** |
| Acculturation | | −.036 |
| Emotional support | | −.161* |
| Number of close friends | | −.177* |
| | | |
| | | |
| F | 3.187** | 7.789*** |
| $R^2$ | .116 | .398 |
| Adjusted $R^2$ | .079 | .347 |
| $\Delta R^2$ | .116** | .283*** |
| | | |

*$p < .05$, **$p < .01$, *** $p < .0001$

## *DISCUSSION*

This study examined depression among a community sample of Japanese American elders. The findings suggest that depression in this population is associated with poor health, fear of dependency, and lack of social support. Japanese American elders, like other elderly groups, are vulnerable to psychological distress in the form of depressive symptoms (Mui, 1996a, 1996c, 1998; Mui & Burnette, 1996). The predictive power of poor perceived health is consistent with the findings of earlier studies using white and other ethnic elderly populations (Berkman et al., 1986; Blazer, Burchett, Service, & George, 1991; Mui, 1996a).

An important finding in this study is the association between fear of dependence and depression. In the bivariate analysis, Japanese elders who were less acculturated (i.e., Japanese-speaking) were more likely to express fear of dependence. Previous studies on Japanese American elders conclude that traditional Japanese culture facilitates dependence among elders because of its emphasis on interdependence (Keifer, 1974). It would seem, therefore, that elders who are less acculturated and prefer to speak Japanese would feel more comfortable with dependence than would their more acculturated counterparts. The findings of this study, however, suggest the contrary. The prospect of having to depend on family is more stressful for less acculturated Japanese American elders. This may be influenced by two factors. First, Japanese-speaking elders in this sample tended to be female, with lower income, and less education. These elders may feel that they lack the resources to reciprocate for the care that they receive from their children. Although caring for elderly parents is upheld as an important value among present-day Japanese Americans (Shibusawa, Lubben, & Kitano, in press), filial obligation is no longer reinforced by traditional social norms. Thus, Japanese American elders cannot automatically expect to be cared for by their adult offspring. In addition, elders who are more acculturated may feel closer to their children because they have fewer cultural differences in the family. Second, in Japanese culture, people who are not able to reciprocate in a helping relationship become indebted and obligated to the care provider (Johnson, 1993). Those who are indebted are not supposed to assert their needs lest they offend the care provider, and they are expected to passively receive assistance even though the help may not be the kind of assistance they desire. Dependency, therefore, may be more stressful among elders who do not have the resources to reciprocate for the assistance since indebtedness can undermine the need for autonomy and self-control.

It is important to note that respondents who did not fear dependency were more likely to have been ill or injured in the preceding three years. This may suggest that fear of dependency is based on anticipation of having to become dependent rather than actually having to be dependent. Elders who experienced injury or illness may have discovered one of two things: that they were not as dependent as they had anticipated, or that intergenerational relationships had not become strained because of their change in physical status.

Elderly Japanese respondents in this study admitted to depressive symptoms at a rate higher than that found in a study among Chinese American elders (Mui, 1996b). Furthermore, research in the Los Angeles area found that elderly Chinese immigrants showed greater moderation and reported fewer physical and mental health problems than the white American elderly (Raskin, Chien, & Lin, 1992). Therefore, it is possible that there are differences between Japanese and Chinese American elders.

Close to 20% of the respondents scored as being mildly depressed, indicating that depression in Japanese American elders is potentially a serious problem, as seen in the high suicide rate. Japanese American elders have the third-highest suicide rate (18.9 per 100,000) following Chinese American (25.9 per 100,000) and white (19.1 per 100,000) elderly (Baker, 1994). The rates of completed suicide among Japanese American elders over 75 years of age are 2.5 times higher than the rates of their white cohorts. The suicide rate among Japanese American men age 85 and over is almost three times higher than the rates of their white cohorts (Baker, 1994).

As this study was limited by a small sample size and the voluntary nature of subject participation, its findings must, therefore, be interpreted with caution. Although age was not associated with depression in the present cross-sectional sample, results might have been different had a longitudinal design been used. In addition, environmental factors such as racial discrimination and safety were not addressed in this study. Future studies on ethnic elders must concern themselves with the social context in which these elders live. The findings of the present study are most appropriately generalizable to mentally capable community-dwelling Japanese American elders.

## *IMPLICATIONS FOR SOCIAL WORK PRACTICE*

The findings of this study provide new directions for culturally appropriate social work interventions with Japanese American elders.

Fear of dependency among this population suggests that social workers must conduct a careful assessment of the Japanese American elders' attitudes toward seeking help. The social worker must be aware of the psychological distress that elders may experience in having to seek assistance from their families. Social workers must explore their elderly clients' fears of dependency and work with them in appraising the extent to which these fears are based in reality. Intergenerational relationships must also be assessed to determine the context of these fears. If the fears are anticipatory, social workers need to help the elder and family discuss concerns about the helping relationship. If the family is not able to provide care, social workers need to minimize the elders' dependency on adult offspring by seeking outside resources for assistance.

Finally, the large proportion of Japanese American elders who were mildly depressed points to the need for active depression prevention programs. Social workers need to find ways to increase and activate social support networks so that elders can develop meaningful social relationships and overcome social isolation. In addition, community education is needed to enable elders, their families, and social organizations such as churches and Buddhist temples, along with primary health care providers, to detect depressive symptoms. Bilingual depression prevention groups for seniors also need to be implemented in the Japanese American community.

## REFERENCES


Antonucci, T., Akiyama, H., & Lansford, J.E. (1998). Negative effects of close social relations, *Family Relations*, *47*(4), 379-384.

Baker, F.M. (1994). Suicide among ethnic minority elderly: A statistical and psychosocial perspective. *Journal of Geriatric Psychiatry*, *27*(2), 241-264.

Berkman, L.F., Berkman, C.S., Kasl, S., Freeman, D.H., Leo, L., Ostfeld, A.M., Coroni-Huntley, J., & Brody, J. (1986). Depressive symptoms in relation to physical health and functioning in the elderly. *American Journal of Epidemiology*, *124*, 372-388.

Blazer, D., Burchett, B., Service, C., & George, L. K. (1991). The association of age and depression among the elderly: An epidemiologic exploration. *Journal of Gerontology*, *46*, 210-215.

Brody, E. (1985). Parent care as a normative family stress. *Gerontologist*, *25*, 19-29.

Brink, T.L., Yesavage, J.A., Lum, B., Heersma, P., Adey, M., & Rose,T.A. (1982). Screening tests for geriatric depression. *Clinical Gerontologist*, *1*, 37-44.

Burr, J.A. & Mutcher, J.E. (1993). Nativity, acculturation, and economic status: Explanations of Asian American living arrangements in later life. *Journal of Gerontology*, *48*(2), 55-63.

Cheung, M. (1989). Elderly Chinese living in the United States. *Social Work, 34*, 457-461.

Chi, I., & Boey, K.W. (1993). *A mental health and social support study of the old-old in Hong Kong (Resource Paper Series No. 22)*. Hong Kong: University of Hong Kong, Department of Social Work and Social Administration.

Clark, M.S. (1984). A distinction between two types of relationships and its implications for development. In J.C. Masters, & K. Yarkin-Levin (Eds.), *Boundary areas in social and developmental psychology* (pp. 241-270). New York: Academic Press.

Damon-Rodriguez, J., Wallace, S., & Kington, R. (1994). Service utilization and minority elderly: Appropriateness, accessibility and accessibility. *Gerontology & Geriatrics Education, 15*, 45-63.

Elo, I.T. (1996). Adult mortality among Asian Americans and Pacific Islanders: A review of the evidence. In K.S. Markeides & M. Miranda (Eds.), *Minorities, aging and health* (pp. 41-78). Thousand Oaks, CA: Sage Publications.

Ishii-Kuntz, M. (1997). Intergenerational relationships among Chinese, Japanese, and Korean Americans. *Family Relations, 46*, 23-32.

Iwamasa, G.Y., Hilliard, K.M., & Kost, C.R. (1998). Geriatric Depression Scale and Japanese American older adults. *Clinical Gerontologist, 19*(3), 13-24.

Johnson, F. (1993). Dependency and interdependency. In J. Bond & P. Coleman (Eds.), *Aging in society: An introduction to social gerontology* (pp. 209-228). London: Sage.

Kagawa-Singer, M., Hikoyeda, N., & Tanjasiri, S.P. (1996). Aging, chronic conditions, and physical disabilities in Asian and Pacific Islander Americans. In K.S. Markeides & M. Miranda (Eds.), *Minorities, aging and health* (pp. 149-180). Thousand Oaks, CA: Sage Publications.

Kao, S-K R. & Lam, M.L. (1997). Asian American elderly. In E. Lee (Ed.), *Working with Asian Americans: A guide for clinicians* (pp. 122-139). New York: Guilford Press.

Kendis, R.J. (1989). *Attitude of gratitude: The adaptation to aging of the elderly Japanese in America*. New York: AMS Press

Kiefer, C. (1974). Lessons from the Issei. In J. Gubrium (Ed.), *Late life communities and environmental policy* (pp.167-197). Springfield, IL: Charles C. Thomas.

Kuo, W.H. (1984). Prevalence of depression among Asian Americans. *Journal of Nervous and Mental Disease, 172* (8), 449-457.

Lam, R.E., Pascala, J.T., & Smith, S.L. (1997). Factors related to depressive symptoms in an elderly Chinese American sample. *Clinical Gerontologist, 17*(4), 57-70.

Lazarus, R.S., & Folkman, S. (1984). *Stress, appraisal, and coping*. New York: Springer.

Le, Q.K. (1997). Mistreatment of Vietnamese elderly by their families in the United States. *Journal of Elder Abuse & Neglect, 9*, 51-62.

Lee, G.R. & Ellithorpe, E. (1982). Intergenerational exchange and subjective well-being among the elderly. *Journal of Marriage and the Family, 44, 217-224.*

Lee, G.R., Netzer, J.K., & Coward, R.T. (1995). Depression among older parents: The role of intergenerational exchange. *Journal of Marriage and the Family, 57*, 823-833.

Lee, M.S., Crittenden, K.S., & Yu, E. (1996). Social support and depression among elderly Korean immigrants in the United States. *International Journal of Aging and Development, 42*(4), 313-327.

Lee, S.M. (1998). Asian Americans: Diverse and growing. *Population Bulletin, 53*, 2-40.

Lubben, J.E., & Becerra, R.M. (1983). Social support among Black, Mexican, and Chinese elderly. In D.E. Gelfand & C.M. Barresi (Eds.), *Ethnic dimensions of aging* (pp. 130-144). New York: Springer.

Matsubayashi, K., Wada, T., Okumiya, K., Fujisawa, M., Taoka, H., Kimura, S. & Doi, Y. (1994). Comparative study of quality of life in the elderly between in Kahoku and in Yaku. *Nippon Ronen Igakkai Zasshi* (Japanese Journal of Geriatrics), *31* (10), 790-799.

Moon, J., & Pearl, J.H. (1991). Alienation of elderly Korean American immigrants as related to place of residence, gender, age, years of education, time in the U.S., living with or without children and with and without a spouse. *International Journal of Aging and Development, 32*(2), 115-124.

Mui, A.C. (1996a). Geriatric Depression Scale as a community screening instrument for elderly Chinese immigrants. International Psychogeriatric, *8*(3), 445-458.

Mui, A.C. (1996b). Depression among elderly Chinese immigrants: An exploratory study. *Social Work, 41*, 633-645.

Mui, A.C. (1996c). Correlates of psychological distress among Mexican American, Cuban American, and Puerto Rican elders in the USA. *Journal of Cross-Cultural Gerontology, 11*, 131-147.

Mui, A.C. (1998). Living alone and depression among older Chinese immigrants. *Journal of Gerontological Social Work, 30*(3/4), 147-166.

Osako, M. (1979). Aging and family among Japanese Americans: The role of ethnic tradition in the adjustment to old age. *Gerontologist, 19* (5), 448-455.

Pang, K.Y. (1995). A cross-cultural understanding of depression among Korean immigrants: Prevalence, symptoms, and diagnosis. *Clinical Gerontologist, 15*(4), 3-20.

Pearlin, L.I., & Schooler, C. (1978). The structure of coping. *Journal of Health and Social Behavior, 19*, 2-21.

Rankin, S.H., Galbraith, M.E., & Johnson, S. (1993). Reliability and validity data for a Chinese translation of the Center for Epidemiological Studies-Depression. *Psychological Reports, 73*, 1291-1298.

Raskin, A., Chien, C.P., & Lin, K.M. (1992). Elderly Chinese and Caucasian Americans compared on measures of psychic distress, somatic complaints and social competence. *International Journal of Geriatric Psychiatry, 7*, 191-198.

Shibusawa, T., Lubben, J., & Kitano, H. (in press). Japanese American Caregiving. In L.K. Olson (Ed.), *Through Ethnic Lenses: Caring for the Elderly in a Multi-Cultural Society*. Boulder, CO: Rowan & Littlefield Publishers.

Stoller, E.P. (1985). Exchange patterns in the informal networks of the elderly: The impact of reciprocity on morale. *Journal of Marriage and the Family, 47*, 335-342.

Tanjasiri, S.P., Wallace, S.P., & Shibata, K. (1995). Picture imperfect: Hidden problems among Asian Pacific Islander elder. *Gerontologist, 35*, 753-760.

Tomita, S.K. (1998). The consequences of belonging: Conflict management techniques among Japanese Americans. *Journal of Elder Abuse & Neglect, 9*(3), 41-68.

Tsai, D.T., & Lopez, R.A. (1997). The use of social supports by elderly Chinese immigrants. *Journal of Gerontological Social Work, 29*, 77-94.

U.S. Bureau of the Census. (1993). *1990 Census of population. Asian and Pacific Islanders in the United States. (1990 CP-3-5).* Washington, DC: U.S. Government Printing Office.

Wong, P.T.P., & Ujimoto, K.V. (1998). The elderly: Their stress, coping and mental health. In L.C. Lee & N.W.S. Zane (Eds.), *Handbook of Asian American psychology* (pp. 165-209). Thousand Oaks, CA: Sage Publications.

Wong, S.S., Heiby, E.M., Kameoka, V.A., & Dubanoski, J.P. (1999). Perceived control, self-reinforcement, and depression among Asian American and Caucasian American elders. *Journal of Applied Gerontology, 18*(1), 46-62.

Yamamoto, J., Machizawa, S., Araki, F., Reece, S., Steinberg, A., Leung, J., & Carter, R. (1985). Mental health of elderly Asian Americans in Los Angeles. *American Journal of Social Psychiatry, 5*, 37-46.

Yamamoto, J., Rhee, S., & Chang, D. (1994). Psychiatric disorders among elderly Koreans in the United States. *Community Mental Health Journal, 30*(1), 17-26.

Yesavage, J.A., Brink, T.L., Rose, T.L., Lum, O., & Huang, V. (1983). Development and validation of a screening scale: A preliminary report. *Journal of Psychiatric Research, 17*, 37-49.

Yu, L.C., & Wu, S.C. (1985). Unemployment and family dynamics in meeting the needs of Chinese elderly in the United States. *Gerontologist, 25*, 472-476.

# Do Ethnic-Specific Long Term Care Facilities Improve Resident Quality of Life? Findings from the Japanese American Community

Nancy Hikoyeda, DrPH, MPH
Steven P. Wallace, PhD

**SUMMARY.** Research on resident/family perceptions of quality of life in residential care facilities for the elderly (RCFEs) has been sparse and has ignored ethnic-specific facilities. This qualitative inquiry compared interviews with Japanese American women in Japanese and non-Japanese RCFEs, family members, and administrators, to examine how ethnic features (e.g., Japanese language, food, staff) meet resident needs/preferences and their influence on the residents' quality of life.

---

Nancy Hikoyeda is affiliated with San Jose State University and Steven P. Wallace is affiliated with the UCLA School of Public Health.

Address correspondence to: Dr. Nancy Hikoyeda, Acting Director, Gerontology Program, San Jose State University, One Washington Square, San Jose, CA 95192-0140 (Email: nhikoyeda@compuserve.com).

The authors thank all of the Japanese American residents, family members, administrators, social services organizations and the RCFEs who made this study possible.

This research was funded in part by a grant from the UCLA/VA/RAND MEDTEP (Medical Treatment Effectiveness Program) Center for Asians and Pacific Islanders and a UCLA Graduate Division Dissertation Year Fellowship to the first author.

[Haworth co-indexing entry note]: "Do Ethnic-Specific Long Term Care Facilities Improve Resident Quality of Life? Findings from the Japanese American Community." Hikoyeda, Nancy, and Steven P. Wallace. Co-published simultaneously in *Journal of Gerontological Social Work* (The Haworth Social Work Practice Press, an imprint of The Haworth Press, Inc.) Vol. 36, No. 1/2, 2001, pp. 83-106; and: *Social Work Practice with the Asian American Elderly* (ed: Namkee G. Choi) The Haworth Social Work Practice Press, an imprint of The Haworth Press, Inc., 2001, pp. 83-106. Single or multiple copies of this article are available for a fee from The Haworth Document Delivery Service [1-800-HAWORTH, 9:00 a.m. - 5:00 p.m. (EST). E-mail address: getinfo@haworthpressinc.com].

Residents and families differed in their preferences and perceptions of quality of life. Residents discussed invisible life process domains such as boredom, socialization, privacy, staff attentiveness/personal qualities, and autonomy. Family members emphasized structural aspects of the homes such as location, cleanliness, costs, home-like qualities, food, and Japanese care.

While ethnic-specific institutions were unique in meeting certain needs (e.g., Japanese-speaking staff), culturally congruent characteristics alone did not provide a desired quality of life for residents, contrary to family perceptions. All institutions, including those with ethnic-specific services, need to integrate resident needs/wishes into their operations, adequate staffing, and meaningful activities to make life worth living. 

**KEYWORDS.** Ethnic residential long term care, quality of life, Japanese American elders

## *INTRODUCTION AND BACKGROUND*

As our population grows older and more diverse, it is anticipated that a growing number of older adults will require assistance with daily activities, resulting in an increased need for residential long term care (LTC). Furthermore, as family structures and roles evolve in ethnic communities, with acculturation and assimilation, it is anticipated that the demand will grow for LTC facilities that meet the personal and cultural preferences of a heterogeneous population.

One LTC setting, residential care facilities for the elderly (RCFEs), has received little attention in the research. RCFE refers to an institutional hybrid that includes two primary housing models. In California, RCFEs may be small custodial board and care homes or the large, rapidly proliferating assisted living facilities (complexes that provide a range of social/medical services in addition to 24-hour supervision). However, little is known about the perceptions or preferences of those who reside in these facilities and nothing has been documented about their ability to meet the needs of a culturally diverse population.

It is anticipated that Asian/Pacific Islander American (APIA) elders will need institutional care due to several trends: continuing immigration of older APIA adults, acceptance of institutionalization due to acculturation and assimilation, and increased knowledge and exposure to information about the availability of LTC facilities (Yeo, 1993). However, APIA families face economic disparities, geographic dispersion, varying personal resources, and shifts in family structure and roles (e.g., smaller support networks), which will impact the need for, and access to, residential settings (Gibson & Jackson, 1987; Jones-Morrison, 1982; Osako, 1979; Tanjasiri, Wallace & Shibata, 1995; Yeo, 1993). Thus, even if family care is preferred, APIA families may be unable to provide the care that is needed or expected.

In California, Japanese Americans (JAs) have developed their own LTC continuum to overcome various service barriers (e.g., racial discrimination) and to meet the need for culturally competent services assuming that they enhance the quality of life of JA residents. This qualitative study systematically examined the perceptions of older JA women residing in Japanese-oriented and non-Japanese RCFEs to determine the unique ways in which the ethnic-specific facilities meet the needs and preferences of the residents and their families and the influence of the ethnic features on resident quality of life.

## *Long Term Care and Ethnic Elders*

The literature on long term care (LTC) and older ethnic minority populations has been quantitative in nature and primarily examines the utilization of LTC services. The strength of these studies is in predicting binary outcomes such as use and non-use of services, or linear relationships such as cost-effectiveness and frequency of visits. Prior investigations have excluded the complex processes, meanings, perceptions, or relationships of those who use the services (Hikoyeda, 2000). No studies were found that examined the quality of services or satisfaction from the perspective of ethnic elders or their families.

Overall, ethnic minority elders experience more health limitations and suffer more socioeconomic disadvantages than comparable whites, but use formal (paid) services less and informal (unpaid) assistance more (Markides & Wallace, 1996). They are believed to have larger and stronger support systems available than comparable whites due to more cohesive family ties (Belgrave, Wykle, & Choi, 1991; Espino, 1993; Manson, 1993; McBride, Morioka-Douglas, & Yeo, 1996; Richardson, 1996). However, it is not clear whether the use of informal care by ethnic families is actually due to a stronger system of informal support or other factors such as economics, personal or cultural preferences, living arrangements, health status, access to care, discrimination, or a combination of these variables (Hikoyeda, 2000; Wallace, Levy-Storms, Kington, & Andersen, 1998).

Historically, institutional LTC settings have been avoided by ethnic families due to discriminatory practices, exorbitant costs, the stigma of family abandonment, fear of social isolation, an emphasis on custodial rather than rehabilitative care, the lack of skilled and adequately paid staff, disregard for ethnic and cultural preferences, and the perception of low quality care (Hing, 1990; Kane & Kane, 1987; Wallace, 1990; Yeo, 1993). There is, however, evidence that utilization may be increasing among African American, Hispanic, and some Asian elders due to the dilution of cultural norms, decreasing discrimination, and changes in the availability of supportive networks (Mui & Burnette, 1994; Yeo, 1993).

### *Quality of Life*

In the literature, quality of life (QOL) has been an elusive, complex concept lacking a theoretical model or a universally accepted definition (Birren & Dieckmann, 1991; Gentile, 1991). QOL indicators have been defined from multiple perspectives that tend to emphasize the structural elements of care such as safety and cleanliness (Kane & Kane, 1987). Current QOL instruments tend to ignore individual perceptions or aspects of normal living (Gentile, 1991; Lawton, 1991). Most relevant to this study, few instruments have been culturally adapted for use in diverse populations. Eurocentric concepts of QOL reflect mainstream American ideals which may or may not accurately represent the perceptions of ethnic elders (Padilla & Kagawa-Singer, 1998).

Due to these shortcomings, a qualitative methodology was used to give insights into the perceptions of QOL from the perspective of Japanese American residents and their families. QOL was approached as a subjective, multifaceted response to daily events that make a life worth living (Birren & Dieckmann, 1991; Gentile, 1991; Mitchell & Kemp, 2000).

### *Japanese American Families*

This inquiry focused on Japanese American (JA) communities. In 1990, 105,932 individuals, or 23% of all Asian Pacific Islander Americans (APIA) over the age of 65 were JAs (U.S. Bureau of the Census, 1990). Among ethnic elders, JAs have the highest proportion of older adults (13%) due to recent low immigration rates and longer residency (Markides & Wallace, 1996). In general, JA elders tend to be long-lived and relatively healthy based on findings from the Honolulu Heart Program, a longitudinal study of 8000 JA males and their families (Yano, Reed, & Kagan, 1985). As a whole, JAs are the most acculturated and assimilated APIA subgroup; however, they exhibit substantial within-group heterogeneity (Kitano, 1993).

To contextualize the LTC needs of JA elders, a brief history of their presence in the U.S. is warranted. JA history consists of four distinct periods (Kitano, 1993): the Immigration period (1890-1924), the Prewar Era (1924-1941), the Wartime Evacuation (1941-1945) (marked by the forced removal of over 120,000 individuals of Japanese descent from the U.S. West Coast into ten relocation camps), and the Postwar Period (1945-present) characterized by resettlement, redress and reparations as a result of relocation, and the labeling of JAs as a "model minority."

Many JA women immigrated in the early 1900s as the wives of male laborers. They entered a harsh environment where they could not speak the language and had few friends. Fortunately, existing JA communities provided the necessary social, educational, cultural, and religious institutions to meet these needs. These women toiled beside their husbands as farmers or shopkeepers, or in menial occupations (e.g., domestics). They endured anti-Japanese hatred even though their children were American citizens.

Ethnic identification and traditional Japanese culture have been central in JA families. For example, generational relationships are so important that each generation has been given a distinct name. *Issei* are the first generation immigrants, *Nisei* are their second generation American-born offspring, *Sansei* are children of *Nisei*, followed by *Yonsei* and *Gosei* (fourth and fifth generations, respectively). *Kibei* are *Nisei* who were educated in Japan and subsequently returned to the U.S. *Shin-Issei* or *Newcomers* refers to post-1965 immigrants (Kitano & Daniels, 1988). *Nikkei* is a recent term that refers to all Americans of Japanese ancestry regardless of generation.

Ethnicity plays a significant role in the behaviors of traditional JA families. Ethnicity refers to social differentiation based on characteristics such as place of origin, a sense of shared peoplehood, cultural symbols, and history (Barresi & Stull, 1993; Spector, 2000). Most JAs have maintained their ethnic involvement in the JA community even though they have become assimilated into American life (Fugita & O'Brien,

1991). Older JAs have continued Meiji-era culture, values, and norms drawn from Confucian, Buddhist, Shinto, and Samurai traditions that dictate how people should behave both individually and as a group. These include a male-dominated hierarchical family structure, a belief in collectivity over individuality, obligation and duty over free will, and interdependence over independence and self-reliance (Kitano, 1993). Women in Japan were raised to be housewives devoted to meeting the needs of their husbands and children (Iwao, 1993). Children were taught filial piety and respect for elders and were expected to care for their parents in their old age. Dependency is not indicative of weakness but is part of a culturally approved behavioral pattern (Shibusawa, 1997).

Kendis (1989) reports that cultural beliefs and ethnic identification contribute to successful aging among older JAs. These include an acceptance of old age and death as part of life, a sense of strength and comfort from successes and adverse experiences, and an orientation of accommodation and acceptance that allow JA elders to adapt to various situations and accept things that cannot be changed. JA elders have specific roles within the family, church, and community that enable them to remain active and maintain a sense of usefulness. They have a revered position in the JA community because of past hardships. These tendencies may be stronger or weaker in different individuals but tend to distinguish older JAs from older EuroAmericans.

Due to these behavioral expectations, JA families may need to reconcile their cultural heritage with those of contemporary American life when decisions involve institutional placement. But JA families may not trust the LTC system because of the way American institutions discriminated against them, especially during the World War II internment. We do not know to what extent aging *Nisei* actually conform to traditional cultural mandates or adopt the dominant EuroAmerican views. Furthermore, as JA family structures change with subsequent generations and other pressures, the cultural and structural influences which have historically reduced LTC use are expected to become more diluted resulting in an increased need for residential LTC (Hikoyeda, 2000).

There were two hypotheses underlying this study. First, ethnic-specific RCFEs meet the needs and preferences of JA residents and families more appropriately than mainstream facilities. Second, ethnic-specific features enhance the perceived quality of life of the JA residents. It was presumed that JA homes provided the most cultural continuity (Atchley, 1999), facilitating the residents' adaptation to the RCFEs and enhancing the quality of their living.

## *METHODOLOGY*

This qualitative inquiry employed a grounded theory analysis of personal interviews and unobtrusive observations in residential care facilities for the elderly (RCFEs). The inductive approach (Strauss, 1987) was considered most appropriate for this study because the unit of analysis was personal perception, experience, and preferences. This study focused on how an ethnically-oriented institutional environment could maximize opportunities for positive experiences for frail JA women.

### *Participants*

Respondents were JA women residing in Japanese-oriented and non-Japanese RCFEs. The women had to be 65 years of age or older, self-identify as JA, and be cognitively able to participate in an interview. A family member or other legal representative (if the resident had no family) was also interviewed. The JA health care community, social service agencies, senior centers, and churches in Northern and Southern California helped to identify RCFEs and recruit residents and families.

Residents included 12 women in Japanese-oriented RCFEs and 14 in non-Japanese facilities. Overall, 10 of the 26 residents were *Issei,* 13 were *Nisei,* and the remainder were *Sansei* and *Shin-Issei.* Residents ranged in age from 75 to 100 years (average age 88 years) and interviews averaged one hour in length.

The perceptions of family members were important because of the role they were assumed to play in the decision for institutional placement and the selection of the facility. Overall, 31 family members/legal representatives were interviewed (15 daughters, 9 sons, 3 daughters-in-law, 1 sibling, 1 spouse, 2 surrogates). One was *Issei,* fifteen were *Nisei,* thirteen were *Sansei,* and one was *Shin-Issei.* Family members ranged in age from 47 to 85 (average age was 65 years) and interviews averaged 95 minutes in length.

### *Facilities*

Four respondents were the administrators of JA facilities. RCFEs located throughout California were included to increase sample size and maximize variations. RCFEs were chosen for this project, rather than nursing homes, in part because most residents were expected to be cognitively intact and capable of responding to interviewers. Additionally, RCFEs are not as tightly regulated as nursing homes, which theoretically, made it possible for them to incorporate more ethnic features. RCFEs were also more prevalent than nursing homes in the JA communities. The recruitment process was initiated using lists from the Community Care Licensing Department to identify Japanese or Asian oriented facilities; however, no residents from these homes volunteered to participate. JA community members were also asked to assist in locating JA residents in RCFEs. Once the facilities were identified, the staff was asked to distribute recruitment flyers and make oral requests for participation. To our knowledge, at least 64 resident/family pairs were asked by staff to participate in the study. However, many of the family members and residents refused to be interviewed. Additionally, a number of residents were more cognitively impaired than family members or staff had indicated which excluded them from participation.

Respondents resided in twenty different RCFEs (six Japanese, fourteen non-Japanese). The Japanese-oriented facilities were located primarily in the greater San Francisco Bay Area. It is noteworthy that eight of the fourteen non-Japanese facilities were, in fact, owned and operated by other Asians (e.g., Chinese or Filipino) who sought only JA clients. These proprietors said it was better for residents if they were all from the same ethnic group. Among the six Japanese facilities, three were nonprofit and three were proprietary while all but two of the non-Japanese homes were for-profit. The facilities were extremely diverse in capacity (five to 100 residents), range and type of activities (no activities to highly structured events), services (minimal to extensive assistance), amenities (large facilities had beauty salons and coffee shops while smaller facilities were simply "home-like") and licensure (two Japanese facilities were unlicensed and operated under a "family cooperative" model).

The question guide consisted of several parts adapted for the two types of facilities, residents, and family members. Demographic data was obtained from all informants. For residents, a six-question screening instrument (J. F. Schnelle, personal communication, June 2, 1997) was used to assess the ability to give informed consent and participate in the interview. Resident functional abilities (Katz et al., 1970) and acculturation level (Suinn, Ahuna, & Khoo, 1992) were assessed but are not reported here. Opened-ended questions were employed to determine how residents and families perceived and defined quality of life and care in the various environments.

### *Interviews*

Overall, 57 interviews, collected over a period of 18 months, were completed in 20 different facilities throughout California. Residents were interviewed in their RCFEs. The majority of family members invited the interviewer into their homes, but others requested meetings in coffee shops, bookstores, and work sites. The first author interviewed all of the English-speaking respondents and personally transcribed the audiotapes. A trained bilingual interviewer from the JA community, fluent in both English and Japanese, was available for respondents who did not speak English or who preferred to use Japanese. Twelve interviews were done in Japanese with the first author as a participant observer. The Japanese interviews were transcribed and translated into English by the bilingual interviewers and verified by one additional bilingual individual.

It was considered extremely important to develop rapport, build trust, and show respect for the JA residents in a culturally appropriate manner. Therefore, training sessions were held with the bilingual interviewers. The sessions addressed qualitative techniques as well as sensitivity to cognitive and physical status (e.g., fatigue or effects of medications), physical deficits such as hearing loss or low vision, and level of discussion such as simplifying questions, length, pace, and content. If the resident became tired or agitated, or if the conversation became unintelligible, the interviewer gave the option of skipping the question or halting the interview. Interviewers were monitored throughout the data collection process and consulted during the analysis phase.

### *Observations*

Twenty hours of unobtrusive and participant observations were completed, by the first author, in the larger Japanese facilities to supplement the personal interviews. Observations were done in 15 to 20 minute blocks and consisted of systematic data gathering to describe the settings, activities, people, routines, social organization, and meaning of phenomena from the perspective of those observed. Specifically, the goal was to see what life was like inside the Japanese facilities by documenting the ethnic characteristics of the homes, observing resident/staff and resident/resident interactions, physical appearance, nonverbal communication, and service attributes, such as activities and visible aspects of "Japanese" care. Nonoccurrences of behaviors or actions were also noteworthy (e.g., the lack of things to do). Administrators were cooperative but extremely protective of their residents (e.g., discouraging visits during particular times of the day) which prohibited unannounced data gathering.

### *Analysis*

Grounded theory analysis was used to formulate explanations and conceptualizations grounded in the narratives, experiences, and perceptions of life in RCFEs elicited from the JA respondents. Extensive fieldnotes and case summaries were prepared after each interview/observation. Data collection, coding, and analysis were done concurrently to maintain flexibility in the process and to incorporate new concepts and emerging themes into subsequent analysis and interviews. Open, axial, and selective coding (Strauss & Corbin, 1990) were used to organize and make sense of the emerging data.

### *Limitations*

There are several limitations to this study. First, the small sample prohibits extrapolation to other RCFE residents and their families. Additionally, only women with families were interviewed and their perceptions may differ from those of males or residents with no families. One also cannot assume that the experiences and perceptions are the same for everyone because of the heterogenous characteristics of the informants and facilities. Some residents were reluctant to discuss the facilities most likely due to the personal nature of the topic or fear of retaliation due to their vulnerability in this setting. The JA residents were considerably more physically and/or cognitively impaired than expected at this level of care so the pool of potential respondents was smaller than anticipated. The voluntary nature of participation was also a limiting factor. In spite of these limitations, the qualitative nature of this investigation was a strength because this information could not have been obtained using conventional quantitative methods.

## *FINDINGS*

While the original study design was intended to compare JA versus generic RCFEs, many of the JAs were in facilities that were not Japanese-oriented, but owned and operated by other Asians. Thus, the homes were actually Japanese-oriented, other Asian-owned, and generic (EuroAmerican). In Japanese-oriented homes, the easily discernible characteristics were expected to provide a better quality of life for the JA elders. Japanese-oriented facilities usually had JA administrators, staff, and volunteers recruited from local JA communities, who were thought to best anticipate the needs and preferences of the JA residents. Additionally, some of the staff members were student interns from Japan. Most staff were monolingual Japanese speakers, thus, Japanese was used in everyday interactions and activities. These homes offered Japanese food at least once a day as well as activities/observances that focused on Japanese celebrations. The facilities also maintained a Japanese "environment," with Japanese dolls and other artifacts on display, as well as Japanese television programs. Several administrators/staff maintained that these homes were based on a "Japanese philosophy" of care. This meant that staff possessed a respect and reverence for elders that influenced their services and caregiving.

The non-Japanese Asian homes shared some of these characteristics. Frequently, residents were all JAs. Staff served foods with Asian flavorings and residents noted that it was not really Japanese food, but it was tolerated. Rice was served (a staple in Japanese diets). Asian proprietors acknowledged the importance of Japanese foods to their JA residents, and in several homes, staff did prepare or were learning to cook some Japanese dishes. Families perceived that the staff in the Asian homes were more respectful towards the JA elders because of a similar cultural upbringing. These facilities also provided Japanese television programs and videos.

The generic facilities operated according to EuroAmerican standards. In most cases, the JA elder was the only Japanese, or Asian, resident and none of the staff were Japanese. Television and activities were in English, and there was nothing Asian about the surroundings. Food typically followed the institutional menu found throughout the U.S., and only American holidays were celebrated.

These were the characteristics that were anticipated in the different facilities. Both continuity theory and cultural congruence would suggest that the more "Japanese" the facility the better the facility would meet resident preferences and enhance quality of life. Family members interviewed also held this perception and, indeed, when searching for an RCFE, they sought a Japanese-oriented facility first.

## *FAMILY PREFERENCES AND PERCEPTIONS ABOUT QUALITY OF LIFE*

All family members admitted they were ethnocentric in their preferences. They believed that "Japanese care" was exceptional because Japanese people were taught early in life to respect and revere their elders. Japanese people were presumed to be more trustworthy, kind, competent, patient, reliable, and accepting of aging than Caucasian workers. Japanese staff were assumed to be more empathetic, exhibiting a genuine fondness for older people. The work ethic was also perceived to be different. Japanese staff were thought to believe that eldercare was a calling, while Caucasian staff looked upon their work as "just a job." If a Japanese home was not available, families turned to non-Japanese-Asian facilities. In general, families said other Asians could be just as caring as Japanese staff because they were raised with similar cultural values including a respect for elders. However, perceptions of the actual quality of Asian staff were mixed since some were described as model caregivers, while others were not considered as clean or trustworthy.

Family members usually had the exclusive decision-making power in selecting homes; only five residents had participated in the selection of the facility. While family members were concerned about the cultural congruence of the RCFE, there were also a number of structural factors that bounded their choice of homes. The most important of these were cost and location.

While most of the JA families interviewed could be classified as middle-class, they had modest resources for paying the high and continually increasing costs of RCFE. Basic charges ranged from $1000-4500 a month in California, and did not include any incidental costs such as prescription medications or incontinence supplies. Families quickly learned that there is no public or private financial assistance available for this level of LTC in California. An exception was one non-profit JA facility that charged residents based on a sliding scale with the remaining costs subsidized by Japanese community fund raisers. Families also discovered that costs are correlated with appearance, maintenance, private rooms, activities, staffing ratios, and other amenities. Even when they were able to afford an RCFE, the most desirable JA oriented facilities usually had waiting lists of several months to years.

Following costs, distance from the family's home to the facility was an important consideration and often required a trade-off. This was important, in part, because most of the families lived in the costly metropolitan regions of San Francisco and Los Angeles, while the least expensive facilities were located in more suburban and rural areas. Distance was a persistent barrier for families, particularly for older caregivers who did not drive or who disliked driving long hours in heavy traffic. Nice residential locations were also desirable, although several facilities were located in deteriorating neighborhoods. Parking was important but lacking in the small urban facilities which dictated the frequency of family visits. Families who lived nearby tended to visit more often and monitored the care more closely.

Other factors in the decision matrix for families could be classified as structural quality of care issues. For example, families preferred a "home-like" environment which was clean and offered appealing food. Home-like characteristics were highly desirable because families believed they provided a family-like environment which enhanced the resident's psychological well-being. Therefore, most families preferred smaller facilities (e.g., converted houses) which had the physical appearances of a family home. Resident rooms frequently displayed personal possessions such as family photographs, drawings from grandchildren and great-grandchildren, and handmade bedspreads. Families preferred homes with fewer residents, because they felt that residents would receive more attention (this was not observed and, in fact, smaller facilities had fewer staff per resident than larger facilities). Families also said they valued personal space and privacy which they assumed (wrongly) would be more prevalent in smaller facilities. Some families justified shared rooms by explaining that they would reduce loneliness and that roommates might help each other. But while the small facilities possessed primary group characteristics such as small size and close proximity, true family characteristics such as boundedness, commitment, and shared affection were absent (see Morgan, Eckert, & Lyon, 1995 for similar findings from generic facilities). Additionally, residents could not use the entire house and were not allowed to have pets.

An essential characteristic of a desirable environment was that it be clean but not sterile. The absence of an odor was thought to be the initial sign of a good home. JA families believed that cleanliness was a Japanese trait and JA homes were cleaner. If the facility was clean and odorless, this was thought to enhance resident morale and symbolized the owner's high regard and respect for the residents.

The other physical characteristic of concern to families was the food. Family members, however, never ate in the facilities and only a few had ever seen the food that was served. Their impressions, therefore, were based primarily on what the facility and residents reported about meals. Families strongly believed that their elders preferred Japanese over American food (although this was not true in several cases). In the JA homes, Japanese food was served at least once a day, and the quality was thought to be superior to meals in generic homes. Of the 20 facilities, only one JA home met with some of the residents, on one occasion, to ask about food preferences.

Families had low expectations for the food served in generic homes, which was described as bland and institutional. Also, several proprietors were criticized for ignoring nutritional guidelines. One 64 year old *Nisei* daughter said:

> One Sunday, I went over there to see what they were eating for meals. I usually don't call ahead, I just go and they were having hot dogs! Hot dogs out of the package–wieners for a Sunday meal and frozen vegetables, a few carrots and a little bit of bread. . . . So I asked the owner the next time I went to visit, 'Why is it that you serve hot dogs for a Sunday dinner, my Mother said you always serve hot dogs on Sunday?' and she said that the person who was taking care didn't know how to cook, and I said 'That's not a good reason.'

In the larger mainstream facilities, the residents were given a choice of entrees for lunch and dinner each day and this was perceived by residents as an important daily task. However, the staff made no effort to satisfy individual tastes for ethnic foods. Families urged residents to adjust to the food rather than asking the homes to accommodate resident preferences. Furthermore, these families compensated, in part, by bringing Japanese food from home or taking residents out to eat.

In summary, family members all expressed a high level of concern for the quality of life of their elderly relative in the RCFE. Families sought care similar to what they themselves would deliver if they were able. They judged the quality of care, however, primarily on visible structural aspects of the facility such as cleanliness, home-like qualities, food, and "Japanese care." Their choice of facilities was also influenced by the constraints of cost and location. Regardless of the ethnic orientation of the facility, families reported peace of mind in their belief that their elders were comfortable and well cared for in their facilities. However, families rarely discussed the facilities with residents and spent relatively little time in them (visits varied from daily to bimonthly, typically for an hour or less). Furthermore, to proprietors, family preferences frequently seemed more important than those of residents.

## *RESIDENTS' PREFERENCES AND PERCEPTIONS ABOUT QUALITY OF LIFE*

Discussions with the JA residents elicited dimensions of satisfaction and quality of life and care that differed from those of family members. Residents emphasized concerns about routine, life process domains such as boredom, socialization, privacy, staff attentiveness/personal qualities, and autonomy. Overall, the JA residents were living lives in marked contrast to their former lifestyles. Most of the women had been active participants in community, religious, and cultural events. Suddenly, their physical and/or mental health had declined and they found themselves needing assistance with mundane activities like dressing, bathing, and cooking. They were forced to abandon the events and activities that made their lives meaningful and move from the familiarity of their homes into facilities where everyday life consisted of ongoing adjustments.

Boredom was a persistent problem in nearly all facilities regardless of ethnic orientation, capacity, or even the presence of organized activities. This was due in part to the structure of the facilities. RCFEs are mandated to provide daily activities to maintain the cognitive and physical functioning of their residents. However, it is left to each facility to determine the degree and the type of activities. Furthermore, regulations are not strictly enforced in small homes with fewer residents. Larger RCFEs hired an activity director who planned various activities while small homes offered little to do, leaving residents to entertain themselves.

Japanese television was a central activity in nearly all the Japanese-oriented and Asian facilities. Typically, residents were seated in front of a loudly blaring television set either asleep or mesmerized by the images on the screen. Staff assumed that residents enjoyed watching television but most residents did not. One 90 year old *Issei* stated, "I have to watch [TV] because there are no other places to be here. But I don't like it." Residents, however, did not disclose their feelings to the caregivers. Furthermore, some residents were reluctant to participate in activities even if they were available and in fact, it was frequently difficult to tell whether a resident preferred to do nothing or whether there was nothing to do.

Several proprietors of Japanese and Asian homes asked that families pay for residents to attend an adult social day care program at a Japanese senior center. Residents who did attend the program seemed happier and more alert than those who did not and this gave residents something to look forward to. Thus, residents had to leave the facilities to find something to do.

One Japanese administrator specifically attributed the lack of activities to Japanese and American philosophical differences. He explained that in Japan, old age signifies a time for rest; therefore, activities were not perceived as necessary. A second Japanese administrator had a somewhat different philosophy but a similar outcome:

> Most of them just watch TV or, I mean, just sitting. We have exercise in the morning. We have volunteer people who come in and take them for a walk if the weather is good. That is about it. The students, on special occasions, they do some kind of art work, basic art work, for holidays. Other than that, we don't have activities. The difficulty is that everybody is different here in abilities. If one person does it, or if we think that person cannot do it, then they get upset. But when they try it, they say 'I don't want to do it' or 'I cannot do it' that kind of thing happens [sic]. But whenever anybody has time, we play with, like this [bean bag], we throw it here and there and paper balloons or we just show Japanese movies on TV. They seem to like that and I guess they watch it.

More significant than the lack of activities was the absence of meaningful tasks, which made residents feel useless. In several small Asian homes, however, residents created their own "work." One woman set and cleared the table at mealtimes, another helped the cook learn to make *sushi*, one offered grace at each meal, while another made her own bed each morning.

The absence of structured activities was compounded by residents' loneliness. Old friends had passed away and the facilities were far from familiar neighborhoods. In shared rooms, roommates were distinct from friends. Additionally, in some Japanese facilities, there were few social interactions because other residents were so cognitively impaired. Thus, close social networks were lacking, except for families. Staff members were too busy to sit and chat and the small Japanese facilities, in particular, appeared short staffed. Japanese caregivers seemed more aloof and stoic rather than tender, which was more congruent with Japanese personality traits but also reinforced the social distance between staff and elders. Caucasian English-speaking staff seemed friendlier, readily laughed out loud, or overtly tried to make residents smile. An 86 year old *Nisei* in a generic home noted that more "friendly" staff-resident relationships were artificial, "They always call you by your first name, as if we knew each other for a long time!" At the same time, residents in all facilities, regardless of ethnic orientation, described good staff as kind, nice, friendly, patient, caring, empathetic, respectful, and helpful. Thus, residents placed a particular value on the attitudes and interpersonal qualities of the staff, desiring those who were friendly and caring, but did not consider them substitutes for family or friends.

Interestingly, residents in non-Japanese homes did not miss other Japanese people. These residents felt that other JAs could be narrow minded and nosy and, in their presence, the residents couldn't be themselves. One 84 year old *Nisei* said:

> No, I prefer this kind [home]. Well, they are easier to live with . . . *hakujins* [Caucasians] care less and we care less about each other. Japanese . . . I guess you haven't had the experience in camp during the war. But it was *urusai,* do you know what *urusai* is? It is a nuisance. They are so petty and all that. I could care less. . . . I like it just like here, this is not too personal and not too indifferent.

Because Japanese culture is other-directed, this comment may help explain why residents in the Japanese facilities were as lonely as those in EuroAmerican homes.

Residents in all facilities preferred private over shared accommodations. Unfortunately, private rooms are more expensive. They are also rare in small RCFEs but a standard amenity in large facilities. Only shared rooms were offered in five of the six Japanese homes and five of the eight Asian facilities, while all six of the mainstream facilities also offered private rooms and bathrooms.

Incompatibility in personalities and interests among roommates was a significant disadvantage of shared quarters. Residents also disliked sharing a room with someone who was demented. However, residents were extremely careful about discussing their roommates because Japanese culture emphasizes the maintenance of harmonious relationships. Private rooms gave residents a sense of freedom and control, as one 95 year old *Issei* said, "I am very happy that I can have my private room. I can think. I can come in and out freely. If I share the room with someone, I feel reluctant to do things my way." Thus, shared rooms were often a source of frustration.

A common thread found in resident interviews were suggestions that residents missed the autonomy they had experienced before their institutionalization. Some residents desired the opportunity to make simple, everyday choices, such as when to go to bed, get up, or take a bath. For example, one resident wanted to bathe daily, but staffing levels in her facility allowed only weekly baths. Regardless of capacity or ethnic orientation, the facilities maintained schedules and work assignments with little room for flexibility in routines that were often determined by staffing patterns and efficiency demands.

Residents in larger mainstream homes seemed more satisfied with their choices than their counterparts in the smaller ethnic-specific facilities. Larger facilities had some choice in meals and activities and private rooms and baths. Thus, the ethnic-specific environment alone was insufficient in meeting all the residents' needs. Except for the monolingual Japanese-speaking residents, the ethnic orientation of the homes did little to normalize the quality of resident living (Hikoyeda, 2000).

The JA residents were bicultural, but tradition-bound in how they responded to their care in both types of RCFEs. For example, residents were very sensitive to family feelings and expectations. They did not complain because their children had selected the facilities, and an inappropriate placement would reflect on the family's decision-making skills and filial responsibility. But the residents were highly adaptive, as one 47 year old *Sansei* daughter said:

> My Mom has a very adaptive personality. She has always, always accepted things and made the best of them. She is very classic, very stoic. I think of her as being typical Japanese. Being stoic, being adaptable, not necessarily changing inside, but accepting the situation around them which you figure they can't change. I think of that as being very Japanese.

In summary, regardless of the ethnic orientation of the homes, residents emphasized the importance of "normal" living. One 86 year old *Nisei* prefaced her comments with, "Of course, it is not like your home." This is consistent with continuity theory, which emphasized social and psychological continuity as much as the environmental and structural continuity of life. The lack of variation in preferences expressed by the residents may be due to a cohort effect as the residents were primarily

*Nisei* and relatively acculturated, and even the *Issei* had been in the U.S. for decades.

Culturally, these residents were taught to defer to authority, avoid confrontations with staff, roommates, and family, and hold back from expressing their true feelings, wishes or needs. This cultural trait (*enryo*) also made most residents reluctant to discuss their facilities and the staff in much depth, making it difficult to obtain extensive information about their preferences. This reluctance was detrimental to the residents because the staff/administrators wanted to make them happy, but their silence led the caregivers and families to believe that the residents were content. In America, this Japanese cultural response works against the interests of the JA residents.

## *DISCUSSION, IMPLICATIONS, AND RECOMMENDATIONS*

### *Discussion*

This study began with the assumption that residential care facilities for the elderly (RCFEs) that incorporated ethnic-specific elements would meet the needs and preferences of Japanese American (JA) residents and families more than generic (EuroAmerican-oriented) facilities. It also assumed, based on continuity theory (Atchley, 1999) and the concept of cultural congruence, that these ethnic-specific features would improve the quality of life of the JA residents.

There were clear structural differences between Japanese-oriented, other Asian, and generic facilities. Japanese-oriented facilities maintained a Japanese feel in the physical environment, used Japanese language in activities and interactions, and the nonprofit JA facilities tapped into the resources of the local JA community. These characteristics attracted JA families, along with assumptions that JA staff would be more respectful and caring than their Caucasian counterparts. While the underlying issues regarding the quality of life were relatively generic among family members (e.g., cleanliness, home-like environment), the way they thought about the issues, interpreted them, and dealt with them were influenced by Japanese cultural values and mores. At times, this was very obvious such as when families interpreted staff as better if they were Japanese. To the extent that families typically preferred the visible characteristics offered by Japanese-oriented homes (which were offered to a lesser degree by other Asian homes), the first hypothesis about the importance of ethnic-specific characteristics *for family members* was supported.

Most significantly, the data reveal that families and residents differed in their preferences and perceptions of quality of life. Residents did not mention the structural or physical aspects of the RCFEs they resided in, except when it impacted their ability to maintain privacy and autonomy of action. Residents of the Japanese-oriented homes did not comment on the culturally familiar environment, while a primary concern of those in generic homes seemed to be the food. All residents were affected by the lack of meaningful activities in many homes, compounded by the loneliness of being separated from life-long friends and family. While residents wanted staff who were friendly and warm, they also expected respect and a social distance that would make it impossible for a staff member to become a pseudo friend or surrogate family member.

Residents of generic homes did not complain about the absence of other JA residents; in fact, some expressed a preference for not being around other Japanese people because there was no desire for social approval. Residents maintained a bicultural, Japanese-American orientation which involved a blending of traditional Japanese values toward family relationships, conflict, and gender roles with American values such as privacy and autonomy. Residents seemed resigned to the various RCFEs although they longed for their "real" homes and former lifestyles. But they rarely discussed these feelings with families because they didn't want to appear ungrateful or be burdensome (Hikoyeda, 2000).

*Implications and Recommendations.* Improving the quality of life in LTC institutions for ethnic elders is much more complex than serving ethnic foods and speaking the native language. Two non-ethnic-specific issues deserve special attention by advocates of LTC reform: boredom and autonomy.

Boredom is a complex issue in residential care. It involves resident abilities and skills, the heterogeneity of interests, available resources, and the mission of the facilities themselves. However, activities have the potential to provide challenge, choices, outside contacts, physical and mental stimulation, therapeutic benefits, and possibly delay deterioration (Morgan, Eckert, & Lyon, 1995). Ironically, the small Japanese-oriented facilities were more likely to have few or no meaningful activities beyond the television, contradicting the assumption that they would provide a better quality of life. The Japanese cultural orientation towards harmonious relationships contributed to facilities offering few activities so that all residents would be treated equally regardless of functional abilities. Perhaps the best solution was presented by the facilities that encouraged residents to use the Japanese senior center's day care program, where a more cognitively homogeneous group engaged in a variety of activities. This could be encouraged in small RCFEs where staffing and case mix make it difficult to design an activity program.

In an RCFE, autonomy means a resident has a right to privacy, to freedom from elder abuse, to voice grievances, and to choose to engage in religious practices and social activities (Regnier, 1996). In reality, autonomous choices are limited due to structural factors (e.g., inadequate staffing), particularly in small facilities. Freedom exists within boundaries, because disabled elders are perceived as dependent and in need of protection, even from themselves. Historically, RCFEs have integrated a home-like environment to facilitate aging in place, creating a pseudo-independence for residents requiring assistance with everyday activities. But within the home-like atmosphere, residents look and dress in a similar fashion, eat at the same time, give up personal possessions and privacy, and develop dependent behaviors (e.g., having to request a glass of water), not unlike inmates in other total institutions (Goffman, 1961). Again, the irony is that the Japanese-oriented homes tended to be smaller and have fewer resources to provide privacy or autonomy. It is difficult to see how this could be improved without additional resources for improved staffing or more volunteers.

Practitioners should also advocate for staff training in RCFEs, including those that are ethnic-specific. Staff could benefit from training on cultural norms and values, acculturation levels, the biopsychosocial aspects of aging, health promotion and disease prevention, mental health issues, family dynamics, trust-building, adaptation, and other caregiving skills to enhance staff competence. Furthermore, to the extent possible, both JA residents and families should be involved in the planning and implementation of residential services and care. There is also a need for policies that make RCFEs more affordable to families and to improve RCFEs for all elders.

The different perspectives of family members and residents presents an important area for practitioners to address. Based on the findings, increased attention should be paid to resident needs and preferences regardless of the RCFEs ethnic orientation or family preferences. Social workers and others need to develop ways to help older JAs, whose culture predisposes them not to complain and to acquiesce to family demands, to communicate their needs and preferences to family members and facility administrators. It is likely that this is an issue for cross-generational (and therefore, to an extent cross-cultural) communications among all Asian groups.

JA families also could benefit from education about normal aging and the biopsychosocial needs of dependent older adults to increase their awareness of factors that contribute to relocation stress and institutional adaptation. They should be encouraged to initiate an ongoing dialogue with their elders about LTC preferences to guide families in the selection of an acceptable facility and give elders some voice in the choice of a home. Consumer education would also help families to navigate the LTC system and provide guidelines regarding services, industry standards, and grievances.

The JA community has been seen by some as a leader in developing ethnically-oriented LTC facilities for the elderly that are culturally congruent and that are assumed to provide a better quality of life. This research found that family members are more satisfied with Japanese-oriented homes because of the Japanese structural characteristics, but that residents do not necessarily appear better off subjectively than those in generic facilities. The findings are an important reminder that continuity for RCFE residents begins with meaningful activities and satisfying social relationships. The basic design and staffing of RCFEs needs to be less institutional and more oriented to individual needs. Ethnic-specific RCFEs were neither necessary nor sufficient for a good quality of life for the majority of JA residents in this study. However, a well-staffed and designed RCFE is *further* enhanced by providing a culturally congruent environment.

## REFERENCES


Atchley, R.C. (1999). *Continuity and adaptation in aging*. Baltimore, MD: The Johns Hopkins University Press.

Barresi, C.M., & Stull, D.E. (1993). *Ethnic elderly and long-term care*. New York: Springer Publishing Co.

Belgrave, L.L., Wykle, M., & Choi, J. M. (1991). *Theoretical approaches to the use of institutionalization by African Americans*. Paper presented at the American Society on Aging, Cincinnati, Ohio.

Birren, J.E., & Dieckmann, L. (1991). Concepts and content of quality of life in the later years: An overview. In J.E. Birren, J.E. Lubben, J.C. Rowe, & D.E. Deutchman (Eds.), *The concept and measurement of quality of life in the frail elderly*. San Diego, CA: Academic Press, Inc.

Espino, D.V. (1993). Hispanic elderly and long-term care: Implications for ethnically sensitive services. In C.M. Barresi & D.E. Stull (Eds.), *Ethnic elderly and long-term care* (pp. 101-112). New York: Springer Publishing Company.

Fugita, S.S., & O'Brien, D.J. (1991). *Japanese American ethnicity: The persistence of community*. Seattle, WA: University of Washington Press.

Gentile, K.M. (1991). A review of the literature on intervention and quality of life in the frail elderly. In J.E. Birren, J.E. Lubben, J.C. Rowe, & D.E. Deutchman (Eds.), *The concept and measurement of quality of life in the frail elderly* (pp. 74-88). San Diego, CA: Academic Press, Inc.

Gibson, R.C. & Jackson, J.C. (1987). The Health, Physical Functioning, and Informal Supports of the Black Elderly. *Milbank Quarterly*, *65*, 421-454.

Goffman, E. (1961). *Asylums*. New York: Doubleday.

Hikoyeda, N.N. (2000). *The role of ethnicity in the quality of life of institutionalized Japanese American Women and their Families*. Doctoral dissertation, University of California, Los Angeles.

Hing, E. (1990). *Long-term care use by Black and White elderly*. Paper presented at the American Public Health Association (APHA), New York, New York.

Iwao, S. (1993). *The Japanese American woman: Traditional image and changing reality*. Cambridge, MA: Harvard University Press.

Jones-Morrison, B. (1982). Sociocultural dimensions: Nursing homes and the minority aged. *Journal of Gerontological Social Work*, *5*(1-2), 127-145.

Kane, R.A., & Kane, R.L. (1987). *Long-term care: Principles, programs, and policies*. New York: Springer Publishing Company.

Katz, S., Downs, T.D., Cash, H.R., & Grotz, R.C. (1970). Progress in development of the index of ADL. *The Gerontologist, Spring*, Part 1, 20-30.

Kendis, R.J. (1989). *An attitude of gratitude: The adaptation to aging of the elderly Japanese in America*. New York: AMS Press.

Kitano, H.H.L. (1993). *Generations and identity: The Japanese American*. Needham Heights, MA: Ginn Press.

Kitano, H. H. L., & Daniels, R. (1988). *Asian Americans: Emerging minorities*. Englewood Cliffs, NJ: Prentice Hall.

Lawton, M.P. (1991). A multidimensional view of quality of life in frail elders. In J.E. Birren, J.E. Lubben, J.C. Rowe, & D.E. Deutchman (Eds.), *The concept and measurement of quality of life in the frail elderly* (pp. 3-27). San Diego: Academic Press, Inc.

Manson, S.M. (1993). Long-term care of older American Indians: Challenges in the development of institutional services. In C. M. Barresi & D. E. Stull (Eds.), *Ethnic elderly and long-term care* (pp. 130-143). New York: Springer Publishing Company.

Markides, K.S., & Wallace, S.P. (1996). Health and long-term-care needs of ethnic minority elders. In J.C. Romeis, R.M. Coe, & J.E. Morley (Eds.), *Applying health services research to long-term care* (pp. 23-41). New York: Springer Publishing Co.

McBride, M.R., Morioka-Douglas, N., & Yeo, G. (1996). *Aging and health: Asian and Pacific Islander American elders*. Stanford, CA: Stanford Geriatric Education Center.

Mitchell, J.M., & Kemp, B.J. (2000). Quality of life in assisted living homes: A multidimensional analysis. *Journal of Gerontology, 55B*, (2), P117-P127.

Morgan, L.A., Eckert, J.K., & Lyon, S.M. (1995). *Small board-and-care homes: Residential care in transition*. Baltimore, MD: The Johns Hopkins University Press.

Mui, A.C., & Burnette, D. (1994). Long-term care service use by frail elders: Is ethnicity a factor? *The Gerontologist*, *34*(2), 190-198.

Osako, M. (1979). Aging and family among Japanese Americans: The role of ethnic tradition in the adjustment to old age. *The Gerontologist, 19*, 448-452.

Padilla, G.V., & Kagawa-Singer, M. (1998). Quality of life and culture. In C.R. King & P.S. Hinds (Eds.), *Quality of life: From nursing and patient perspectives* (pp. 74-92). Boston, MA: Jones and Bartlett Publishers.

Richardson, J. (1996). *Aging and health: Black American elders (2nd Edition).* Stanford, CA: Stanford Geriatric Education Center.

Shibusawa, Tazuko. (1997). Attitudes towards dependency and receiving support among the Japanese elderly. Doctoral dissertation. University of California, Los Angeles.

Spector, R.E. (2000). *Cultural diversity in health and illness* (5th ed.). Upper Saddle River, NJ: Prentice Hall Health.

Strauss, A.L. (1987). *Qualitative analysis for social scientists.* Cambridge: Cambridge University Press.

Strauss, A., & Corbin, J. (1990). *Basics of qualitative research: Grounded theory procedures and techniques.* Thousand Oaks, CA: Sage Publications.

Suinn, R.M., Ahuna, C., & Khoo, G. (1992). The Suinn-Lew Asian self-identity acculturation scale: Concurrent and factorial validation. *Educational and Psychological Measurement, 52*, 1041-1046.

Tanjasiri, S.P., Wallace, S.P., & Shibata, K. (1995). Picture imperfect: Hidden problems among Asian Pacific Islander elderly. *The Gerontologist, 35*, (6), 753-760.

U.S. Bureau of the Census. (1990). *Census of the population and housing-guide: General population characteristics* (pp. 19-48). Washington, DC: U.S. Department of Commerce, U.S. Bureau of the Census.

Wallace, S.P. (1990). Race versus class in the health care of African-American elderly. *Social Problems, 37* (4), 517-534.

Wallace, S.P., Levy-Storms, L., Kington, R., & Andersen, R.A. (1998). The persistence of race and ethnicity in the use of long-term care. *Journal of Gerontology: Social Sciences, 53B:2*, S104-S112.

Yano, K., Reed, D.M., & Kagan, A. (1985). Coronary heart disease, hypertension and stroke among Japanese American men in Hawaii: The Honolulu Heart Program. *Hawaii Medical Journal, 44*, 297-325.

Yeo, G. (1993). Ethnicity and nursing homes: Factors affecting use and successful components for culturally sensitive care. In C.M. Barresi & D.E. Stull (Eds.), *Ethnic elderly and long-term care* (pp. 161-177). New York: Springer Publishing Company.

# Leisure Activity, Ethnic Preservation, and Cultural Integration of Older Korean Americans

Eunja Kim, PhD
Douglas A. Kleiber, PhD
Nancy Kropf, PhD

**SUMMARY.** For immigrant groups, leisure activity has the potential both to increase familiarity with a new culture and to preserve cultural history and identity. Using a qualitative case study design, this research analyzed leisure activities of six older Korean Americans to determine both personal and cultural meanings of leisure. From a personal perspective, leisure was used to create two effects for the older adults: *Ki-Bun-Chun-Whan*, which is the experience of a shift in emotional atmosphere as a result of engaging in activities; and self-development activities, which provide the older adults with opportunities for learning or growth. Cultural meanings of leisure activities included the re-creation of Koreanness and the reliance on familiar patterns to create a sense of security in a still-strange land. Thus, with the individuals studied in this investigation, leisure activities were used more often for continuity and ethnic preservation than for cultural integration. Social workers can use

---

Eunja Kim, Douglas A. Kleiber, and Nancy Kropf are affiliated with the University of Georgia.

This project was partially funded by the University of Georgia Gerontology Seed Grant program (1999-2000).

[Haworth co-indexing entry note]: "Leisure Activity, Ethnic Preservation, and Cultural Integration of Older Korean Americans." Kim, Eunja, Douglas A. Kleiber, and Nancy Kropf. Co-published simultaneously in *Journal of Gerontological Social Work* (The Haworth Social Work Practice Press, an imprint of The Haworth Press, Inc.) Vol. 36, No. 1/2, 2001, pp. 107-129; and: *Social Work Practice with the Asian American Elderly* (ed: Namkee G. Choi) The Haworth Social Work Practice Press, an imprint of The Haworth Press, Inc., 2001, pp. 107-129. Single or multiple copies of this article are available for a fee from The Haworth Document Delivery Service [1-800-HAWORTH, 9:00 a.m. - 5:00 p.m. (EST). E-mail address: getinfo@haworthpressinc.com].

 

leisure activities as avenues to increase knowledge and social participation, but they should also take into account the need to preserve cultural and collective identity in older immigrants. 

**KEYWORDS.** Leisure activity, older Korean Americans, immigrants, ethnic preservation, cultural integration

Being involved in leisure activities in social settings is particularly important for immigrants because it serves to connect them, in spite of the disruptive effects of their shift in life circumstances, to the "social worlds" of others (Kelly, 1996). In this way immigrants may gain familiarity with their new environment and/or rediscover and cultivate histories, cultures, and identities. People negotiate, define, and produce ethnic boundaries, identities, and cultures through social interaction inside and outside their ethnic communities (Nagel, 1994). The nature of leisure makes it an agreeable context for such processes (Stokowski, 1994) and provides an arena for intervention to help preserve and strengthen both social connectedness and self-identification.

Like other social behaviors, leisure activities need to be recognized as culturally specific. As Kelly (1996) acknowledged, leisure is distinguished not by time and activity, but by the particular use of time and the meaning of the activity. Because of cultural differences in meanings, activity forms, and values, different ethnic groups may practice and be shaped by different leisure experiences. Leisure provides a context in which individuals develop new identities and/or strengthen existing ones (Kelly, 1983; Kleiber, 1999); and these are tasks that are particularly important to immigrants. Although there is some understanding about how immigrants in general assimilate into the host society (e.g., Gordon, 1964; Hurh & Kim, 1984; Yinger, 1981), research has not been conducted to determine how expressing actions and social interactions of daily life influences cultural integration and ethnic preservation.

Examining how leisure pursuits relate to cultural integration and ethnic preservation of older Korean Americans has practical implications as well. As older Asian American populations continue to increase, social workers need to design and implement programs and interventions that are based upon the experiences, strengths, and accomplishments of these older adults, their families and their communities (Browne & Broderick, 1994; Dhooper, 1991; Fong & Mokuau, 1994; Tsai & Lopez, 1997). Damron-Rodriguez (1998) refers to this as promoting an "appreciation of the elder's strengths won from a life lived" (p. 53). For social workers, an assessment of leisure activities and pursuits provides a method to understand the fit between an individual's personal and social worlds. The analysis of leisure activities of older Korean Americans that follows was conducted to determine both the personal and cultural significance of such activities. Before turning to the details of the current investigation, however, it is necessary to consider the immigration experience in a broader context.

## *IMMIGRATION: CONTINUITY AND CHANGE*

When people move from their homeland, the process and depth of acculturation into the new culture are based upon several factors. One is age, since the point at which immigration occurs is likely to influence the tendency to use activities to preserve ethnic identity or to facilitate acculturation to the host culture. Acculturation is likely to occur more easily in younger people, whose lives are yet to unfold in the new culture, than with older immigrants who have left more of their lives in their country of origin. For the latter, the past may be more significant than the future. Their daily patterns may change in accommodating to a different culture, language, and environment, but maintaining certain activities or interests in which they have engaged in the past may be especially important.

From a gerontological perspective, the aging process itself influences leisure choices and activities. Atchley (1989) asserted that people in later life attempt to preserve and maintain internal and external structures of their lives. This sense of *continuity* links an individual to the past through his or her personal history. According to Atchley, continuity can be either internal or external. Internal continuity is the integration of inner changes with one's past and a recognition of the relationship between old and the new selves (Lieberman & Tobin, 1983). External continuity is reflected in the structure of physical and social environments, role relationships, and activities that are maintained over time. Atchley (1999) highlighted long-term patterns of external continuity in terms of living arrangements, household composition, marital status, income adequacy, and primary modes of transportation. Atchley

(1987) found that relationships maintained with close friends, parents, and adult offspring were particularly important among older people. Thus, continuity of activities, relationships, and environments provides older people with the practical advantage of stability in spite of other changing and challenging circumstances. Maintaining an interest in preferred enjoyable activities contributes to both external and internal continuity.

Although there is clearly a preference for continuity in late life, discontinuity can be a source of growth and adaptation for people of all ages. Change is part of growing, learning, and adapting. This is particularly true in the case of adult immigrants. Change in social and physical environments caused by immigration may contribute to a disruption in both internal and external continuity, but discontinuity in roles, relationships, and social support may lead adult immigrants to adapt to changing circumstances in ways that are growth-producing. For instance, having breakfast at McDonald's with only Korean-speaking friends may nevertheless reflect a degree of acculturation, and slight variations in traditional Korean activities may also demonstrate accommodation to the new environment. Further investigation is thus needed to reveal how external and internal continuity are preserved in the context of immigration changes and if and how discontinuity in activity patterns contribute to adaptation and cultural integration.

For immigrants who are suddenly disconnected from familiar people and resources, family relations and living arrangements in a new culture are also very important in shaping the course of everyday life. For instance, older Korean Americans living with their adult children and grandchildren may develop a sense of belonging and recognition through family activities and interactions, though living in a residential area within American neighborhoods may isolate this population from other Koreans. In contrast, older Koreans living with other older Koreans in the same apartment complex may preserve their Koreanness more effectively than those who live in American neighborhoods, while the latter may be more acculturated to the host culture as a result of their living arrangements. Older Koreans living in the same apartment complex have more opportunities to interact with other Koreans, by speaking in Korean, watching Korean TV programs, singing Korean music, and sharing Korean food. All these cultural activities may remind them of who they are and to whom they belong in a foreign country. According to Kim (1981), this phenomenon is particularly common among first generation Korean immigrants with a strong desire to maintain part of their own culture. Such activities may or may not replicate those in which they engaged prior to immigration.

We may ask then, how do immigrants choose leisure activities or adapt them once they come to the United States? What are the driving forces in their decision processes? And perhaps most important, what impacts do such choices have on maintaining a sense of self or creating a new sense of self and place? The purpose of this study was to explore daily activities and interactions of older Korean Americans and the relationship of these activities and interactions to ethnic identity preservation and/or cultural integration. This topic is important to social workers since they often strive to help immigrants become part of US culture without diminishing the ties to their traditional cultural norms and practices.

Within this research, first generation older Korean immigrants are of particular interest because they have lived in both Korea and the United States long enough to know both cultures. Using a qualitative analysis three main research questions were explored: (1) What are the meanings that older Korean Americans associate with leisure (*Yeo-Ga*) and other social activities?; (2) How are leisure activities (*Yeo-Ga Whahl-Dong*) and social interactions related to previous (pre-immigration) lifestyles and to ethnic preservation in older Korean Americans?; and (3) How do leisure activities and interactions contribute to the cultural integration of older Korean Americans in the United States?

## *METHOD*

This study used the qualitative case study method to address the three research questions (Yin, 1994). Qualitative case studies are particularistic, descriptive, heuristic, and inductive (Merriam, 1988). A case study approach examines "a phenomenon in its natural setting, employing multiple methods of data collection to gather information from one or a few entities (people, groups, or organizations)" (Benbasat, Goldstein, & Mead, 1987, p. 370). According to Yin (1994), case studies rely on systematic interviewing, direct observation, primary documents, secondary documents, and cultural and physical artifacts as the main sources of evidence. The sources of data used for this study were interviews, time diaries, and field notes.

Six Korean participants over the age of 65 were recruited from the metropolitan area of Atlanta, Georgia, in the United States. Although no official census records are available on the Korean American population in Atlanta, the Korean American Association in Atlanta currently estimates about 50,000-60,000 Koreans residing in the area. The Korean American Welfare Center in Atlanta considered about 10% of the Korean population as older Koreans over 65 years old. The six participants recruited for this study had lived in the U.S. for at least 15 years at the time of data collection. The latter requirement was based on evidence that the longer people live in a strange culture, the more they acculturate (Hurh & Kim, 1984). This criterion thus selected for Korean Americans who have lived in the U.S. long enough to have adapted to the host culture to some extent. It also separated first-generation Korean American citizens and permanent residents from other types of residents such as short-term visitors.

First-generation immigrants with some level of English fluency were solicited for the research. The level of English fluency was measured by whether or not they could communicate minimally with Americans to ask directions, order food, greet American neighbors, etc. A diversity of living arrangements and gender were also considered in selecting the participants. Three males and three females were selected. Of these six, four were living in a residential area with American neighbors while two were living in a senior housing apartment complex with some Korean neighbors. Three participants (two males, one female) lived with a spouse, two (one male, one female) with children, and one (female) lived alone. The level of education the participants had acquired suggested their social status as middle to upper-middle class: Three males had higher than college degrees and three females had high school degrees.

The long interview method (McCracken, 1988) was used because it depends less on participant observation and extended contact. In-depth, semi-structured, open-ended conversational interviews (with voice recording), time diaries, and field notes were the primary sources for data collection. The long interview was arranged with the participants at their homes. In general, each interview took an intensive period of two to four hours, along with informal conversations when the first author stayed overnight at participants' home by their invitation. Several formal and informal follow-up interviews in person or by phone were conducted as needed. For instance, when formal interviews were interrupted because of personal circumstances of the participants, a makeup was arranged. The first author conducted all interviews over a period of four months, maintaining a journal to record her own reflections, as well as comments concerning non-taped verbal and nonverbal behaviors, and notations about the environment (cf. Patton, 1990).

Since data analysis in qualitative research is an ongoing process (Taylor & Bogdan, 1984), initial data analysis started after the biographical information was collected from each participant. The participants were asked to complete a daily time diary for one week, which consisted of "when, where, with whom, and what" to plainly describe the leisure activities that occurred during that week. The time diary data were used to provide "talking points" for the interviews. Interviews were conducted in Korean and audio-taped. All audio-taped data were transcribed in the language (mostly Korean) spoken in the interviews. The best way to keep the meaning of what was said in the original data was to avoid translating and to use the original Korean transcripts for data analysis. However, specific sentences and paragraphs of Korean transcription were later translated to English to provide direct quotations that illustrate the research findings and interpretations. To increase trustworthiness of the data, interpretations of research findings were shared with co-authors and with participants as a form of member-checking (Guba & Lincoln, 1989). The credibility and rigor of the research was further strengthened by an additional source. A Korean fellow researcher who has been educated in both Korea and the United States assisted in exploring cultural interpretations of the data.

The constant comparative method (Glaser & Strauss, 1967) was applied for the data analysis. The basic strategy of the method was to constantly compare data from one time to the next and from one participant to another. For this study we first employed a "within case" analysis method, looking for consistency and differences in meanings portrayed by each participant, and then a "cross-case" analysis to identify shared categories and subcategories. Accordingly, the codes and categories generated for each case were developed as a result of considering each subsequent case.

## *FINDINGS*

The analysis of leisure activity among older Korean Americans in this study revealed both personal and cultural leisure meanings though the personal also had cultural characteristics. The distinction was essentially that the personal served mainly individual psychological interests while the cultural meanings were thus associated with ethnic preservation and cultural integration. In the personal group, two general categories were distinguishable: *Ki-Bun-Chun-Whan* and self-development. *Ki-Bun-Chun-Whan* has particular Korean connotations associated with escape and positive affect. We will examine these personal meanings first and then discuss the cultural meanings and significance of the activities in which the older Korean Americans engaged. The categories for cultural leisure meanings were (1) recreating Koreanness and (2) accommodation to the host culture: dancing between the old and the new. The report concludes with a discussion of the contributions of both personal and cultural meanings of ethnic preservation and cultural integration.

### *Ki-Bun-Chun-Whan*

Although there is no research that has explored the relationship between *Ki-Bun-Chun-Whan* as a form of leisure in Korean society, this study suggests that for older Korean Americans *Ki-Bun-Chun-Whan* is a meaningful part of their daily leisure activities. This is an "emic" category (Geertz, 1983) in that it was offered by a participant and consistently recognized by other participants. Literally, "Ki-Bun" means "a state of mind, or atmosphere" and "Chun-Whan" means "change or shift." Therefore, *Ki-Bun-Chun-Whan* can be interpreted as a "shift in emotional atmosphere." A similar expression people often use is "*Ba-Ram-Ssoi-Da*," meaning "go out to get exposed to fresh air or atmosphere."

Activities people use for *Ki-Bun-Chun-Whan* range from spontaneous, unplanned, and solitary activities to planned, organized group activities. *Ki-Bun-Chun-Whan* enables one to escape from a routine life, reduce stress, and become refreshed and rejuvenated. People achieve Ki-Bun-Chun-Whan in active, social, and collective activities (i.e., drinking, singing, and dancing in a social gathering) but also in passive, personal, and solitary activities (i.e., reading and singing alone).

One participant (Olivia) stated that she sometimes enjoys singing alone for *Ki-Bun-Chun-Whan*. Nevertheless, she admited that "it is better to have *Ki-Bun-Chun-Whan* with other people than by yourself" because "it is better to talk and laugh with others." This statement suggests that social interaction may contribute effectively to *Ki-Bun-Chun-Whan* even though it can occur alone as well. As one of the participants (Charles) put it, *Ki-Bun-Chun-Whan* in a social gathering is epitomized in "becoming elated and losing one's inhibition . . . dancing, playing around, having fun, making jokes, and then sharing funny stories." Common to such expressive patterns is the emotional uplift that they bring. *Ki-Bun-Chun-Whan* makes people feel better and causes them to forget about other stressful aspects of life. But there are a wide variety of ways this is accomplished.

*Ki-Bun-Chun-Whan* can be differentiated in terms of both social interaction and motivation. As a casual form of leisure activities (low motivation), an individual can experience *Ki-Bun-Chun-Whan* with different degrees of social interaction. To take the example of window shopping, participants spoke of window shopping alone with no interest in socializing with other people in the activity, while in other cases they shopped with neighbors where there was a shared purpose. Regardless, window shopping in this study was a common source of *Ki-Bun-Chun-Whan*, relieving boredom and creating some distance from the concerns of every day living. One participant identified window shopping and watching videotapes as activities she does alone when she gets bored with the day, while others pointed to shopping with others as a source of *Ki-Bun-Chun-Whan*.

*Ki-Bun-Chun-Whan* is often found in more meaningful and expressive activities (high motivation) than shopping or watching television. Traveling seemed to create opportunities for more meaningful experience whether it was done alone or with others. *Ki-Bun-Chun-Whan* was also identified as the experience of becoming intensely involved in some activities such as game playing. One of the best sources of *Ki-Bun-Chun-Whan* was a social gathering in which people get together to eat and share stories with each other. One of the female participants remarked:

> Since we have been friends for a long time, we make all kinds of jokes with each other. By doing that, we reduce stress. Wives laugh at husbands' loud conversation. They just laugh and laugh. That's what we do in our gathering. I feel most comfortable when I meet my friends. We are like family. We discuss and share anything with each other without hesitation . . . (Sunny)

Singing was another regular source of *Ki-Bun-Chun-Whan* for several of the participants, but when it was done socially it also contributed to the experience of *Jeong* which is a sense of closeness with others. Emily described this feeling:

> . . . While singing you remember happenings from the past. It's good, you know . . . You feel good while singing. But, singing alone is a different story. You feel good when you socialize and have fun with friends . . . You feel close *Jeong* by doing it. You feel *Jeong* through close interactions and relationships with oth-

ers. After social gatherings with neighbors, you find yourself feeling closer *Jeong* to them. (Emily)

When *Ki-Bun-Chun-Whan* was intense it resulted in a very absorbed state of consciousness akin to what Csikszentmihalyi (1990) called "flow" where everything else (e.g., time and oneself) is forgotten. Most often this occurred while involved in a similar kind of overt action such as playing *Mah-Jong*, but sometimes it occurred simply in watching others (e.g., Korean videotapes or one's grandchildren). Emily recalled her husband's comment in the past that he would forget everything from work as soon as he saw his grandchildren "and their playful tricks" when they had lived in an extended family setting several years ago:

> Our granddaughter has many talents. When she reached the age of four, after coming back from her school, she would have grandpa and grandma sit and pretend to be their teacher. We used to have fun in that way with our family members. Because of such fun with our grandchildren, we would easily get rid of our stress and fatigue from the hard work in the store . . .

### *Self Development*

Unlike *Ki-Bun-Chun-Whan*, the immediate experience of uplift, engagement, and escape is less important to some activities than the planned outcomes that are sought. They are chosen primarily for some advantage they provide for self-development. People choose certain activities because they provide an opportunity for intellectual, physical, psychological, or spiritual growth through the acquisition of knowledge, information, different perspectives, or spirituality rather than being simply a transcendence of every day life. In some cases, participants engaged intentionally in various activities for their educational value. The most common and frequent activities performed for self-development by participants were reading, watching TV, and traveling. While these are all done for *Ki-Bun-Chun-Whan* in some cases, they are also intentionally instrumental. For instance, traveling is an opportunity for changing oneself, as Olivia acknowledged:

> When you stay home all the time you envision only a small world, but you achieve wider perspectives when you go to foreign countries to observe how they live. You open your eyes and ways of thinking through traveling. You gain different perspectives from

> people who don't travel at all and always stay home . . . I find a lot of changes in my life after coming back from traveling. I live with a lot of stresses at home, but traveling around other countries among different people, I feel relaxed . . . and proud of myself and want to tell somebody about my trip and experiences (laugh).

Reading is done to collect information and knowledge to keep up with the changing society. For instance, Charles spoke about reading as his hobby through which he cultivates his life philosophy and feelings of happiness. He noted that it is a source of personal discipline rather than *Ki-Bun-Chun-Whan* for him: "I may have been a useless human being, but when I read, I feel that I am a very significant person. It stimulates my interests . . ." One of the women (Olivia) noted that she reads the Korean newspaper for information on health and listens to radio programs to learn English: "I usually get up at 7 am. The first thing I do in the morning is to turn on the radio. There is an English program called 'pop English' from which I learn a lot." One of the other women also indicated that by keeping up with Korean and American news through a Korean radio channel, she felt she kept in touch with both the old world and the new.

> . . . Yes, I turn on that [Korean Radio] channel for the whole day at home. I just listen to the news or other programs, but there is no special program that I favor . . . I listen to the Korean language. By listening to Korean news, I get Atlanta news or Korean news as if I am in Korea . . . I listen to the radio always. That helps me not to develop suffocating feelings that I don't need to feel like I am blind or confined . . . I know what is going on in Korea as well as in Atlanta. I like it . . . the news is in Korean, talking about both American news and Korean news. (Sunny)

Olivia further emphasized the significance of keeping up with information and knowledge in relation to acquiring self confidence. Olivia admited in the following statement that learning helped her become confident and independent.

> If you don't know what is going on in the world, it is depressing. You have to know so that you can communicate with others. If you don't know, you cannot participate in the conversation. Knowing is power. You accumulate confidence when you know more. It is better to spend your time for self-improvement. You should know

more to be confident of yourself, and others will acknowledge and respect you.

In sum, these older Korean Americans experienced *Ki-Bun-Chun-Whan* through various daily leisure activities and sought self-development through some of the same or other activities. In the next section the focus moves from the individual, social, and psychological meanings of activities to the cultural meanings that are derived in the context of *Yeo-Ga* (leisure). As will be seen, activities are often chosen because of their potential for creating *Jeong*, a feeling of closeness that makes individuals feel re-connected to their "Koreanness" and secure in a still-strange environment. At the same time, some of the self-development activities referred to above (e.g., listening to English language programs) contribute to cultural integration as well.

### *Re-Creating Koreanness*

In this section, the cultural implications of daily leisure activities are examined by which older Korean Americans re-create their sense of "being Korean" or their "Koreanness." Three categories suggested by the data were re-building *Jeong* (attachment/care), re-enforcing collective identity, and seeking familiarity.

*Rebuilding Jeong*. This category encompasses attachment and closeness older Korean Americans feel, develop, and strengthen in interaction with other Koreans in various leisure activities. The Korean word *Jeong* has no English equivalent but contains a unique cultural meaning and refers to a special interpersonal bond of trust and closeness. *Jeong* is slowly developed through a period of interaction, adding other elements such as attachment, empathy, and care. According to Kim (2000), *Jeong* brings about special feelings in relationships including togetherness, sharing, and bonding. *Jeong* is what makes us say "we" rather than "I," "ours" rather than "mine." Koreans consider *Jeong* an essential element in their daily life. Involvement in leisure activities, particularly social, cultural, and collective gatherings promote these elements of *Jeong*. Several Korean terms and concepts that are closely related to the category of "rebuilding Jeong" will be introduced later in this section.

*Jeong* can be developed not only by family members and friends, but by any Koreans who share the idea of Koreanness. Sharing *Jeong* among Korean immigrants seems to be a significant source of unity and identification with each other while living in a foreign country. However, people share deeper *Jeong* with family members or close friends. Sunny described her social interaction with close Korean friends whom she met every month for over 10 years.

> . . . We meet once a month, just an informal social gathering with close friends. We call each other and one of our members will say, "I will invite our group for next month." No fixed date is set for every month. Someone else will take a turn for the next month. . . . We get together at a restaurant or the house of the invitor who will treat the group to a meal. . . . Sometimes, we go to Florida for a vacation . . . we have been meeting once a month for the last 10 years.

The primary purpose of the informal gathering is to socialize but the regularity of it suggests something more meaningful. Charles speaks to the value of socializing in more formal *Kye* meetings. *Kye* is a very common social gathering in Korea within which people satisfy their needs for financial support ("Money Kye") and social interaction ("Social *Kye*"). Exchanging information on any happenings in the community is another purpose of the social gathering. Charles acknowledged *Kye* as distinctively Korean:

> Like the Joy Luck Club, the *Kye* meeting is a cultural tradition for us to socialize. . . . It provides a motive to socialize. It's necessary in our society. It's part of our culture and lifestyle in our daily lives. That's the *Kye* meeting. . . . Without this gathering, we seldom have an opportunity to communicate with other Koreans . . .

In addition to reproducing *Jeong*, *Kye* and other social gatherings serve as a way to reconnect with the past and restore internal continuity, as Sunny noted:

> In Korea, we used to visit our neighbors all the time, this house or that house, but here in the States, we don't have that opportunity. So, when we get together, we like to talk about our lives in the past in Korea.

The informal gathering that took place in Korea that Sunny recalled is referred to as *Ma-Sil-Ka-Gi*. *Ma-Sil-Ka-Gi* is an activity that commonly takes place in agricultural societies where people settle down in the same place for generations. In the rural area of Korea, people would visit their neighbor's house after supper without any invitation or notice in advance. They would spend most of the time talking, but dancing and drinking could follow. As Korean society became modernized, the pure form of *Ma-Sil-Ka-Gi* virtually disappeared in the urban area, but it is still reproduced in different forms of activities that demonstrate similar meanings.

Emily talked about a young man in her church who was a former (Korean) national diver and who volunteered to give swimming lessons to older Koreans in the church out of "*Hyo*" (filial piety) to his mother living far away. Because of the feeling of *Jeong*, he identified other Korean elderly with his own parents. Feelings of *Jeong* with the motherland are also expressed by Charles while listening to music from the past: "It takes me back to feelings and memories of my childhood that I had forgotten and now seldom think about . . . It's reminiscence."

In the case of John, a feeling of attachment toward his motherland is unconsciously expressed by his act of hanging a Korean national flag on the wall in the living room. Although John considers the national flag simply as a decoration, his bonding (*Jeong*) to the motherland is revealed in his behavior without his being aware of it. Involvement in religious practice on a regular basis is another influential factor in building *Jeong* with other Korean church members, as Emily noted:

> In our church we often met with church members to socialize and had fun without getting involved in social *Kye*. We did not get involved in any social *Kye* like other people who miss other Koreans, meet, and socialize. Other people might need it, but we did not have much to do with it. . . . We often had social gathering with our church members. We like it much more than social gatherings with other friends. . . . Maybe because we see each other every Sunday and keep in close touch . . .

*Re-Enforcing Collective Identity.* Older Korean Americans identify with other Koreans and create a sense of security by being members of a Korean community. They interact and socialize with each other by sharing the same culture, tradition, values, language, and physical appearance. Invigorating in ways referred to in the section *Ki-Bun-Chun-Whan*, various leisure opportunities promote the sense of belonging and community for older Korean Americans. These include traveling, attending Korean senior school, or observing Korean traditional holidays. Traveling is an important activity through which older Koreans experience mixed and complicated feelings of who they are. By traveling together Koreans are reminded of the non-Korean world "out there" and conversely of their own common culture through the reactions of others to them. Participants often possess two views of their own identity: legal and cultural. Older Korean Americans are well aware of their legal status as American citizens. However, they also know that they are Korean. In exposing themselves to others through travel Koreans acknowledge their own identity as Korean. Olivia offered a specific example:

> While traveling, people ask me 'What's your nationality?' I say, 'I am Korean.' . . . Although I acquired American citizenship, I am originally Korean. . . . Who would think me American? My skin color is different. Americans have white skin color and yellow hair, shouldn't I have it, too? . . . Even in my apartment, if somebody would ask my nationality, then I would say, 'I am Korean.' Who would believe me as American? Nobody. I've been recognized as Korean. Look, our skin color is different from Americans. . . . With lack of fluent English language ability, how could you say you are American?

This statement points out Olivia's awareness of her different physical appearance and lack of fluency in English. Differences in physical appearance may influence Korean immigrants to sustain their ethnic identity, not by choice but by psychosocial pressure. Language barriers also contribute to ethnic identification. As expressed in Olivia's statement, to be truly American, one should possess an American accent and fluency in English, in addition to an American appearance. One participant (Emily) emphasized that "Americans are different in physical appearance. They have a big nose, blonde hair, and different shapes of eyes, everything is different." Like others, Emily limits her definition of the term "American" to that segment of the American population which possesses these physical characteristics. The limiting itself is self-defining.

Observing Korean holidays also reminded Korean Americans of their original culture and traditions and provided an opportunity to get together with other Koreans who understand and share the meaning and significance of the holiday celebration.

> A couple on the 6th floor invited us for dinner to celebrate "January Full-moon day." They make '*O-Gok-Bab*' (rice with five different grains). . . . Everyone in the building will come. . . . After dinner, we might watch Korean videotapes. The husband of the dinner invitor always rents about ten videotapes with his own

> money for us. That's why we all can watch them all the time . . . (Olivia)

By watching Korean videotapes at the gathering, older Korean Americans experienced the same language, culture, and understanding of the stories. Emily explained that she watches Korean videotapes because she shares the same nation and race. In addition, attending Korean senior school reassured Olivia of some cultural stability in this foreign land. She recalled her feelings of the first day at the senior school:

> When I attended this senior school for the first time I was very moved by the fact that I can take a Korean music class here in another country. Staying at home everyday alone I had nobody to talk and laugh with, but now I am at the school, sitting in a music class, singing and thinking, 'This is great' . . .

Another source of collective identification was through organized sports clubs such as mountain climbing. John shared his experience of being a member of a mountain climbing club. The purpose of joining a sports club for John seems to be more for the activity itself, rather than for an opportunity for social interaction with other Koreans. He was very aware of being older than other club members, which prevented active interaction with them. Thus, *Jeong* was not particularly generated in this case, but a sense of collective identity was reinforced nonetheless:

> Here we (Korean Americans) have a mountain climbing club. With the club members on weekends, I go to mountains nearby. The one-day course starts in the early morning for 4-5 miles and then back home after lunch. I've done it for three years. . . . We have about 20-30 members as a group climbing once every month . . . . Everybody in the club is young . . . I don't hang out with other young members. I just go to the mountain with the group. After coming back from mountain climbing, I seldom get together with them to visit their houses.

*Seeking Familiarity*. Some of the interview responses suggested that some leisure activities had less to do with asserting Koreanness than with falling back on it for familiarity and continuity. Language familiarity reinforces older Korean Americans' tendency to continue listening to Korean radio channels and audio tapes, watching Korean videotapes, and reading Korean newspapers and books, and interacting with other Koreans by speaking only in Korean. Various quotations illustrate these tendencies. Sunny admitted that "the first thing [I] do in the morning is to turn on the Korean radio channel . . . I like it very much. I can listen to the Korean news broadcast in Korean in my car. I love to listen to Korean news. In fact, we older people like to listen to all Korean radio programs." Some older Koreans, according to Sunny, would call a radio program in which callers are invited to sing on the phone.

Familiarity with language extended to watching Korean videotapes with other older Koreans. Watching Korean videotapes with Korean neighbors was a very common daily activity among those older Korean Americans living in the same senior housing apartment complex and became the focus of their congregating. Olivia said, "My Korean friend living across the hall always asks me to come to her apartment to watch [Korean] videos and laugh together . . . " Charles explains why watching Korean videotapes is a popular activity among older Korean Americans:

> The reason the elderly enjoy watching videotapes is that these programs show how they lived out their lives in the past. . . . The stories on tapes make them reflect on their life experiences . . . they re-visit their *Han-Kuk-Jeok-In-Geot* (Koreanness) in viewing the videotapes.

Preference for the familiar also influences the choice of restaurants for older Korean Americans. Sunny explained why she prefers Chinese restaurants over American restaurants in the following statement:

> First of all, I cannot go to an expensive and formal American restaurant because of language barriers. I cannot. We have many Korean restaurants as well as Chinese restaurants. When you go to a Chinese restaurant, you find people working in the restaurant speaking Korean very well. . . . I don't feel uncomfortable going to the Chinese restaurant because I used to eat Chinese food that I like in Korea.

Going to a Korean church is another way of maintaining the comfortable support of other Koreans. Emily gave her own reason for going to a Korean church: "I like Korean church . . . I like it because we can speak Korean, meet friends, and when we meet, we can hold each other's hands. That's what I like about going to Korean churches."

Another way to keep social interaction with Koreans is to attend formal or informal social gatherings. Tim explained the birth of *Kye* meetings after immigration: "In the beginning, we organized this *Kye* meeting for those who are very lonely, and who want to meet and enjoy themselves together once a month." Tim admitted that he was not interested in *Kye* meetings in the past in Korea, but in the U.S. "we seldom find a place for social gatherings, so we organized *Kye* for a meeting place to socialize with each other once a month."

Regardless of the efforts and determination of immigrants, particularly the first generation, to acculturate into the host society, the older Korean Americans in this study re-created their Koreanness by re-building *Jeong*, re-enforcing collective identity, and seeking familiar forms of the old culture. Nevertheless, it is also clear that they made accommodations to their host culture in the course of daily living, and leisure activities were a mechanism for this as well.

## *ACCOMMODATION TO THE HOST CULTURE: DANCING BETWEEN THE OLD AND THE NEW*

Although lifestyles and daily activities of older Korean Americans in this study are predominantly colored by the traditions, culture, language, and food of their motherland, there is no doubt that these people have struggled to fit between the two cultures. The tuning in to English language radio and the listening to Atlanta news on Korean stations are examples of accommodation, done as much out of personal interest as necessity. Sunny spoke of overcoming her homesickness during the early immigration period and learning to know and enjoy America after living here for 15 years, and John described a similar realization:

> Since I was not raised in the U.S. I couldn't say I know American culture, but after living here for over 30 years, I could not say that I *don't* know much about American culture. Either statement could be considered untruthful to someone else.

In beginning to live independently from her son, Olivia learned that "living alone means freedom. . . . Nobody bothers you if you jump around dancing or singing in your own space." This statement also demonstrates the experiences of independence brought about by living arrangements.

While we have established the place of watching TV and shopping in *Ki-Bun-Chun-Whan*, watching American TV provides an exposure to the host culture as well.

> I don't watch American TV much, but sometimes I watch wrestling or skating. Wrestling looks very scary, beating each other with objects like iron chairs or lifting and throwing a woman . . . I just watch it because it draws my attention. . . . They look like beasts rather than human beings. I don't enjoy watching, but it is entertaining. The other evening, I happened to turn on the channel and watched for quite a long time . . . (Olivia)

Olivia distinguished entertainment from enjoyment in her statement by saying that she was entertained by the program, but she did not enjoy it. She seemed to take the role of spectator rather than participant in the activity. Nevertheless, watching American wrestling on TV was one way to get familiarized to the host culture. Going window shopping was another example that demonstrated the involvement in the activity as a spectator. Sunny shared her experience of going window shopping at a mall with her husband. They walked around with other Americans but were not fully engaged in the interactions: "We would sit there and watch Americans . . . watch them pass by because now we are not afraid of doing it."

Food is one of the most difficult habits to adjust to in another country, for adults in particular (Bourdieu, 1984). Nevertheless, several participants admitted that their meal habits, especially breakfast, have changed somewhat, after living in the States for a long time. One participant (Sunny) acknowledged her changes by saying that "Well, I like milk and cereal, so I feel I have changed." Another participant (John) prefered to go to McDonald's and to read American newspapers while having lunch there. Generally, though, the examples of using leisure for cultural accommodation and integration in the six individuals discussed in this investigation were far fewer than examples of ethnic preservation.

## *DISCUSSION*

Obviously, leisure is not an isolated aspect of life or culture, but derives from complex social and interpersonal relationships and interactions. The nature of leisure is apparently connected to the meaning of community, social relationships and interactions, and the relationships between individuals and their environments (Stokowski, 1994). One simple way to portray individuals' experiences in a new culture is to observe the dynamics of daily activities and interactions, which often occur in leisure contexts. This study examined the personal and cultural meanings of leisure experience of a group of older Korean immigrants. In this study, leisure (*Yeo-Ga*) was used personally to create two effects: *Ki-Bun-Chun-Whan* and self-development. *Ki-Bun-Chun-Whan* is a feeling of refreshment and transcendence that was found in a wide variety of activities. But some of the same activities, as well as others, were used for intellectual, physical, psychological, or spiritual growth and for familiarization with the host culture.

From a cultural perspective, leisure activities and social interactions were used more often for continuity and ethnic preservation than cultural integration. Older Korean Americans in the study maintained a high level of attachment to their ethnic identity. While physical and cultural differences perpetuated a feeling of strangeness, they used a wide variety of activities to reinforce their Koreanness and restore their sense of place. As Min (1991) stated, most Korean immigrants speak the Korean language, eat Korean food, and practice Korean customs most of the time. Many are affiliated with at least one Korean organization and are involved in active informal ethnic networks. Through networks such as churches, business organizations, alumni organizations, and senior schools, most Korean Americans maintain and strengthen social interaction with other Koreans.

## *IMPLICATIONS FOR SOCIAL WORK*

These findings suggest several implications for social work practice. Even though all of the participants in this study had lived in the U.S. for 15 years or more, a continued tension exists between being "Korean" and being "American." Part of this challenge is based on the differences between the more individually-oriented American culture and the traditional Asian value of collectivism (Balgopal, 1999). For these older adults, there is a strong desire to remain connected to that part of themselves and their history that is uniquely Korean. A wide variety of activities described in this research indicate a will to preserve their cultural identification. These included recreating traditional Korean activities in the U.S. (e.g., *Kye*), celebrating traditional holidays (e.g., January-Full-Moon Day), and establishing Korean social institutions (e.g., Korean American churches). Such activities should be viewed as a way to preserve cultural heritage and provide opportunities to retain

"Koreanness." In addition, these memberships and activities serve as points of contact between Korean community and the formal services that currently exist for older adults (Choi & Tirrito, 1999).

Although somewhat less commonly, older Koreans also used leisure activities as a way to learn more about and connect to the American culture. In certain cases, "Americanizing" their lives simplified their daily habits such as with the woman who discovered that she enjoyed cereal and milk for breakfast. In other cases, activities were intentionally instrumental, such as enhancing English language skills or learning about U.S. forms of recreation.

Several of the participants reported that participation in American culture continues to be difficult. Barriers to social participation and access to services must be addressed for Koreans and other ethnic/racial groups. Within this research participants reported alienation based upon their physical characteristics (skin and hair color) as well as language. However, the "double jeopardy" of being an older person of color was also evident. Being an older adult appeared to add another dimension since difference involves both cultural and age distinctions. This fact was reflected in comments from the older mountain climber who felt apart from the younger climbing group, even though they were Korean.

As the number of older adults continues to increase, social workers will be working with clients from a variety of cultural, ethnic, and religious backgrounds. In this study, research on leisure activity of older Korean Americans provided significant information about how daily activities are used to strengthen cultural connectedness and preserve ethnic identity. By assessing and understanding how older adults choose to spend their time, practitioners can determine some of the challenges that older adults are facing as well as the strategies that are being used to manage these tensions. In addition, this type of analysis provides a rationale for creating social programs and interventions that have a special meaning in the lives of older adults, whatever their cultural and social backgrounds.

## REFERENCES

Atchley, R. C. (1987). *Aging: Continuity and change* (2nd Eds.). Belmont, CA: Wadsworth.

Atchley, R. C. (1989). A continuity theory of normal aging. *The Gerontologist, 29*(2), 183-190.

Atchley, R. C. (1999). *Continuity and adaptation in aging: Creating positive experiences*. Baltimore, MA: The Johns Hopkins University.

Balgopal, P. R. (1999). Getting old in the U.S.: Dilemmas of Indo-Americans. *Journal of Sociology and Social Welfare, 26*(1), 51-68.

Benbasat, I., Goldstein, D. K., & Mead, M. (1987). The case research strategy in studies of information systems. *MIS Quarterly*, September, 369-386.

Bourdieu, P. (1984). *Distinction: A social critique of the judgment of taste*. Cambridge, MA: Harvard University.

Browne, C., & Broderick, A. (1994). Asian and Pacific Island elders: Issues for social work practice and education. *Social Work, 39*(3), 252-259.

Choi, G., & Tirrito, T. (1999). The Korean church as a social service provider for older adults. *Arete, 23*(2), 69-83.

Csikszentmihalyi, M. (1990). *Flow: The psychology of optimal experiences*. New York: Harper & Row.

Damron-Rodriguez, J. A. (1998). Respecting ethnic elders: A perspective for care providers. *Journal of Gerontological Social Work, 29*(2/3), 53-72.

Dhooper, S. S. (1991). Toward an effective response to the needs of Asian Americans. *Journal of Multicultural Social Work, 1*(2), 65-81.

Fong, R., & Mokuau, N. (1994). "Asian Americans": Periodical literature review on Asians and Pacific Islanders. *Social Work, 39*(3), 298-305.

Geertz, C. (1983). Thick description: Toward an interpretive theory of culture. In M. Emerson (Eds.), *Contemporary field research: A collection of readings*. (pp. 37-59). Prospect Heights, IL: Waveland.

Glaser, B. G., & Strauss, A. L. (1967). *The discovery of grounded theory*. Chicago: Aldine.

Gordon, M. M. (1964). *Assimilation in American life*. NY: Oxford University Press.

Guba, E. G., & Lincoln, Y. S. (1989). *Fourth generation evaluation*. Newbury Park, CA: Sage.

Hurh, W. M., & Kim, K. C. (1984). *Korean immigrants in America: A structural analysis of ethnic confinement and adhesive adaptation*. Cranburry, NJ: Associated University Presses.

Kelly, J. R. (1983). *Leisure identities and interactions*. UK: George Allen & Unwin.

Kelly, J. R. (1996). *Leisure*. Needham Heights, MA: Allyn & Bacon.

Kim, I. (1981). *New urban immigrants: The Korean community in New York*. Princeton, NJ: Princeton University Press.

Kim, L. I. (2000). To name our feelings: Searching out Korean psychology, ethos and emotions. *Korean Quarterly, 3*(4), 10-13.

Kleiber, D. (1999). *Leisure experience and human development*. New York: Basic Books.

Lieberman, M. A., & Tobin, S. S. (1983). *The experience of old age: Stress, coping, and survival*. New York: Basic Books.

McCracken, G. (1988). *The long interview*. Newbury Park, CA: Sage.

Merriam, S. B. (1988). *Case study research in education: A qualitative approach*. San Francisco, CA: Jossey-Bass.

Min, P. G. (1991). Cultural and economic boundaries of Korean ethnicity: A comparative analysis. *Ethnic and Racial Studies, 14*(2), 225-241.

Nagel, J. (1994). Constructing ethnicity: Creating and recreating ethnic identity and culture. *Social Problems, 41*(1), 152-176.

Patton, M. (1990). *Qualitative evaluation and research methods.* Newbury Park, CA: Sage.

Stokowski, P. A. (1994). *Leisure in society: A network structural perspective.* NY: Mansell.

Taylor, S. T., & Bogdan, R. (1984). *Introduction to qualitative research methods: The search for meaning.* NY: John Wiley & Sons.

Tsai, D. T., & Lopez, R. A. (1997). The use of social supports by elderly Chinese immigrants. *Journal of Gerontological Social Work, 29*(1), 77-94.

Yin, R. K. (1994). *Case study research: Design and methods.* Thousand Oaks, CA: Sage.

Yinger, J. (1981). Toward a theory of assimilation and dissimilation. *Ethnic and Racial Studies, 4,* 249-264.

# Conceptions of Dementia Among Vietnamese American Caregivers

Gwen Yeo, PhD
Jane Nha UyenTran, MSW
Nancy Hikoyeda, DrPH
Ladson Hinton, MD

---

Gwen Yeo is Director Emerita and Director of Special Projects, Stanford Geriatric Education Center, Stanford University School of Medicine. Jane Nha UyenTran is Research Assistant, Center For AIDS Prevention Studies, Health Studies for People of Color, University of California, San Francisco. Nancy Hikoyeda is Director, Gerontology Program, San Jose State University. Ladson Hinton is affiliated with UC Davis Medical School, Sacramento, CA.

Address correspondence to: Ladson Hinton, MD, Department of Psychiatry, UC Davis Medical School, Sacramento, CA 95817 (E-mail: ladson.hinton@ucdmc.ucdavis.edu).

The authors express their sincere appreciation to Quyen Kim Le, MS, for her assistance with interviewing, transcribing, and translating some of the interviews.

This work was partially supported by a pilot project grant from the Harvard University's Center on Culture and Aging, one of six Exploratory Centers for Research on Health Promotion in Older Minority Populations, funded by the National Institute on Aging, Sue Levkoff, PhD, Director. The opportunity to conduct this study of the conceptions of dementia and caregiving among Vietnamese families in the San Francisco Bay Area presented itself through the generous support of Drs. Arthur Kleinman and Sue Levkoff of the Harvard Center on Culture and Aging. They offered the Stanford Geriatric Education Center at Stanford University the option of developing a pilot project to apply the methodology used in the Boston Area to study African American, Chinese American, Irish American, and Puerto Rican American families to Vietnamese Americans in the San Francisco/San Jose area under the direction of Dr. Ladson Hinton who helped direct the research at Harvard.

[Haworth co-indexing entry note]: "Conceptions of Dementia Among Vietnamese American Caregivers." Yeo et al. Co-published simultaneously in *Journal of Gerontological Social Work* (The Haworth Social Work Practice Press, an imprint of The Haworth Press, Inc.) Vol. 36, No. 1/2, 2001, pp. 131-152; and: *Social Work Practice with the Asian American Elderly* (ed: Namkee G. Choi) The Haworth Social Work Practice Press, an imprint of The Haworth Press, Inc., 2001, pp. 131-152. Single or multiple copies of this article are available for a fee from The Haworth Document Delivery Service [1-800-HAWORTH, 9:00 a.m. - 5:00 p.m. (EST). E-mail address: getinfo@haworthpressinc.com].

 

**SUMMARY.** Understanding cultural conceptualizations of dementia and caregiving can assist health and social service providers to work more effectively with elders and their families. Interviews with nine Vietnamese American family caregivers in the San Francisco Bay Area were tape-recorded, transcribed and then content-analyzed for dementia labels and attributions. Labels fell into three main categories: (1) *lẩn* and closely related folk idioms that refer to age-cognitive decline and confusion in older adults, (2) folk and professional terms that refer to medical illness, and (3) folk and professional terms for mental illness or craziness. Attributions fell into four categories: (1) normal age-related, (2) physiological, (3) psychosocial, and (4) spiritual/religious. An additional theme that emerged from the analysis was the sense of obligation for family members to care for elders and the reluctance to use outside supportive and long term care services. 

**KEYWORDS.** Vietnamese, caregivers, dementia, attributions

## *BACKGROUND*

Understanding cultural variations in the meaning of cognitive impairment and behavior change in old age is important for developing culturally competent approaches to research (Hazuda et al., 1997; Henderson, 1990; Hinton et al., 2000) and clinical care (Valle, 1998; Yeo, 1996). Conceptions of dementia, the labels and attributions that families hold, may influence a range of illness behaviors, including self-care, help-seeking, and treatment compliance. Informed by an understanding of patient and family interpretations of the illness, the clinician will be better able to assess families, negotiate a treatment plan, establish rapport, and engage patients and their families in successful treatment.[1] Despite the importance of this topic for clinical care and research, relatively little is known about how patients and their families view dementing illness, particularly among minority populations such as Asian Americans, African Americans, and Latinos. This information is especially important for clinicians working with members of ethnic minority groups who view dementia in ways that differ from the biomedical model of disease.[2]

Qualitative methods were used for this pilot study because there are no previous studies of Vietnamese caregivers of dementia-affected elderly. The goal of this study was to elicit conceptions of dementia held by Vietnamese caregivers of elderly with dementia. More specifically, what labels do caregivers use to describe dementia and what attributions do they make to its causes? How are these understandings similar to, or different from, the biomedical model? What are the implications for the practice of clinically competent care? We also describe attitudes towards use of formal supportive services, particularly nursing homes, which emerged as a prominent theme in several interviews and have direct relevance to clinical care.

### *Demographic and Historical Background of Vietnamese Americans*

Triggered by the end of the Vietnam War, a large Vietnamese Diaspora has been created throughout the world over the past 25 years. The first large exodus of Vietnamese migration to the U.S. occurred following the fall of Saigon in 1975. This initial "wave" included many South Vietnamese military officers, government officials, and professionals who were evacuated by air and by boat during and shortly after the Communist takeover. Overall, this first group of refugees was largely ethnic Vietnamese Catholics who tended to be better educated and more affluent than Vietnamese who migrated later. The second "wave" of migration, beginning in 1978 when hostilities erupted between Vietnam and China, included ethnic Chinese and ethnic Vietnamese, often escaping on small boats where they were vulnerable to pirate attacks and the elements. From the early 1980s through the 1990s, special programs for family reunification (i.e., Orderly Departure Program) and for political detainees (i.e., reeducation camp survivors) resulted in migration of large numbers of Vietnamese to the U.S., many of whom were older adults. The influx of older adults through these programs and the aging of earlier immigrants from prior waves have resulted in an exponential growth in the number of Vietnamese elders in the U.S. For example, between 1989 and 1992, 16,021 people age 60 and over immigrated from Vietnam to the U.S. By 1995, there were an estimated 41,500 persons aged 65 and over of Vietnamese ancestry residing in the U.S. (Young and Gu, 1995; Yeo, Hikoyeda, McBride et al., 1998).

While the ethnic Vietnamese population in the U.S. was only 600,000 in 1990, it is now fast approaching 1 million. More than half of the Vietnamese population in the U.S. resides in California. Many older Vietnamese Americans have experienced severe discrimination since their arrival in America, as well as adjustment to radically different lifestyles in which culturally defined expectations of deference and care in old age are not always met. Younger members of families often struggle to try to meet their elders' expectations of filial piety in the face of economic situations that require employment of all of the adults, and lack of available extended family support that would have been available in Vietnam. No information is available on the prevalence of dementia among Vietnamese elders in the U.S., but anecdotal reports from local social service agencies serving the Vietnamese American population indicate that, as with most populations, caregiving of frail elders is a common challenge for these families.

### *Previous Empirical Studies of Lay Conceptions of Dementing Illness*

An emerging literature of largely small scale qualitative studies suggests both cross-ethnic similarities and differences in the way that family caregivers view dementing illness (Braun et al., 1996; Elliott et al., 1996; Fox et al., 1999; Henderson et al., 1996; Hinton et al., 2000; Ortiz et al., 1999). Only one study focused on Vietnamese. Braun and her associates conducted focus groups and individual interviews with members of the Vietnamese community in Hawaii (Braun et al., 1996). Participants were selected based on a number of criteria and included key informants, but not Vietnamese caregivers of elders with dementia. Braun concludes that for Vietnamese, dementia is often viewed as a normal part of the aging process, and often is not a priority for families compared with other challenges they face, and that families are quite open to the use of formal services. A number of key idioms or labels are mentioned, including *lẩn*, which translates as "confusion."

Braun's findings are augmented by studies of Chinese and Chinese-Americans, because of the intertwining of Chinese and Vietnamese cultures (Elliott et al., 1996; Hicks and Lam, 1999; Hinton and Levkoff, 1999; Guo et al., 1999; Hinton et al., 2000). For example, traditional Vietnamese views of mental and physical health may be influenced by concepts derived from traditional Chinese medicine, and from moral/religious traditions such as ancestor worship, Taoism, Confucianism, and Buddhism. A study of dementia in China concluded that dementia is less alarming to many Chinese families (compared with European Americans) because it is viewed as a normal outcome of the aging process (Ikels, 1998). Hinton and Levkoff (1999), in their cross-cultural study of caregivers in Boston, observed that while Irish-American and African-American family caregivers often experienced dementia as a loss of the personhood or self of the afflicted person, Chinese families rarely experienced dementia in these terms. Instead the focus for Chinese families was on moral obligations to provide care and on dementia changes as a normal part of the aging process. More recent studies have suggested that the stigma of mental illness may be an important factor in Chinese-American families caring for someone with dementia (Guo et al., 1999; Hinton et al., 2000). Hinton et al. (2000) suggests that in a cross-cultural context the labeling of dementia symptoms may be best understood as the result of an interaction of biologically-based symptoms, disease severity, interactions with the medical system, and sociocultural context of family care.

In summary, available literature reflecting the cultural influences on Vietnamese families suggests they may be less familiar with biomedical labels such as Alzheimer's disease or dementia, and more likely to view dementia-related changes as normal than non-Vietnamese Americans. To our knowledge, ours is the first empirical study of Vietnamese caregivers of elders with dementia, allowing us to begin to test the general assumptions in the literature directly.

## *METHODS*

The research was a qualitative study of ten family caregivers of elders with dementing illness, all of whom were born in Vietnam. A convenience sample of subjects was recruited through multiple community agencies serving Vietnamese Americans in the San Francisco area, including primary care clinics, adult day health centers, and religious organizations. To be eligible for the study, caregivers needed to be self-identified as Vietnamese or Vietnamese-American and to be an adult family caregiver of an elder (i.e., age 60 or above) who had been diagnosed with dementia or who was suffering from significant memory loss or confusion. If the elderly care recipient had not been formally diagnosed with dementia, the signs and symptoms (as reported by the caregiver) were reviewed by the geropsychiatrist (Dr. Hinton) to determine whether they met DSM-IV criteria for probable dementia. All but three of the caregivers identified agreed to participate in the study.

Nine structured interviews were conducted with ten caregivers (one included both a son and husband of the elder) by trained bilingual/bicultural interviewers in the caregivers' homes lasting approximately two hours. All of the interviews were conducted in Vietnamese based on the respondents' choice. One interview was excluded because the elder's symptoms did not fit the criteria for dementing illness. The following analysis focuses on the remaining eight interviews with nine family caregivers.

## *RESULTS*

### *Demographic Characteristics of Caregivers and Elders*

The nine caregivers who were interviewed had the following relations to the five women and two men for whom they were caring: one was a wife, two were husbands, two were sons, three were daughters, and one was a son-in-law's niece. In two cases, two caregivers for the same elder were included in the study because they had both been heavily involved in caregiving responsibilities. Ages of the caregivers ranged from 28 to 72, and the elders ranged from 52 to 82. Two of the caregivers were no longer living with their elders at the time of the interview; one elder was in a nursing home, and one was living with another family member, who was also interviewed. Although questions regarding religion were not asked directly, issues of spiritual support and belief emerged in a number of the interviews. Catholicism was the dominant religious affiliation, but two respondents described Taoist and Buddhist beliefs and practices.

The median household size was five individuals, with a range from two to ten. In several cases the household included family members outside the nuclear family relationship, such as nephews. When asked to choose a response that best described their financial situation, four chose the statement "I barely have enough or do not have enough," two chose "I do not have enough," and two said "I have enough and sometimes more"; one caregiver chose not to respond. Income figures ranged from less than $5,000 for two respondents to $50,000-$75,000 for one person. Most respondents had a high school education or a little less; the exceptions are one daughter who had attended law school, and an older husband who identified his education as "able to read and write." Caregivers reported their current occupations as electronics, *au pair*, barber, business woman, janitor, and student; the two husbands were retired and no prior occupation was given. One elder had graduated college, but the rest had elementary or middle school education. Previous occupations were listed for all of the elders, including the older women in their 70's and 80's; all but two were in business, one had been a farmer, and one a housekeeper. We now present our qualitative analysis of dementia labels, attributions, and attitudes towards use of formal long-term care and support services.

## *Labels*

An exploration of the different types of labels and their usage provides an important window on the meanings of dementia-related symptoms within the context of Vietnamese culture. Our analysis revealed a rich variety of labels for dementia falling into three main categories: (1) *lân* and closely related folk idioms that refer to cognitive decline and confusion in older adults, (2) folk and professional terms that refer to medical illness and (3) folk and professional terms for mental illness or craziness.

*Lân and related terms*: In Vietnamese culture, it is recognized that older adults may lose some of their mental acuity and sometimes become forgetful and confused. This is often accepted as a normal part of the aging process. Cognitive decline in older adults is understood through the folk idiom of "*lân*," which roughly translates as "confused." This term emerged as a prominent label in six of the eight interviews. Within the context of Vietnamese culture, an older man (*ong*) or woman (*ba*) who exhibits forgetfulness was said to be *lân roi,* meaning to be "confused already" or "become confused." Another related expression found in the interviews is *lân lon,* meaning confused and mixed-up. In their descriptions of the elderly care recipients considered to be *lân,* caregivers emphasized cognitive symptoms of dementia such as forgetting names of children or other relatives, not recognizing family members, and forgetting how things work. While its use is not exclusively reserved for older adults, the term *lân* is most commonly used to refer to elderly. The close connection between the later stages of life and mental confusion is expressed by the well-known phrase *gia lân,* meaning old and confused, which was used by several of our informants. According to this conception of old age, memory loss is normal and expected, not pathological. As one 51-year old caregiver stated, her mother was "just confused" and "not sick."

*Folk and professional terms for medical or physical illness*: Another group of caregivers used biomedical labels to explain their relative's illness. Here caregivers had clearly adopted the descriptive language of health care providers that is less stigmatizing than the lay terms connoting mental illness. For example, two caregivers referred to their relative as having suffered a "stroke," a term they said their doctor had used. Use of the stroke label was often accompanied by references to pathological processes in the brain, such as clogged arteries or shrinkage. Some caregivers used the term brain disease (*benh nao*). Only one caregiver used the term Alzheimer's disease: "The only thing I remember is that the doctor used the word Alzheimer a lot." Other caregivers referred to their relative's illness using terms that bear less resemblance to professional medical terms but refer to the pathology, such as old age illness and confusion illness.[3]

Interestingly, several caregivers who used these folk and professional illness labels also used the term *lân*. For example, *lân* was used by several caregivers together with illness labels such as "brain disease" and stroke, as described in more detail in the following paragraph. Our data suggest that the idiom *lân* can be used in a variety of situations to label a spectrum of severity of cognitive impairment, from what is considered to be "normal" age-related forgetfulness to severe, pathological memory loss. Thus our findings differ from Braun's findings based on research with non-caregivers, in which she suggests that the use of the term *lân* is reserved for those with normal age-related memory loss.

*Folk and professional terms for mental illness:* In two interviews, caregivers used lay or professional terms that connote mental illness. The Vietnamese equivalent of "crazy," which is "*dien,*" was used in describing the behavior of demented elders by two of the caregivers interviewed. During one interview, the term was used by the caregiver to implicitly note his mother's state of mind: "*Dien roi, sao ma minh biet* . . . ?" ([She is] already crazy, so how should she know?) In other instances, *dien* was used to describe or imply the elder's behavior, rather than the elder herself: "They're ill and to make them upset, who knows, they might turn around, be crazy and beat us to death." Both situations are significant in that *dien* is a stigmatizing term that carries negative connotations, and is usually used to denote people whose behavior is beyond the pale of acceptable social mores. Furthermore, its use can also signify lack of respect or have a derisive quality.

Other caregivers used more formal terms for mental illness to describe their elders' diagnoses. For example, one woman whose father often had severe angry outbursts said that she attributed his "hot" (*nong*) temperament to the following: "I just think that my father is mentally ill (*binh than kinh*). He just talks nonsense, stories that aren't so and he says they are." *Binh than kinh* is a formal Vietnamese term for mental illness that is quite stigmatizing, unlike the idiom of *lân*. In other parts of the interview, the same caregiver used the term *binh tam than*, another Vietnamese term for mental illness. In one other interview, a 78-year old husband, when asked if he considered his wife to suffer from *lân*, replied: "I think that at her age, it can't yet be *lân*. If she were 80, almost 90, then it would be normal, something all old women and men have. But she is only 72." This caregiver views her condition as abnormal because of her relatively young age.

It was our observation that caregivers who used the terms *dien* or *binh tam than* seemed to be more distressed and burdened compared with others we interviewed. One son expressed the following about caring for his ill mother: "I think it's only because she's my mother. Because if anyone were to hire me for however much money to take care of a crazy man or woman who has lost her memory, I wouldn't dare do it." The increased burden expressed by these caregivers may be due, in part, to the difficult nature of some of the behavioral problems they described, such as aggression. It is also possible that caring for an older adult who has been labeled as being mentally ill may be more burdensome because of the social stigma that may attach, not only to the afflicted individual, but also to the family itself. For example, among more traditional Vietnamese families it is common to discourage marriage into a family with a history of mental illness for fear that it may be inherited. One caregiver said, "There are people, if they have a crazy family member, they are very ashamed, they want the person to just die." Another caregiver alluded to the need to "save face" within the community and among peers by not allowing the elder's condition to become more widely known. The importance of stigma has also been described among Chinese Americans (e.g., Elliott et al., 1996; Guo et al., 1999).

### *Attributions*

In our analysis of the interviews, four main categories of dementia attributions emerged: normal aging, physiological factors, psychosocial factors, and influences related to spiritual beliefs or fate. We now describe each of these categories and their relationship to Vietnamese culture and history. While these categories are described separately, it is important to emphasize that individual caregivers often drew on attributions from two or more categories during the course of their interview.

*Normal aging*. As described above, a prominent theme that emerged in these interviews was that dementia changes were part of the normal process of aging. This was supported by statements from numerous caregivers, such as a 42-year old caregiver who said, "Being confused is part of natural aging, or course." Speaking of her mother, one caregiver told us, "She is old so she has to be confused." The theme of old age as a return to childhood also emerged: "The old become like children."

Four of the nine caregivers interviewed went on to connect their view of memory loss and aging to their homeland in some way. Memory loss and confusion was declared to be normal in Vietnam with statements such as, "Forgetting is normal in Vietnam, it is not really a disease; it is very normal," or "It's normal in Vietnam now, many people have this sickness." One 51-year old daughter developed a rationale for the normalization of the condition by saying, " I don't think memory is necessary. If she has it, she will have worries. If she did not remember anything, she was very happy. If she remembered the past, it makes her sad."

Some caregivers, such as the husband described above, viewed these changes as abnormal when they occurred prematurely. Three others questioned the assumption that the condition was part of normal aging, even as they were making the attribution. For example, a 42-year old caregiver said, "Being confused is part of natural aging, of course. But many times, people who aren't old are also confused–Then there are a lot of people like my maternal grandfather, who at 90 something years of age up to the minute he died was still sharp-minded. He hardly forgot anything."

*Physiological factors.* The second attributional category was that memory loss and confusion were a result of physiology, such as problems with the circulatory system, heredity, or medications. It is significant that caregivers who were able to use biological explanations as points of reference to explain their elder's illness expressed less concern regarding stigma. This was particularly the case if the elder's illness was due to reasons such as multiple strokes. Caregivers were then usually able to discuss their elder's illness at length in terms conveyed by health care providers, while caregivers who did not have the benefit of a diagnosis, tended to discuss their elders' illness by referring to the elder's inappropriate or distressing behavior.

Several caregivers mentioned brain shrinkage (*teo oc*), and linked this to conversations with health care providers in which they had been told about the results of "x-rays." A 56-year old daughter who had been told that her mother's brain scans showed atrophy, believed that indulging her mother's penchant for overeating played a role in the elder's current condition. The caregiver framed her concern by saying, "The children and grandchildren loved Elder too much, gave-in/coddled her, pitied her, let her eat a lot so that Elder's heart suffocated."

Explanations focusing on the role of the circulatory system were commonly used such as blood pressure, or "arteries get clogged and suffocate, then the heart will suffocate." One 34-year old son explained his theory of how problems with the circulatory system caused his mother's illness:

> In the old days we ate too much fat, it stayed in the brain blood vessel, then ate too much salt that caused high blood pressure. Viet Nam called that a high blood vessel, then when the time comes, with one strong excitement or fall, then it breaks the brain blood vessel.

Medications were also indicated by two caregivers. According to one 78-year old husband,

> The aches and pains did cause her to lose her memory, of course. It's because of too much pain, that's why, and the medication. I think that the medications caused this and that to manifest in the body system. And the Western medications, there are many types that cause too much harm.

While it is prudent to note that all medications have some sort of negative and positive side-effects, the context of this caregiver's statement involves a different perspective on how the body functions than that commonly held by Western medical providers. This caregiver later discussed his opinion of Western medications and their tendency to upset the body's overall balance by causing it to be overwhelmed by properties that produce too much "heat." The resulting imbalance caused by his wife's pain medications were believed by this caregiver to have been a factor in the onset of his wife's dementia.

Another physiological theme was heredity, but there did not seem to be agreement on its role. One caregiver said the problem was definitely in the genes, another said it was not, and one was not sure.

*Psychosocial factors.* There were a number of respondents who described the cause of dementia as a result of emotional trauma or social relationship problems. More specifically, caregivers expressed the view that difficult life events, such as the indiscretions of an unfaithful husband, financial woes, difficulty adjusting to life in the U.S., loss of family support, led the elder to experience pathological states, such as "worrying too much" (*lo nhieu qua*), "thinking too much" (*nghi nhieu qua*), or simply to a state of loneliness and isolation.[4] The emphasis was on thinking too much about upsetting things, such as difficult life events and situations over which people have little control, situations that occur all too frequently in the life experiences of refugees. For example, a

42-year old wife said, "This condition can be caused by doing a lot of thinking, mental exhaustion." A male caregiver in his late thirties spoke of how emotional stress exacerbated his mother's hypertension and led to stroke: "It seems that this sickness is being created by many reasons. First is high blood pressure which we normally don't talk about, but getting a sudden shock, falling or getting upset about something that breaks the blood vessel [is significant]."

One of the three male caregivers also referred to the perceived role of stress in bringing on dementing illness when he said, "I think that perhaps my wife worries too much, fears too much and so it turns out like this." The same male caregiver also explained the onset of his wife's illness as such: "According to my understanding–I don't know if it's correct or not–I think the major reason is that people are worried, fearful, and so they get this illness; they think too much, are sad and upset too much and will therefore develop this illness." A 51-year old daughter said:

> If we let ourselves worry all the time, or become sad to the point that we cannot sleep, our mind will be overworked, and when we get old, it will surely give you problems. But if we know how to take care of our lives, do not let things get to us, then I think nothing will happen.

The two previous caregiver statements reflect the perception that not only does excessive worry cause dementing illnesses, but that these illnesses can be prevented by controlling, to some extent, one's mental and emotional processes. Implicit in the statements is the belief that ill people may have brought on their dementing illness because they were not able to successfully cope with life's stressors: "It only happens to people who do not know how to take care of their minds." This is culturally syntonic, given the fact that Vietnamese beliefs regarding connection between the mind and body is strongly influenced by Buddhist and Taoist philosophies, both of which endorse meditation and emotional discipline for mental and physical health. An example of this teaching is found in the following translation of Chuang Tzu, whom Eastern lore views as the incarnation of Lao Tzu, founder of Taoism: "No sight, no hearing; in silence embrace your spirits and your body will become spontaneously sound. Be calm, be pure, do not overburden your body . . . and you will enjoy Long Life! . . . I keep the One so as to remain in harmony!" (Schipper, p. 149). The human body is viewed as the microcosm of a universe in constant struggle for balance, such that too much of anything–for instance, food, stress, heat, cold, sorrow or joy–results in imbalance, and therefore, illness.

The emphasis on internal balance may also have its roots in traditional Chinese medicine, wherein opposites such as hot (*yang*) and cold (*yin*) need to be kept in balance. A 47-year old daughter caring for her father who sometimes became violent and abusive, spoke of his outbursts as when he became "heated" or "hot." Another 34-year old caregiving son expressed views that parallel the 47-year old daughter's perspective, saying, "[She] feels like she's doing something that causes the sons to lose harmony." Both statements reflect the intertwined manner in which this particular group of Vietnamese view the relationship between maintaining emotional stability and good health.

Other psychological attributions were that elders were feeling one or more of the following: uselessness, loneliness, fearfulness, worry, sadness, self-pity, and/or being upset or homesick for Vietnam. The effects of loneliness were described by this 42-year old caregiver:

> Many people in Vietnam look forward to quickly coming to the U.S. When here, they're disappointed, wishing to return. For people with resources to go back that's fine, but many people can't go back because they've sold their homes and have no relatives still there. That situation makes it easy to get sick.

Several caregivers expressed the same thought by comparing the differences in lifestyles found here and in Vietnam. One sentiment mentioned often, even by the younger caregivers, was the difficulty many Vietnamese elders face in adjusting to new cultural values. In the following passage a caregiver explains the link between cultural dislocation and dementia among older Vietnamese:

> For example, my son does many things I don't like, I want him to follow me, but I must understand not to restrict him like that. In the past or in Vietnam that's okay, over here to do that is bad, not right . . . The elders who came here, some of them go mad . . . because they don't understand this . . . Before coming here from Vietnam, you must understand, to see it over here is quite a shock. For you to demand them to revere, respect you like old times in Vietnam, that doesn't exist now. Over here, kids come first, are the priority. Elders start at the bottom.

In addition to a perceived "loss of respect" by a younger generation that appears to be adopting American values much too quickly, elders may face social isolation. The effects of loneliness were described by this son-in-law's niece who was currently caring for the Elder after she was transferred from the house of the daughter and son-in-law:

> Over there at my uncle's house everybody works. There's nobody home, nobody for her to talk to. None of them are close. With every passing day, her feelings become more stagnated and dried-up. So it was partly due to that that Elder's problems with being confused and disoriented increased and became worse. Elder could no longer sleep and her mind went flat/became paralyzed.

In a poignant way, these dementia attributions provide a window on difficult but common aspects of the refugee experience common among older Vietnamese in the U.S.[5]

*Spiritual/Fate*. Since Vietnam has a strong tradition of folk healing and metaphysical beliefs regarding health, it is not surprising that some of the illness explanations offered by caregivers involve a mystic or religious component. As with the psychosocial attributes of illness, caregivers sometimes fused information they were given by medical providers with metaphysics to better fit their cosmology and spiritual beliefs.

One particularly interesting explanation with metaphysical components was the belief of a 78-year old husband who said: "My partial understanding is that in Vietnam this woman (his wife) was rich and well-off, so the spirit took over/possessed her and caused her to be in pain and ill. She is taken over/possessed by this thing and that thing." This caregiver believed that his wife's condition was retribution for her abundance of wealth and good fortune. The caregiver practiced a mystical form of Taoism, and this attribution of his wife's illness was in keeping with Taoist edicts against excesses of any sort, be they positive or negative. As such, while this caregiver continued to rely on Western medical providers, he was also having his wife seen by geomancers and spiritual mediums, with the hope that the spirits would be "exorcised" or placated, and his wife returned to "balance" and good health. This is again, a valuable insight into myriad cultural practices that will affect help-seeking behavior and inform the decisions caregivers and their families make regarding treatment.

Other caregivers had fatalistic attitudes reminiscent of both Christianity and Buddhism. These caregivers tended to place strong emphasis on the will of a higher spiritual authority or the theory of karma. Oftentimes, these attributes took the form of giving in to fate or God's will. One caregiver spoke of her father as a "person who is near death/closer to the ground, further away from the sky." She went on to say, "[The] Creator can take him back anytime he pleases and the family will accept it." Another caregiver who professes fundamentalist Christianity but cannot completely shed her Eastern roots, viewed her mother's illness as a matter of fate: "Everybody has a number and destiny." In both cases, the caregiver's attribution of illness helped them cope with their caregiving tasks and put the enormity of the job into perspective.

In summary, the conceptualizations of dementing illness the Vietnamese caregivers expressed revealed multiple cultural strands. They bridged many influences, from the scientific biomedical explanations common to Western medicine, such as stroke and hypertension, to aging itself, to spiritual and religious causality, to health beliefs common in Asian cultures, all mixed with unique individual ideas based on their own experiences. There were some unique physiological conceptualizations not found in gerontology, such as the brain going flat or wearing out from too much work.

### *Use of Formal Supportive or Long-Term Care Services*

Although preferences and experiences in seeking help from service providers in the U.S. were not systematically explored in the interviews as a primary issue, several of the caregivers expressed attitudes that increase our understanding of the way they perceive the process of seeking relief from some of their burden. In their interviews, caregivers often discussed their attitudes towards use of formal services, particularly nursing homes. One emergent theme related to this was the duty and obligation of the family to care for elderly. While this general attitude can be found across cultural groups, in these interviews it is shaped by traditional cultural values, such as filial piety and ancestor worship, which are at the core of Vietnamese culture.

Filial piety, a part of Vietnam's heritage influenced by Chinese culture, emphasizes the enormous debt that the younger generation owes to the older from which flows the felt obligation to care for older family members (Jamison, 1994). The importance of deference and obligation of the younger towards the older family members is also reinforced by the practice of ancestor worship, which is based on a concept of the family unit that transcends time and space, connecting the living with their ancestors in a chain of being. It is therefore not surprising that in this set of interviews, caregivers spoke often of their duty to care for older family members and "set an example" for the younger generation. It also leads to a reluctance to rely on formal supports, such as long-term care, as revealed by this 34-year old son who was one of the primary caregivers for his mother:

> The American doctor suggested the nursing home. He said, "The reason America has nursing homes is for people like you." But I came home and thought that Asians cannot do that. It seems kind of cruel to the old woman. It's not Asian's tradition. There are four more younger siblings in Canada–If I can't take care of her over here, they will come here illegally to take care of her.

Another daughter who was struggling with caring for an abusive father refused to have outside help or services, maintaining it was not necessary because she and her family could care for him alone, no matter what. "I don't need help from an outsider," she said.

To avoid "help from an outsider," family caregivers in need of help often turned to other relatives, almost always women, to assist with "hands-on" care. This tendency reflects traditional Vietnamese gender roles, in which women are expected to provide this type of care to dependent older family members, whereas men are expected to assist more in the realm of decision-making and financial support. One example was the daughter who arranged for her mother to be cared for by her husband's niece, who was already caring for her own mother. The 34-year old son who was separated from his wife, in discussing his perspective of what would happen in the future, said, "Cannot bathe, wash herself?–I don't dare to think about that. This home ought to have one or two girls; her sickness needs to have a girl." While traditional Vietnamese gender roles dictate women are the primary caregivers to disabled older adults, the reality "on-the-ground" is that this does not always occur. For example, fragmentation of the family and geographic dislocation may lead to the lack of an identified female family member, resulting in the identification of a male family caregiver.

While traditional Vietnamese values tend to discourage use of non-family long-term care services, this option is being used by some Vietnamese families in the U.S. How do such families reconcile their behavior with cultural norms? One caregiver we interviewed who had placed her mother in a nursing home discussed at length her reasons for doing so. Her case is now discussed more fully because it illustrates the tremendous burden she felt and how she came to this decision.

Ms. N was a 51-year old unmarried woman with seven siblings who had been given the primary responsibility for caring for her 71-year old mother. She and her mother were sponsored for immigration in 1991 by one of her older brothers who was already living in the U.S. After their arrival, the mother's confusion became increasingly severe, and she became incontinent of bowel and bladder. They lived with a brother for a year, then they moved into to an apartment. While the daughter was trying to earn her own living, she had to stay up with her mother at night because of her wandering. The mother's legs were very weak, so that the daughter had to lift her to get her to the bathroom. The daughter lost almost 20 pounds. She joined a Christian church in the U.S., in part so that her mother would have visitors. The daughter told of her struggle trying to decide whether or not to put her mother in a nursing home. She told the interviewer,

> I am not avoiding hard work, but I compare the benefit between me taking care of her at home, and the hospital (nursing home). The hospital is operating 24 hours a day, with 3 shifts, each shift works 8 hours. While for me, the most I can give is 15 hours a day. I still need 7-8 hours of sleep, I need to go to the restroom, I have to eat, take a shower, go shopping. Within those times if something happens to my mother and she dies, nobody will know how hard I take care of her. I will regret that too. If I know that I can only spend 15 hours for my mother, why should I want to when the hospital can spend 24 hours on her. They also have doctors, medical specialists. How can I do better than 20 people in a hospital?–At that time I discussed with my church, asked them to pray for my problem, if Jesus agrees to put my mother in the nursing home, then the hospital will accept her. If they accept her, my brother will agree to sign the admission papers. If the hospital does not accept her, that means Jesus does not want her there. Or if the hospital accepts her, and my brother does not want to sign the papers, I will gladly keep my mother.

The very difficult conflict this caregiver was experiencing in reconciling the cultural expectations of parent care with the reality of her enormous felt burden were evident. It was extremely difficult for her to reach out for assistance, even when she knew that there was help available. In this case the idea that her brothers or others might think she was not working hard enough to take care of her mother seemed impossible for her to accept. In order for her to justify the decision to place her mother in a nursing home, she relied on receiving a spiritual confirmation that she was doing the right thing.

## DISCUSSION AND CONCLUSIONS

To work effectively with ethnically diverse older clients and their families, social workers and other clinicians should have an understanding of the sociocultural context of caregiving (Dilworth-Anderson and Anderson, 1994; Hinton et al., 1999). Understanding Vietnamese family explanatory models of dementia can help to establish rapport and to build a foundation on which to negotiate a treatment plan (Hinton and Kleinman, 1996). This study provides a window on the cultural labels and attributions that Vietnamese caregivers may draw on to make sense of dementia changes. In this small study, it is clear that Vietnamese caregivers often understand dementia in ways that deviate substantially from the biomedical model. How families view dementia changes (e.g., viewing dementia as "normal aging" versus stigmatized mental illness) may profoundly impact the subjective quality of their caregiving experience.

One avenue for future research is to explore in more detail how these different "modes" of experiencing dementia are linked to caregiver outcomes and other health care indicators, such as utilization of nursing homes and formal services. One hypothesis that emerges from our interviews is that families who understand dementia via traditional Vietnamese views of mental illness may experience increased burden and be less likely to use formal services because of concerns about shame and "loss of face." One caregiver in our study, for example, alluded to the need to "save face" within the community and among peers by not allowing her elder's condition to become more widely known. Language barriers that prevent less acculturated Vietnamese from being exposed to anti-stigma campaigns regarding mental illness in the U.S., may result in increased stigma compared with more acculturated Vietnamese or non-minority caregivers. It is important for social workers to be able to identify these situations and to intervene in culturally appropriate ways to reduce caregiver burden and distress.

What is also apparent, even in this relatively small qualitative study, is that there is substantial intraethnic variation in the views of dementia and use of formal services, such as nursing homes. Constructs such as acculturation (Valle, 1998) or behavioral ethnicity (Harwood, 1996) may help providers understand this diversity. Valle (1998) emphasizes the importance of cultural mapping, including assessing the client's position on the continuum of acculturation, to be able to assess some of the significant differences among caregivers from the same ethnic population. Eliciting the explanatory models in work with Vietnamese clients may help to identify where on the acculturation spectrum they are located. One of the experiences shared by almost all of the Vietnamese caregivers we interviewed was exposure to Western medical care. Thus, as a group these caregivers demonstrate a range of conceptions of dementia, from the biomedical (e.g., stroke) to alternative, lay conceptualizations (e.g., normal aging or mental illness). In considering the ways this study might inform the practice of social work and other health care providers, it important for providers to recognize the potential differences and not to stereotype all Vietnamese caregivers.

Although obvious as a starting point in a helping relationship, understanding clients' conceptualizations of their problems may not always be easy in cross-cultural interactions. For service providers who do not share the culture-specific beliefs and values of their clients, it may take time and effort to become familiar with those important underlying assumptions which the clients bring to the relationship. Being able to recognize, acknowledge, and perhaps integrate the clients' understanding and beliefs in the therapeutic relationship is believed to increase the level of trust and the compliance with the recommendations of the health or social service practitioner (Berlin and Fowkes, 1983; Handelman & Yeo, 1996).

To work effectively with diverse families of elders with dementia it is also important for service providers to understand the degree to which caregivers perceive the burden of caregiving and how this is culturally shaped. In contrast to the findings of Braun et al. (1996), in which the members of their focus group indicated that caring for elders was not seen as "something special or burdensome," several of the caregivers in our study expressed indicators of burden that were sometimes considerable even though they uniformly accepted it as their responsibility. For example they reported having to cope with the following types of behaviors from their elders: being slapped and hit, having a knife drawn on them, demanding to eat over and over again, refusing to eat unless she was entertained, dealing with urinary and/or fecal incontinence, wandering, yelling and screaming. Health and social service providers working with Vietnamese families struggling with the effects of dementing illness would do well to take into account not only the families' understanding of their elders' conditions and the burdens they face, but also the family members' assumptions about how the elders' care should be provided. In these interviews, with the exception of medical care, that assumption strongly endorsed the norms of filial piety and family care, even to the exclusion of non-family care in the home.

In summary, however, knowledge of the stories and metaphors the caregivers use to make sense of the struggles they face can be the first step in the helping process. Understanding their conceptualizations of dementia, their expectations of family care, and the burdens they face, can help in diagnosis and communication, establishing trust, and negotiating acceptable interventions. That understanding can also assist agencies with appropriate outreach for their services to ethnic communities.

## NOTES

1. For published guidelines for eliciting family perspectives in chronic illness, see Kleinman, 1988, and Hinton and Kleinman, 1996.

2. Contemporary views of the impact of ethnic or minority status on sociocultural processes in dementia can be found in social gerontology and medical anthropology (e.g., Dilworth-Anderson and Anderson, 1994; Kramer and Barker, 1994; Henderson, 1994; Hinton et al., 1999; Valle, 1998). One common theme in much of this work is the emphasis on contextual factors and intraethnic diversity that moves beyond a now out-dated view of ethnic groups as mini-cultures within the larger, host society).

3. A number of families said that their doctors had not communicated to them a diagnosis or explanation for their elderly relative's condition. One caregiver said, "The doctor does not give diagnosis, just pills." Another said, "The doctor didn't really state the problem clearly. I also spoke with the psychiatrist and it was also the same thing. He just said the mind is completely stressed-out; it's careless/clumsy, that's all."

4. Handelman and Yeo (1996) found that the most common chronic illness among the Cambodian elders interviewed was severe headaches accompanied by dizziness. The most common term that was used to explain their view of the cause for that condition was *pruiy chiit kiit chraen*, which is best translated as extreme sadness from thinking too much. Usually that thinking was related to the disturbing memories of the elders' experiences under Khmer Rouge in Cambodia and worry over the loss of their loved ones. The similarity between these two Southeast Asian populations view of the effect on brain function of worry and excessive thinking about problems is noteworthy.

5. These are well described in extended narratives of Vietnamese refugees in a book-length monograph (Freeman, 1990).

## REFERENCES

Berlin, E.A. & Fowkes, W.C. (1983). A teaching framework for cross-cultural health care–application in family practice. In Cross-cultural Medicine (special issue) *Western Journal of Medicine*, *139*(6): 934-938.

Braun, K., Takamura, J., & Mougeot, T. (1996). Perceptions of Dementia, Caregiving, and Helpseeking among Recent Vietnamese Immigrants. *Journal of Cross-Cultural Gerontology 11*: 213-228.

Demographic Research Unit (1997). California Current Population Survey Report. March 1997 Data. Sacramento, CA: Demographic Research Unit, State of California.

Dilworth-Anderson, P., & Anderson, N.B. (1994) Dementia Caregiving in Blacks: A Contextual Approach to Research. In E. Light, G. Niederehe, and B.D. Lebowitz (Eds.) *Stress Effects of Family Caregivers of Alzheimer's Patients.* New York: Springer.

Elliott, K.S., Di Minno, M., Lam, D., & Tu, A.M. (1996). Working with Chinese Families in the Context of Dementia. In Yeo, G. & Gallagher-Thompson, D. (Eds.) *Ethnicity and the Dementias.* Washington, DC: Taylor and Francis.

Fox, K., Hinton, W.L., & Levkoff, S. (1999). Take up the Caregiver's Burden: Stories of Care for Urban African-American Elders with Dementia. *Culture, Medicine, and Psychiatry, Special Issue 23(4)*: 501-529.

Freeman, J. (1990). *Hearts of Sorrow.* Berkeley, CA: University of California Press.

Guo, Z., Levy, B., Hinton, W.L., Weitzman, P.F., & Levkoff, S.E. (1999). The power of labels: Recruiting dementia-affected Chinese-American elders and their caregivers. *J Mental Health and Aging* 6(1): 103-111.

Handelman, L. & Yeo, G. (1996). Using Explanatory Models to Understand Chronic Symptoms of Cambodian Refugees. *Family Medicine, 28*: 271-276.

Harwood, A.H. (1991). Introduction. In A. Harwood (Ed.) *Ethnicity and Medical Care.* Cambridge: Harvard University Press.

Hazuda, H. P. (1997). Minority issues in Alzheimer disease outcomes research. *Alzheimer Disease and Associated Disorders, 11 Suppl* 6: 156-61.

Henderson, J.N. (1990). Anthropology, Health, and Aging. In R.L. Rubenstein (Ed.) *Anthropology and Aging.* Dordrecht, Netherlands: Kluwer Publishing.

Henderson, J.N. (1994). Ethnic and Racial Issues. In J.F. Gubrium & A. Sankar (Eds.) *Qualitative Methods in Aging Research.* New York: Sage.

Henderson, J.N. (1996). Cultural dynamics of dementia in a Cuban and Puerto Rican population in the United States. In Yeo, G. & Gallagher-Thompson, D. *Ethnicity and the Dementias.* Washington, DC: Taylor & Francis.

Hicks, M., H.R., & Lam, M. (1999) Decision-Making within the Social Course of Dementia: Accounts by Chinese-American Caregivers. *Culture, Medicine, and Psychiatry, Special Issue* 23 (4): 415-452.

Hinton, W.L., & Kleinman, A. (1996). Cultural Issues in Primary Care Medicine. In J. Noble, H. Green, J. Heffernan, W. Levinson, & G. Modest (Eds.), *Primary Care Medicine CD-ROM*, Mosby-Yearbook.

Hinton, L. & Levkoff, S. (1999). Constructing Alzheimer's: Narratives of lost identities, confusion, loneliness in old age. *Culture, Medicine, and Psychiatry, Special Issue 23(4)*: 453-75.

Hinton, L., Levkoff, S., Fox, K. (1999) Examining the relationships among Aging, Ethnicity, and Family Dementia Caregiving. *Culture, Medicine, and Psychiatry, Special Issue 23*(4): 403-413.

Hinton W.L., Guo, Z., Hillygus, J., & Levkoff, S.E. (2000). Working with culture: A qualitative analysis of barriers to the recruitment of Chinese-American family caregivers for dementia research. *Journal of Cross Cultural Gerontology* 15: 119-137.

Ikels, C. (1998). The experience of dementia in China. *Culture, Medicine and Psychiatry*, Sep, 22(3): 257-83.

Jamieson, N.L. (1994). *Understanding Vietnam*. Berkeley, CA: University of California Press.

Kleinman, A. (1988). *The Illness Narratives: Suffering, Healing, and the Human Condition*. New York: Basic Books.

Kramer, B.J., & Barker, J.C. (1994). Ethnicity in the Elderly. *Journal of Cross-Cultural Gerontology*. 9: 403-417.

Levkoff, S., & Hinton, L. (Eds.). (1999). Aging, Ethnicity, and Dementia: Family Caregiving. *Culture, Medicine, and Psychiatry, Special Issue 23(4)*: 403-529.

Ortiz, A., Simmons, J., & Hinton, W.L. (1999). Locations of Remorse and Homelands of Resistance: Notes on Grief and Sense of Loss of Place among Latino and Irish American Caregivers of Demented Elders. *Culture, Medicine, and Psychiatry, Special Issue* 23(4): 477-500.

Schipper, K. (1993). *The Taoist Body*. Berkeley and Los Angeles, CA: University of California Press.

Valle, R. (1998). *Caregiving Across Cultures: Working with Dementing Illness and Ethnically Diverse Populations*. Washington, DC: Taylor and Francis.

Yeo, G. (1996). Background. In Yeo, G., & Gallagher-Thompson, D. (Eds.) *Ethnicity and the Dementias*. Washington, DC: Taylor and Francis.

Yeo, G., Hikoyeda, N., McBride, M., Chin, S-Y., Edmonds, M., & Hendrix, L. (1998). *Cohort Analysis as a Tool in Ethnogeriatrics: Historical Profiles of Elders from Eight Ethnic Populations in the United States*. Stanford Geriatric Education Center Working Paper #12, Stanford, CA: Stanford Geriatric Education Center.

Young, J.J. & Gu, N. (1995). *Demographic and Socio-Economic Characteristics of Elderly Asian and Pacific Island Americans*. Seattle, WA: National Asian Pacific Center on Aging.

# Elder Mistreatment Among Four Asian American Groups: An Exploratory Study on Tolerance, Victim Blaming and Attitudes Toward Third-Party Intervention

Ailee Moon, PhD
Susan K. Tomita, PhD
Staci Jung-Kamei, MSW

**SUMMARY.** Using 14 statements, this study examined similarities and differences among four groups of elders (American-born Chinese Americans, American-born Japanese Americans, first-generation Korean Americans, and first-generation Taiwanese Americans) with regard to tolerance for elder mistreatment behaviors, tendency to victim blame, and attitudes toward reporting elder mistreatment. The American-born groups were more likely to be tolerant of verbal abuse, less likely to

Ailee Moon is Associate Professor, Department of Social Welfare, UCLA School of Public Policy and Social Research, 3250 Public Policy Building, Box 951656, Los Angeles, CA 90095-1656 (E-mail: aileem@ucla.edu). Susan K. Tomita is Clinical Associate Professor, Harborview Medical Center, School of Social Work, 359760 Harborview Medical Center, 325 Ninth Avenue, Seattle, WA 98104 (E-mail: tomita@u.washington.edu). Staci Jung-Kamei is Director of MSW Program Admissions, Department of Social Work, California State University, Los Angeles (E-mail: sjung@exchange.calstatela.edu).

[Haworth co-indexing entry note]: "Elder Mistreatment Among Four Asian American Groups: An Exploratory Study on Tolerance, Victim Blaming and Attitudes Toward Third-Party Intervention." Moon, Ailee, Susan K. Tomita, and Staci Jung-Kamei. Co-published simultaneously in *Journal of Gerontological Social Work* (The Haworth Social Work Practice Press, an imprint of The Haworth Press, Inc.) Vol. 36, No. 1/2, 2001, pp. 153-169; and: *Social Work Practice with the Asian American Elderly* (ed: Namkee G. Choi) The Haworth Social Work Practice Press, an imprint of The Haworth Press, Inc., 2001, pp. 153-169. Single or multiple copies of this article are available for a fee from The Haworth Document Delivery Service [1-800-HAWORTH, 9:00 a.m. - 5:00 p.m. (EST). E-mail address: getinfo@haworthpressinc.com].

 

blame the elderly parents for causing the mistreatment by their grown children, and more favorable toward reporting elder mistreatment to the authorities. The Korean Americans differed significantly from the other three groups: They had a greater tolerance for financial exploitation, were more likely to blame the elder as the cause of the mistreatment, and not favorable toward reporting and outside intervention. Among all participants, tolerance for elder mistreatment was strongly associated with victim blaming and not favoring reporting and outside intervention. The large percentages of "Don't know" and "It depends" responses to the statements among all four groups indicate that these groups are unfamiliar with the problems of elder mistreatment. 

**KEYWORDS.** Elder mistreatment, tolerance, victim blaming, third party intervention and reporting, four Asian American groups

## *INTRODUCTION*

Elder mistreatment is a national problem, yet little is known about mistreatment among Asian Americans. Anecdotal information and qualitative data from other exploratory studies indicate Asian Americans are aware of victims among friends, relatives or neighbors in their own ethnic circles (Anetzberger, Korbin, & Tomita, 1996; Chang & Moon, 1997; Tatara, 1998; Tomita, 1998a), but they are not a part of the currently small percentage of Asian American victims who are reported to regulatory agencies (National Center on Elder Abuse, 1998). In this field, definitions, policies and intervention techniques have been based on information and research conducted mostly in English among Caucasian Americans.

Recent studies indicate that variability in ethnic groups' perceptions of elder mistreatment may compound reporting rates (Brown, 1989; Moon, Tomita, Talamantes, Brown, Y. Sanchez, Benton, C. Sanchez, & Kim, 1998; Moon & Williams, 1993). Also, underreporting may be due to culturally specific elder mistreatment behaviors not falling into commonly known categories (Chang & Moon, 1997; Kaneko & Yamada, 1990; Tomita, 1998b), and because victims may not realize that mistreatment acts committed against them are reportable. For example, in another study involving Korean Americans, on average they were reported to be less sensitive to or more tolerant of abusive situations than African American and Caucasian respondents. In response to one of 13 scenarios of elder mistreatment, in which the son threw a frying pan at the mother for the third time after the mother burnt some food, only 60% of the Korean American participants perceived the incident to be abusive compared to 100% of the African American and 97% of the Caucasian participants (Moon & Williams, 1993). A good deal more needs to be done to better understand victims whose cultural values affect their perceptions of elder abuse and ability to obtain help.

Moon and Benton (2000) studied tolerance of elder abuse, tendency to victim blame, and attitudes toward third-party intervention among African American, Korean American, and Caucasian elderly. They found that while African American and Caucasian elderly were remarkably similar in their responses, Korean American elderly differed significantly from the other two groups in their tolerance for medical mistreatment, financial exploitation and neglect, tendency to victim blame, and attitudes toward reporting elder abuse. Korean American elderly were the least sensitive, or most tolerant of, possible elder abuse, were significantly more likely than the other two groups to blame the victims for the occurrence of elder abuse, and they held significantly more negative attitudes toward the involvement of persons outside the family in elder abuse incidents, as well as toward reporting of such incidents to the authorities. As a possible explanation of this pattern of study findings, the authors noted that "the vast majority of African American and White elderly studied were born in the U.S. and, therefore, shared a common native culture, whereas all of the Korean American elderly in the study were immigrants" (Ibid., 298).

Given this background, this study focuses on four Asian American ethnic groups of elderly and examines the degree to which they (1) tolerate elder mistreatment, (2) blame the victim, and (3) are likely to report it to agencies and law enforcement. The study also explores the extent to which the Asian American groups varied in their responses and whether the variations could be associated with their ethnicity and the degree of acculturation, or adaptation to the dominant American culture, which in this study is defined as the country of birth and the length of time the participants have been in the United States.

## METHODOLOGY

### Sampling and Data Collection Methods

In 1997, as part of a multicultural study of elder mistreatment (Moon et al., 1998), face-to-face interviews were conducted with 95 Korean Americans in Los Angeles County, California and 53 Japanese Americans in Seattle, Washington. In 1999, for the purpose of the current study, 50 Chinese Americans and 80 Taiwan Americans were interviewed in Los Angeles County, California. Eliminating five Japanese first-generation Americans for comparison purposes, the remaining 48 Japanese Americans and 50 Chinese Americans were U.S.-born, while all of the Korean and Taiwan Americans were born in their respective countries of origin. This resulted in 273 participants who were 60 years old and older.

Purposive and convenience sampling methods were employed to recruit study participants. For heterogeneity of the sample, recruitment of study participants took place in a number of community-based sites, including ethnic grocery stores, senior citizen centers, churches, temples, drug stores, barber shops, and beauty salons. Depending on the participants' preference, interviews were conducted in Cantonese, Japanese, Korean, Mandarin, or English, and lasted 20 to 25 minutes. Participants were provided $10.00 for their time.

Participants were read 14 statements that represented elder mistreatment (eight items), victim blaming (two items), and attitudes toward reporting the mistreatment (four items). Eight items used to assess respondents' tolerance of potential elder mistreatment cover several types of mistreatment, including physical, verbal, psychological and medical mistreatment, neglect, and financial exploitation. The statements are a part of an original instrument consisting of 20 statements that was developed by a group of multicultural researchers in the field of elder mistreatment (Moon et al., 1998). Standard translation methods of back-translation and committee consensus were used. For each statement, participants were asked to answer with one of four choices: Agree, Disagree, Don't know, It depends.

### Data Analysis Method

Frequency distribution and the chi-squared test of independence were used to examine group differences for each of the 14 statements. In addition, responses to the eight statements reflecting potential elder mistreatment were recoded and totaled in order to provide an overall tolerance scale score. A score of one was assigned when respondents disagreed with the statement, for example: "It is okay for an adult child caregiver to tie down a physically or mentally impaired parent in bed," and therefore had low tolerance for the behavior. A score of two was assigned to "Don't know" and "It depends," and meant the respondent was neither tolerant nor intolerant. A score of three was assigned when respondents agreed with the statements, indicating high tolerance. Therefore, the tolerance scale score, based on eight statements, ranged from 8, the lowest tolerance, to 24, the highest tolerance for mistreatment.

Similarly, responses to two statements measuring tendency to victim blame and four statements measuring attitudes toward third party intervention were recoded and added so that higher scale scores reflected greater tendency to victim blame and to favor third party intervention. Possible scores ranged from 2 to 6 for the former, and from 4 to 12 for the latter. One-way ANOVA analysis was used to examine the four group differences in the mean scores for each of the three scales. Finally, Pearson's product-moment correlation (r) technique was used to study the strength and direction of association between tolerance, victim blaming, and attitudes toward third party intervention.

## *RESULTS*

### *Sociodemographic Characteristics*

As shown in Table 1, the majority of respondents were female, currently married, and were living with someone. The average age of the respondents was approximately 73 years except for the Chinese Americans, who were significantly younger with a mean age of 67.5 years. The Chinese Americans were more likely to be married, living with someone, rate their health as very good or good, have a college education, and had the highest monthly incomes.

While the Chinese Americans and Japanese Americans were born in the U.S., the Korean Americans had been in the U.S. for an average of 13.6 years, and the Taiwan Americans for an average of 17.0 years. This suggests that these two groups immigrated to the U.S. when they were in their mid- or late-fifties or early-sixties, and brought with them the cultural values of their country of origin. The Korean and Taiwanese

TABLE 1. Sociodemographic Characteristics of the Sample

| Demographic characteristics | U.S. Born | | Non-U.S. Born | | $\chi^2$ or F-Value |
|---|---|---|---|---|---|
| | Chinese American (N = 50) % | Japanese American (N = 48) % | Korean American (N = 95) % | Taiwanese American (N = 80) % | |
| Gender | | | | | |
| Female | 56.0 | 46.8 | 62.1 | 55.0 | |
| Male | 44.0 | 53.2 | 37.9 | 45.0 | 0.38[a] |
| Age (Mean) | (67.5) | (73.4) | (73.3) | (73.6) | (10.30)[b]*** |
| 60-64 years old | 34.0 | 8.5 | 8.4 | 12.7 | |
| 65-69 years old | 36.0 | 19.1 | 21.1 | 16.5 | |
| 70-74 years old | 16.0 | 25.5 | 29.5 | 26.6 | |
| 75 years old or older | 14.0 | 46.8 | 41.1 | 44.3 | |
| Average Year in the U.S. | N/A | N/A | 13.6 | 17.0 | 2.91[b]* |
| Marital status | | | | | |
| Married | 80.0 | 62.5 | 58.9 | 62.5 | |
| Separated/Widowed/Divorced/ Never married | 20.0 | 37.5 | 41.1 | 37.5 | 6.75[a] |
| Living arrangement | | | | | |
| Living alone | 14.0 | 39.6 | 33.7 | 21.5 | |
| Living with someone | 86.0 | 60.4 | 66.3 | 78.5 | 11.31[a]** |
| The number of living children (Mean) | 2.8 | 2.7 | 4.0 | 3.8 | 11.17b*** |
| Self-rated health status | | | | | |
| Very good | 40.0 | 12.5 | 6.3 | 13.8 | |
| Good | 56.0 | 52.1 | 24.2 | 38.8 | |
| Fair | 2.0 | 31.3 | 34.7 | 41.3 | |
| Poor | 2.0 | 4.2 | 25.3 | 6.3 | |
| Very poor | 0.0 | 0.0 | 9.5 | 0.0 | 92.94[a]*** |
| Years of formal education completed(Mean) | 16.0 | 14.3 | 8.0 | 11.6 | 44.81[b]*** |
| Total monthly income | | | | | |
| Under $599 | 4.7 | 4.3 | 44.1 | 40.6 | |
| $ 600-$1,199 | 20.9 | 21.7 | 49.5 | 39.1 | |
| $1,200-$1,799 | 14.0 | 26.1 | 4.3 | 5.8 | |
| $1,800 or more | 60.5 | 47.8 | 2.2 | 14.5 | 111.03[a]*** |

* $p < .05$; ** $p < .01$; *** $p < .001$
[a] Chi-square statistics; [b] F value obtained from one-way ANOVA

Americans also were more likely than the U.S.-born participants to be low income, have less education, and have more children.

## *Tolerance for Potential Elder Mistreatment*

Table 2 shows that no significant differences were found between the four groups in three of the eight statements measuring tolerance for potential elder mistreatment. Most respondents of all four groups disagreed with the statement, "Among elderly couples, occasional hitting of the other person is okay." While no significant differences were found in the responses to the statement, "When adult children feel too much stress in caring for their elderly parents, it is okay to calm the parents with medication," roughly one-fifth of respondents except for Tai-

TABLE 2. Respondents' Tolerance for Elder Mistreatment by Ethnic Group[a]

| Items | Chinese American (N = 50) | | Japanese American (N = 48) | | Korean American (N = 95) | | Taiwanese American (N = 80) | | $\chi^{2b}$ |
|---|---|---|---|---|---|---|---|---|---|
| | Agree (%) | Disagree (%) | Agree (%) | Disagree (%) | Agree (%) | Disagree (%) | Agree (%) | Disagree (%) | |
| 1. Among elderly couples, occasional hitting of the other person is okay. | 0.0 | 100.0 | 10.4 | 85.4 | 3.2 | 96.8 | 2.6 | 93.6 | 8.7 |
| 2. It is okay for an adult child caregiver to tie down a physically or mentally impaired parent in bed. | 4.0 | 64.0 | 14.9 | 63.8 | 9.5 | 78.9 | 0.0 | 88.6 | 13.1** |
| 3. When adult children feel too much stress in caring for their elderly parents, it is okay to calm the parents with medication. | 18.0 | 60.0 | 14.9 | 40.4 | 21.1 | 67.4 | 6.3 | 64.6 | 6.1 |
| 4. It is okay for adult children to yell occasionally at their elderly parents. | 30.0 | 50.0 | 20.8 | 58.3 | 8.4 | 87.4 | 5.1 | 71.8 | 24.0*** |
| 5. It is okay for an adult child to use his/her elderly parent's money for himself/herself. | 8.0 | 54.0 | 10.4 | 66.7 | 45.3 | 37.9 | 12.7 | 58.2 | 35.1*** |
| 6. When adult children borrow money from their parents, it is okay not to pay it back, even if the parents ask for the money. | 0.0 | 94.0 | 2.1 | 91.7 | 37.9 | 50.5 | 8.9 | 69.6 | 53.8*** |
| 7. It is okay for an adult child caring for bedridden elderly parents to leave them alone occasionally for a few hours. | 38.0 | 22.0 | 29.2 | 18.8 | 37.9 | 29.5 | 6.3 | 75.9 | 46.0*** |
| 8. When elderly parents continue to reject food, it is okay for adult children to force them to eat. | 20.0 | 66.0 | 14.6 | 68.8 | 35.8 | 60.0 | 13.9 | 41.8 | 6.7 |

* $p < .05$; ** $p < .01$; *** $p < .001$

[a] The percentages in the table are based on a total N. However, since percentages are reported only for "Agree" and "Disagree," they may not add to 100% due to the exclusion of "Don't know" and "It depends" responses.

[b] Chi-square statistics were calculated based on "Agree" and "Disagree" responses only.

wanese Americans (6%) indicated such behavior as acceptable. Last, the statement regarding forcing the elderly parent to eat did not yield significant differences, but a large percentage (36%) of Korean Americans tolerated this behavior.

Significant group differences were found in the remaining five statements. The Korean Americans and Taiwanese Americans were more likely to disapprove (79% and 89%, respectively), compared to U.S.-born Chinese Americans (64%) and Japanese Americans (64%), the behavior of an adult child caregiver who ties down a physically or mentally impaired parent in bed. Similarly, the Korean and Taiwanese Americans were significantly less likely to tolerate adult children yelling occasionally at their elderly parents (8% and 5%, respectively), compared to Chinese Americans (30%) and Japanese Americans (21%). Financial abuse was most tolerated by Korean Americans, while the Chinese and Japanese Americans did not tolerate an adult child using the parents' money for himself or herself, and none of the Chinese Americans and only one Japanese American respondent agreed that it was okay for adult children not to pay back borrowed money. Taiwanese Americans (6%) were least tolerant of leaving bedridden elderly parents alone occasionally for a few hours, while roughly one-third of the respondents of the other three groups tolerated this behavior.

As interesting as the differences noted above were the large percentages of "Don't know" and "It depends" among the eight statements. The majority (52%) of Japanese Americans answered "Don't know" or "It depends" to the statement about leaving parents alone occasionally for a few hours. In addition, almost one-half (45%) of the Japanese Americans responded with "Don't know" or "It depends" to the statement, "When adult children feel too much stress in caring for their elderly parents, it is okay to calm the parents with medication." Similarly, 38% of Chinese Americans answered "Don't know" or "It depends" to the statement, "It is okay for an adult child to use his/her elderly parents' money for himself/herself."

### *Tendency to Victim Blame*

Both statements in Table 3 measuring the tendency to blame the victim for the elder mistreatment yielded significant differences among the groups. The Korean Americans had the greatest tendency to victim blame, and the Chinese Americans and Japanese Americans strongly disagreed with the victim blaming statements. For example, 43% of Korean Americans, compared to 11% of Taiwanese Americans, and 6% of Chinese Americans and Japanese Americans agreed that many elderly people are badly treated because they did something wrong to deserve it. Similarly, nearly one-third of Korean Americans agreed that elderly parents who abused their children deserve abuse from their grown-up children, while none of the Chinese Americans and only one Japanese American agreed with the statement.

Compared to the other groups, a large percentage of the Taiwan Americans (24%) answered "Don't know" or "It depends" to the statement, "Many elderly people are badly treated because they did something wrong to deserve it."

TABLE 3. Respondents' Tendency to Victim Blame by Ethnic Group[a]

| Items | Chinese American (N = 50) | | Japanese American (N = 48) | | Korean American (N = 95) | | Taiwanese American (N = 80) | | $\chi^{2b}$ |
|---|---|---|---|---|---|---|---|---|---|
| | Agree (%) | Disagree (%) | Agree (%) | Disagree (%) | Agree (%) | Disagree (%) | Agree (%) | Disagree (%) | |
| 1. Many elderly people are badly treated because they did something wrong to deserve it. | 6.0 | 80.0 | 6.4 | 83.0 | 43.2 | 40.0 | 11.4 | 64.6 | 48.3*** |
| 2. Elderly parents who abused their children deserve abuse from their grown-up children. | 0.0 | 96.0 | 2.1 | 87.5 | 30.5 | 62.1 | 10.0 | 75.0 | 35.9*** |

* $p < .05$; ** $p < .01$; *** $p < .001$
[a]. The percentages in the table are based on a total N. However, since percentages are reported only for "Agree" and "Disagree" responses, they may not add to 100% due to the exclusion of "Don't know" and "It depends" responses.
[b]. Chi-square statistics were calculated based on "Agree" and "Disagree" responses only.

## *Attitudes Toward Third-Party Intervention and Reporting Elder Mistreatment*

As with the other two areas discussed above, significant differences were found among the groups' responses to three of the four statements regarding third party intervention and reporting, as shown in Table 4. Although the majority of respondents supported third party intervention (Statement 1) and reporting of known elder abuse or neglect incidents to the authorities (Statement 2), a considerable percentage of respondents, especially Korean Americans (39% and 25%), did not. With regard to the first statement, 62% of the two American born groups, and 54% of Korean Americans were in favor of persons outside the family getting involved, with the Taiwan Americans (70%) having the greatest tendency to favor third party intervention.

If the third party intervention meant reporting known elder mistreatment to authorities, such as the police and social service agencies, considerably greater percentages of respondents, with the exception of Taiwanese Americans, seemed to support third party intervention by the appropriate authorities. Nevertheless, significantly higher percentages of Korean Americans (25%) and Taiwanese Americans (28%), compared to American born groups (0% of Chinese Americans and 13% of Japanese Americans) still felt the neighbor should not report the mistreatment to social service agencies and the police.

TABLE 4. Respondents' Attitude Toward Third-Party Intervention and Reporting of Elder Mistreatment by Ethnic Group[a]

| Items | Chinese American (N = 50) | | Japanese American (N = 48) | | Korean American (N = 95) | | Taiwanese American (N = 80) | | $\chi^{2b}$ |
|---|---|---|---|---|---|---|---|---|---|
| | Agree (%) | Disagree (%) | Agree (%) | Disagree (%) | Agree (%) | Disagree (%) | Agree (%) | Disagree (%) | |
| 1. When an elderly person is abused or neglected by a family member, persons outside the family should not get involved. | 22.0 | 62.0 | 19.1 | 61.7 | 38.9 | 53.7 | 15.0 | 70.0 | 12.1*** |
| 2. When a neighbor knows that an elderly person is being abused or neglected by a family member, the neighbor should not report it to such authorities as social service agencies and the police. | 0.0 | 90.0 | 12.5 | 77.1 | 25.3 | 68.4 | 27.5 | 67.5 | 18.3*** |
| 3. When a neighbor suspects that an elderly person is being abused or neglected by a family member, the neighbor should not report it to such authorities as social service agencies and the police until s/he is absolutely sure about it. | 56.0 | 40.0 | 52.1 | 33.3 | 64.2 | 31.6 | 47.5 | 35.0 | 1.8 |
| 4. Reporting elder abusers to such authorities as social service agencies and the police will destroy the abusers' lives. | 4.0 | 84.0 | 12.5 | 64.6 | 49.5 | 37.9 | 26.9 | 53.8 | 41.5*** |

* $p < .05$; ** $p < .01$; *** $p < .001$
a. The percentages in the Table are based on a total N. However, since percentages are reported only for "Agree" and "Disagree" responses, they may not add to 100% due to the exclusion of "Don't know" and "It Depends" responses.
b. Chi-square statistics were calculated based on "Agree" and "Disagree" responses only.

The majority of respondents, ranging from 48% of Taiwanese Americans to 64% of Korean Americans, also felt the neighbor should not report the mistreatment until the neighbor was absolutely sure about it (Statement 3). This finding clearly suggests the respondents' reluctance or disapproval of reporting suspected mistreatment to authorities. In addition, one-half (50%) of the Korean Americans and 27% of the Taiwanese Americans felt strongly that reporting abusers to authorities would destroy the abusers' lives. Conversely, only a few of the U.S. born Chinese Americans (4%) and Japanese Americans (13%) agreed that reporting abusers would destroy their lives.

### *Summary of Tolerance, Victim Blaming and Attitudes Toward Reporting*

Utilizing the mean and range of scores, Table 5 summarizes each group's tendency to tolerate mistreatment behaviors, victim blame, and favor third party involvement and reporting. Range of scores for each category reflects the lowest and highest average score received on any of the statements within that category. As discussed earlier, possible scores ranged from 8 to 24 for tolerance, from 2 to 6 for victim blaming, and from 4 to 12 for attitudes toward reporting. Respondents with higher scores were more tolerant of mistreatment, more likely to victim blame, and more supportive of third party intervention and reporting.

For example, for the eight statements in the Tolerance category, the Chinese Americans' responses ranged from 8 (the lowest possible level of tolerance) to 18 out of a possible 24 points. None of the groups had total scores approaching 24 for elder mistreatment, and the large standard deviation values indicate considerable within group variations. With the lowest mean score of 11.0, the Taiwanese Americans were significantly least tolerant of the eight behaviors described, and the Korean Americans with the mean score of 12.9 were the most tolerant. The U.S. born groups showed remarkably similar mean tolerance scores (12.1 for Chinese Americans and 12.3 for Japanese Americans).

In the other two categories, again, the Korean Americans differ from the other groups. With regard to victim blaming, the Korean Americans with the mean score of 3.7 were significantly more likely to victim blame and had a large standard deviation. Conversely, the Chinese and Japanese Americans with mean scores of 2.3 and 2.4, respectively, were less likely to victim blame and had a smaller standard deviation. Also, in the attitude toward reporting category, the Korean Americans were least favorable toward reporting and outside intervention and had the largest standard deviation. On the other hand, the Chinese and Japanese Americans were more favorable toward outside involvement.

### *Relationship Between Tolerance, Victim Blaming and Attitude Toward Reporting*

Finally, Table 6 shows the relationship between the three categories, tolerance, victim blaming and attitude toward reporting among all of the participants ($N = 272$). A significant positive relationship was found between tolerance and victim blaming ($r = 0.23$, $p < .01$). At the same time, a significant negative relationship was found between tolerance

TABLE 5. Summary of Tolerance, Victim Blaming and Attitude Toward Reporting by Ethnic Group

| | Total | Chinese American | Japanese American | Korean American | Taiwanese American | F-Value[a] |
|---|---|---|---|---|---|---|
| Tolerance (8 items) | | | | | | |
| Score range | 8-20 | 8-18 | 8-19 | 8-20 | 8-20 | |
| Mean | 12.1 | 12.1 | 12.3 | 12.9 | 11.0 | |
| SD | 2.7 | 2.4 | 2.6 | 2.8 | 2.4 | 7.63*** |
| Victim Blaming (2 items) | | | | | | |
| Score range | 2-6 | 2-4 | 2-5 | 2-6 | 2-6 | |
| Mean | 3.0 | 2.3 | 2.4 | 3.7 | 2.8 | |
| SD | 1.3 | 0.6 | 0.8 | 1.5 | 1.1 | 22.5*** |
| Attitude toward Reporting (4 items) | | | | | | |
| Score range | 4-12 | 6-12 | 6-12 | 4-12 | 4-12 | |
| Mean | 9.0 | 9.9 | 9.4 | 8.1 | 9.1 | |
| SD | 2.2 | 1.7 | 2.0 | 2.4 | 1.9 | 9.44*** |

[a] One-way ANOVA analysis. *** $p < .001$

TABLE 6. Relationship Between Tolerance, Victim Blaming, and Attitude Toward Reporting (N = 272)

| | Tolerance | Victim Blaming | Attitude Toward Reporting |
|---|---|---|---|
| Tolerance | 1.00 | | |
| Victim Blaming | 0.23** | 1.00 | |
| Attitude Toward Reporting | − 0.22** | − 0.28** | 1.00 |

** Correlation is significant at the 0.01 level. (2-tailed)

and attitude toward reporting ($r = -0.22$, $p < .01$), and between victim blaming and attitude toward reporting ($r = -0.28$, $p < .01$).

## *CONCLUSION AND DISCUSSION*

Significant differences were found between the U.S.-born Chinese and Japanese Americans and the first generation Korean and Taiwanese Americans, perhaps due to their current subscribed norms and length of time in the United States. The U.S.-born Asians were more likely to tolerate yelling at elderly parents, but less likely to tolerate financial exploitation than the Korean and Taiwanese Americans. The U.S.-born Chinese and Japanese Americans also tended not to victim blame, and were more favorable toward reporting elder mistreatment.

The first-generation Korean Americans were most likely to tolerate financial abuse, least likely to tolerate yelling at elderly parents, had the greatest tendency to victim blame, were least likely to favor reporting the mistreatment, and felt reporting abusers would destroy the abusers' lives. For the Korean Americans, their responses indicate a strong adherence to the concept of filial piety ("hyo" in Korean), which has always dictated the Korean parent-child relationship (K. Lee, 1989; Sung, 1995), while among the Chinese and Japanese Americans, who traditionally have had an equally strong sense of filial piety (Tomita, 1998; Wong, 1988), subscription to this may have diminished as the younger generations replace it with such norms as independence and individualism.

Korean norms dictate that children should respect, obey, and engage with their parents in a polite and respectful manner. As the parents age, sons especially are expected to care for the parents physically, emotionally and financially in a willing manner. In turn, the parents share their income and savings as if equal access to their funds by their children is expected. In addition, the elder's tolerance for financial abuse may be related to the traditional patriarchal property transfer system in Korean society. Under this system, sons, even after marriage, enjoy exclusive family inheritance rights. Although the passage of the 1989 Korean family law granted equal inheritance rights to daughters and sons, the long-standing precedent of the son's entitlement to family wealth and property still prevails in both Korean and Korean American families. This tradition has tended to promote an adult son's financial dependence and exploitation of the elderly parent (Chang & Moon, 1997).

Focusing on the Taiwanese Americans, their responses did not show a pattern, and were not similar to those of either the U.S.-born or the Korean American group. While they joined the Korean Americans in disagreeing with physically restraining an elderly parent in bed, unlike any of the other three groups, the Taiwanese Americans were intolerant (76%) of leaving a bedridden parent alone occasionally. Yet, 44% responded with "Don't know" or "It depends" to the statement indicating it was okay to force parents to eat when they rejected food. Given the variation in their responses, it is impossible to make any conclusions about the Taiwanese Americans and their relationship to elder mistreatment. This is the first exploratory study on elder mistreatment known to include Taiwanese Americans and conducted in Mandarin.

Due to their mixed responses to the four statements related to reporting and outside intervention, it is unknown if Taiwan Americans, due to their relatively recent arrival, are more or less similar to their Korean American counterparts. In Korea and Taiwan, child and elder abuse are not public issues but confined to the family, and responses to the problems by such response systems as law enforcement and child and adult protective services are not yet fully established. Not knowing what the U.S. response agencies are capable of doing for the family may have contributed to the Korean and Taiwanese Americans' responses in this study. Future researchers are encouraged to study Taiwanese Americans in greater depth in order to understand their notions of treatment of the elderly.

The large percentages (40%-50%) of "Don't know" and "It depends" responses for some of the statements indicate that the respondents had difficulty relating to the phenomenon of elder mistreatment and what constituted an act of mistreatment. The Chinese and Japanese Americans' high rate of "Don't know" or "It depends" responses to two of the eight elder mistreatment statements could be due to their inability to answer without more information about the social context. This idea is supported by Hayashi and Kuroda's (1997) work on comparing the ways people from different cultures respond to questionnaires. They note that the Japanese are non-absolutists who do not respond readily to polarized statements. Instead, they pay attention to the entire social context rather than just to the individual, and their response to a particular situation or individual depends on their assessment of all the other social contextual variables at hand. Nevertheless, such large percentages in these response categories raise the notion that there is a strong possibility that within these groups, a potential exists for tolerating what are considered by many to be elder mistreatment behaviors. The wide range of within-group scores and large standard deviations indicate tremendous variation in the responses, and it could be that depending on the participants' exposure to the phenomenon of elder mistreatment and other intervening cultural variables, Asian Americans' attitudes and understanding of the problem will be as varied as the American population as a whole.

## *LIMITATIONS OF THE STUDY*

This was an exploratory survey with many limitations. Although the study assured some degree of heterogeneity by recruiting participants in various settings, its convenience sampling process may have recruited persons who were of the same socioeconomic background and who possessed similar cultural values. All of the participants were recruited in Los Angeles or Seattle, and it may be that Asian Americans living in other parts of the country would have responded differently. The uneven and small sample size among the groups is another reason for the non-generalizability of the study results. The lack of consistent patterns between those who were U.S.-born and not U.S.-born suggests the need to replicate the study on a larger, more representative sample of elders. For example, it would be helpful to practitioners to understand why most of the Japanese Americans (45%) chose "Don't know" or "It depends" regarding calming the parents with medication, and 15% were tolerant of tying a parent down in bed while no other group responded in a similar way. The data analysis did not control for gender, so it is unknown if the Asian American women, who traditionally are known to suffer quietly, were more likely to victim blame than the men. Last, in the absence of multiple measures of acculturation, the use of country of birth and number of years in the U.S. offers little insight into the process of how acculturation influences the perceptions of elder mistreatment, victim blaming and attitudes toward reporting.

## *IMPLICATIONS FOR SOCIAL WORK PRACTICE*

Despite these limitations, results from this study have important implications for policy makers and practitioners. First, the four groups had significantly different responses to five of the eight descriptions of elder mistreatment, and a significant percentage of respondents did not favor reporting the mistreatment. This implies that practitioners should keep in mind that there is a substantial difference even among Asian American elderly regarding tolerance of elder mistreatment and that the way clients may respond to one form of mistreatment may differ depending on the type of mistreatment experienced. The finding also implies that many Asian Americans do not recognize common forms of mistreatment, and may not understand the reporting process as a venue of support, much less know where and whom to call. This finding supports the findings in Moon and Evans-Campbell's (1999) comparison study of Korean Americans and Caucasian elders, which found that Korean Americans were significantly less aware of resources of help, including their county's elder abuse hotline and adult protective services.

Second, regardless of ethnicity, those who were tolerant of the elder mistreatment statements tended to victim blame, and were not favorable toward reporting. Relatedly, those who victim blamed were not favorable toward reporting. It could be that those who victim blame may also refuse or interfere with outside involvement. In order for successful interventions to occur, a concurrent process of countering the beliefs that support victim blaming and tolerance for mistreatment through community education must take place. In clinical settings, it would be helpful for practitioners to keep in mind the diversity of beliefs and be sensitive to the possibility that their elderly Asian clients may be dealing with abusive behavior but will not reveal it due to self-blame feelings about the situation. Furthermore, practitioners could help clients understand the process of reporting, the benefits to the victim if they reported the incident, and the realistic consequences for the perpetrator.

Finally, understanding how elder mistreatment is perceived and manifested among Asian American elderly allows practitioners to provide appropriate clinical interventions. Their help-seeking behaviors will depend in part on their degree of commitment to the group, whether it is family or community (E. Lee, 1997). Sometimes, an admission of being victimized will occur only if these victims ascertain that the perpetrators and families will not be affected negatively by the report. As a result, in the assessment phase, practitioners must explore the elder's degree of collective self or commitment to the perpetrator (Tomita, 2000). Elders who feel oppressed or who want attention from other family members often must remain silent (Reinharz, 1994). The assessment process must allow for more time in order for elderly victims to warm up to the process of speaking up and having their reports validated by the practitioner without any notion of self-blame. In some cases, admission of mistreatment may be obtained by using non-verbal and non-straightforward styles of communication (Tempo & Saito, 1996), and empowerment may be possible through teaching victims the "language of feelings" (Masaki & Wong, 1997).

The results of this study clearly support the need to incorporate culture in designing effective policy, education, and intervention strategies when dealing with elder mistreatment.

## REFERENCES

Anetzberger, G., Korbin, J. & Tomita, S. K. (1996). Defining elder mistreatment in four ethnic groups across two generations. *Journal of Cross-Cultural Gerontology*, *11*, 187-212.

Brown, A. (1989). A survey on elder abuse at one Native American tribe. *Journal of Elder Abuse & Neglect*, *1*(2), 17-37.

Chang, J. & Moon, A. (1997). Korean American elderly's knowledge and perceptions of elder abuse: A qualitative analysis of cultural factors. *Journal of Multicultural Social Work*, *6*(1/2), 139-154.

Hayashi, C. & Kuroda, Y. (1997). *Japanese culture in comparative perspective*. Westport, CT: Praeger.

Kaneko, Y. & Yamada, Y. (1990). Wives and mothers-in-law: Potential for family conflict in post-war Japan. *Journal of Elder Abuse & Neglect*, *2*(1/2), 87-99.

Lee, E. (Ed.) (1997). *Working with Asian Americans: A guide for clinicians*. NY: The Guilford Press.

Lee, K. K. (1989). *An analysis of the structure of the Korean family, 11th Ed.*, Seoul, Korea: Il-Ji Publishing Co.

Masaki, B. & Wong, L. (1996). Domestic violence in the Asian community. In E. Lee (Ed.). *Working with Asian Americans: A guide for clinicians* (pp. 439-451). NY: The Guilford Press.

Moon, A. & Benton, D. (2000). Tolerance of elder abuse and attitudes toward third-party intervention among African American, Korean American, and White elderly. *Journal of Multicultural Social Work*, *8*(3/4), 283-303.

Moon, A., Tomita, S., Talamantes, M., Brown, A., Sanchez, Y., Benton, D., Sanchez, C., & Kim, S. J. (1998). *Measures toward elder mistreatment and reporting: A multicultural study*. A report submitted to the National Center on Elder Abuse, February.

Moon, A. & Evans-Campbell, T. (1999). Awareness of formal and informal sources of help to victims of elder abuse among Korean Americans and Caucasian elders in Los Angeles. *Journal of Elder Abuse & Neglect*, *11*(3), 1-23.

Moon, A. & Williams, O. (1993) Perceptions of elder abuse and help-seeking patterns among African-American, Caucasian-American, and Korean-American elderly women. *Gerontologist*, *22*(3), 386-395.

Reinharz, S. (1994). Toward an ethnography of "voice" and "silence." In E. Trickett & R. Watts (Eds.). *Human diversity: Perspectives on people in context*, (pp. 178-200). San Francisco, CA: Jossey-Bass.

Sung, K. (1995). Measures and dimensions of filial piety in Korea. *Gerontologist*, *35*(2), 240-247.

Tatara, T. (Ed.) (1998). *Understanding elder abuse among minority populations*. Philadelphia: Brunner/Mazel.

Tempo, P. & Saito, A. (1996). Techniques of working with Japanese American families. In G. Yeo & D. Gallagher-Thompson (Eds.). *Ethnicity and the dementias* (pp. 109-122). Washington, DC: Taylor & Francis.

Tomita, S. K. (2000). Elder mistreatment: Practice modifications to accommodate cultural differences. *Journal of Multicultural Social Work*, *8*(3/4), 305-326.

Tomita, S. K. (1998a). The consequences of belonging: Conflict management techniques among Japanese Americans. *Journal of Elder Abuse & Neglect*, *9*(3), 41-68.

Tomita, S. K. (1998b). Exploration of elder mistreatment among the Japanese. In T. Tatara (Ed.). *Understanding elder abuse in minority populations* (pp. 119-139). Philadelphia, PA: Brunner/Mazel.

Wong, M. (1988). The Chinese American family. In C. Mindel, R. Habenstein & R. Wright, Jr. *Ethnic families in America: Patterns and variations* (pp. 230-257). NY: Elsevier Science Publishing Co.

# A Profile of Asian/Pacific Islander Elderly in Home Health Care

Ji Seon Lee, PhD
Timothy R. Peng, PhD

**SUMMARY.** This study explores the differences in patient characteristics, home health service use, and discharge outcomes between Asian/Pacific Islanders (API) (n = 408) and White elderly home health care patients (n = 2,480) with a primary diagnosis of diabetes, hypertension or cardiovascular disease. Outcomes Assessment Information Set and administrative data from a large urban home health agency located in the Northeast were used for analyses. Overall, API elders were more likely to be dually eligible for Medicare and Medicaid; entered with greater dependencies; and received more home health aide services than White elders. However, White elders reported greater anxiety and were more likely to live alone. 

---

Ji Seon Lee is Assistant Professor, Fordham University, Graduate School of Social Service; Hartford Geriatric Social Work Faculty Scholar; Associate Director of Research, Ravazzin Center for Social Work Research in Aging; Research Associate, NIMH Center for Hispanic Mental Health Research, 113 West 60th Street, New York, NY 10023. Timothy R. Peng is Research Associate, Center for Home Care Policy and Research, Visiting Nurse Service of New York, 5 Penn Plaza, New York, NY 10001.

[Haworth co-indexing entry note]: "A Profile of Asian/Pacific Islander Elderly in Home Health Care." Lee, Ji Seon, and Timothy R. Peng. Co-published simultaneously in *Journal of Gerontological Social Work* (The Haworth Social Work Practice Press, an imprint of The Haworth Press, Inc.) Vol. 36, No. 1/2, 2001, pp. 171-186; and: *Social Work Practice with the Asian American Elderly* (ed: Namkee G. Choi) The Haworth Social Work Practice Press, an imprint of The Haworth Press, Inc., 2001, pp. 171-186. Single or multiple copies of this article are available for a fee from The Haworth Document Delivery Service [1-800-HAWORTH, 9:00 a.m. - 5:00 p.m. (EST). E-mail address: getinfo@haworthpressinc.com].

 

**KEYWORDS.** Asian/Pacific Islanders, elderly, home health care, service use

## *HOME HEALTH SERVICE USE AMONG ASIAN PACIFIC ISLANDER ELDERLY*

Asian Pacific Islanders (API) are projected to be among the fastest growing segment of the elderly population in the next 30 years, but little is known about API elders who utilize home health services (Administration on Aging, 1999) compared to other minority elders. Home health care has gained increased popularity among the elderly as a means to remain independent in the community following an acute illness or to address the service needs of a severe chronic condition. As the fastest growing Medicare benefit, the average annual increase of Medicare home health was 28% per beneficiary between 1990 and 1996 (Komisar, 1997). In October of 2000, a Prospective Payment System (PPS) was implemented in Medicare home health care, under which participating home health agencies receive capitated payment per episode of care, similar to the Diagnosis Related Group system used to reimburse Medicare inpatient care services. Identifying patient characteristics that may influence service use and outcomes among home health users has become increasingly important to both policy makers and service providers under PPS. For social work, the shift to PPS provides a unique opportunity for improved integration of social work services into home health service delivery, which may help in the effective response to consumer needs. Social workers have traditionally helped patients and families deal with illness and the recovery process through various services, including counseling for psychosocial issues, the coordination of services, and advocacy for patient rights. These social work roles may be further emphasized under the rules of PPS, which explicitly encourage agencies to strive for improvement of patient outcomes and smoother transitions into and out of care.

This study explores the differences between API and White elders in home health care on their (1) socio-demographic characteristics, (2) home health service use, and (3) discharge outcomes. Identifying unique characteristics and service use patterns among API elders can help inform social workers, service providers, and policy makers to develop appropriate care plans and target resources efficiently under PPS.

## *BACKGROUND*

Minority elderly are projected to represent 25% of the elderly population in the United States by 2030, a rise from 16% in 1998 (AoA, 1999). Between 1998 and 2030, the White elderly population is projected to increase by 79%, while the API elderly population is projected to increase by 323% (AoA, 1999). In recent years, these projections have made researchers and policy makers increasingly aware of the growing diversity across the elderly population. However, as stated in Healthy People 2010 (United States Department of Health and Human Services, 2001), there exists only limited evidence-based knowledge on health disparities between different racial and ethnic groups.

The projected increase in the proportion of minority elderly, among other things, has led to a growing interest in minority populations among researchers of long term care services. Studies have shown that African-American, Latino, and API elders typically are less likely than White elders to use nursing home care (Chee & Kane, 1983; Espino & Burge, 1989; Morrison, 1982; Stuttlesworth, Rubin & Duffy, 1982; Weissert & Cready, 1988). Yet, at the same time, community-based services are often less used by minority elders. African-American elders have been shown to use less formal in-home care compared to White elders (Wallace, Andersen, & Levy-Storms, 1993). Latinos have also been found to use fewer services than non-Latino Whites (Green & Monahan, 1984). Guttman and Cuellar (1982) found that API elders used significantly fewer social services than even Latino and Black elders.

Other studies have focused on patient knowledge of community-based services to explain the differences in general health service utilization rates (Holmes & Holmes, 1983; Moon, Lubben, & Villa, 1998; Spence & Atherton, 1991). Holmes, Teresi, and Holmes (1983) have shown that African American and Puerto Rican elders were less knowledgeable about available services compared to White and Mexican American elders. Nevertheless, some studies suggest that race is not a significant factor in predicting general health and social service use (Wallace, Levy-Storms, & Ferguson, 1993; Wolinsky et al., 1983).

Compared to other minority elderly groups, however, research on API elders has been very limited in scope. Most research has focused on social service utilization (Guttman, & Cuellar, 1982) and barriers to general health services utilization (Chang & Moon, 1997; Koh & Bell, 1987). Little is known about home health service utilization among API elders.

The neglect of API elders in research has been largely attributed to the lack of systematic data on API elders in readily available national datasets (LaVeist, 1995). Yu and Liu (1994) suggest that the difficulty in finding a representative sample of a diverse API population is the primary reason for the lack of available data. The limited data that are available on API elders depict API elders to be healthier than other older population groups (Gelfand, 1994). Prior research has shown API elders to have a lower level of prevalence in all major disease categories (Liu & Yu, 1985) and lower mortality rates than Whites (Yu, Chang & Liu, 1984). However, this healthy picture of API elders can be misleading. Tanjasiri, Wallace, and Shibata (1995) argue that aggregate analysis of data on API elders blurs substantial differences across API groups with respect to socioeconomic and health status. Length of time since immigration in particular contributes to the "bipolar nature" of socioeconomic and health status (Lin-Fu, 1988). The grouping of various API ethnic groups into a single category, combined with the difficulty of finding sufficiently large representative samples, limits the generalizability of the available research on service utilization among API elders.

Although the current study does not disaggregate the diverse ethnic groups among the APIs, it does consist of a large enough sample to provide information on API elders and their home health service use. Accurate data on actual service utilization and discharge outcomes afford a unique opportunity to examine the profile of a population of frail API elderly. This study contributes to building the knowledge base of API elders receiving home health care by describing their sociodemographic profile and exploring their home health service utilization and outcomes.

## *METHODS*

### *Study Design and Sample*

This is a descriptive study of patients admitted to a large urban home health care agency located in the Northeast during the 12 months of 1999. The area in which this home health agency is located is characterized by 2.03% API elders and 84.96% White Elders (U.S. Census Bureau, 2001). Among API elders, 44.64% were male and 55.36% female compared to 39.22% and 60.77% respectively among White elders

(U.S. Census Bureau, 2001). The top API groups represented in this area are Chinese, Asian Indian, Korean, Filipino and Japanese.

Data from initial Outcomes Assessment Information Set (OASIS) and other routinely collected administrative records are used for analyses. The OASIS is a comprehensive assessment tool that includes indicators of a patient's physiological and functional status (Shaughnessy, Crisler, & Schlenker, 1998). The Health Care Financing Administration has mandated that as of October 2000, home health service providers must collect OASIS assessments on their patients as a condition of participation in the Federal Medicare program. Initial OASIS assessments are conducted by home health nurses during the first visit following referral and admission into home care.

The sample consisted of patients over 64 years of age, self-identified as API (n = 408) or White (n = 2,480) who were admitted to home care with primary diagnosis of diabetes, hypertension or cerebrovascular disease (CVD) in 1999. These conditions represent the top three diagnoses for admission to home health care among API elders at this home health agency during 1999 (see Table 1). For those patients who were admitted to the agency more than once during 1999, only the first admission was included in the sample. Across both groups, eligible patients had a median readmission rate of once during 1999. To avoid right-censoring of utilization estimates, patients who were admitted in 1999 but for whom discharge information was not yet recorded as of June 2000 were not included in the sample.

### *Measures*

*Demographics*. Demographic information obtained from OASIS records includes patient age, sex, insurance status, and living situation. Insurance status is categorized by Medicare-only, Medicaid-only, dually eligible for both Medicare and Medicaid, or other. The measure of living situation categorizes patients into those who live alone and those who do not. Administrative data is used to determine referral sources–hospitals as opposed to those who were self or physician referred.

*Physical and psychological functioning*. Indicators of patients' physical functioning was obtained from OASIS measures of activities of daily living (ADLs) and instrumental activities of daily living (IADLs). Summary scores indicating whether patients were dependent on another person performing ADL activities (grooming, dressing upper body, dressing lower body, bathing, toileting, transferring, ambulation, and feeding, with scores ranging from 0 to 8 dependencies) and IADL activ-

TABLE 1. Sample Distribution by Primary Diagnosis

| | Diabetes | | Hypertension | | CVD | | Total | |
|---|---|---|---|---|---|---|---|---|
| White | 758 | 84.3% | 1,055 | 87.6% | 667 | 85.0% | 2,480 | 85.9% |
| API | 141 | 15.7% | 149 | 12.4% | 118 | 15.0% | 408 | 14.1% |
| Total | 899 | 100.0% | 1,204 | 100.0% | 785 | 100.0% | 2,888 | 100.0% |

ities (meal preparation, transportation, laundry, housekeeping, shopping, and telephone use, with scores ranging from 0 to 6 dependencies) were computed.

Measures of patients' cognitive functioning, confusion, and levels of anxiety were also obtained from OASIS assessments. The measures of cognitive functioning and confusion ranged from 0 to 4, with higher numbers indicating poorer functioning and greater confusion, respectively. The measure of anxiety ranged from 0 to 3, with higher numbers indicating higher levels of anxiety. These measures were designed as rough case-mix adjusters for use in the analysis of patient outcomes (Shaughnessy, Schlenker, & Hittle, 1994), and have not been validated for the elderly API population. The actual items associated with each measure are presented in the Appendix.

*Utilization and outcomes.* Utilization of home health care services was obtained from patient administrative records. Services examined in this study were: total number of skilled nursing visits provided for each patient, total number of social work visits provided, and total number of hours of home health aide services provided. Skilled nursing and home health aide services represent the vast majority of home health services typically used by home health care patients (Mauser & Miller, 1994).

Patient outcome is measured by discharge status at the end of the episode of care provided by the agency. As discharge to self or community care is the desired "ideal" goal of non-palliative home health care provision, patients who were discharged to self or community care are compared to those who were discharged due to: hospitalization, institutionalization (e.g., skilled nursing facility, nursing home), death, admission to hospice care, or unknown (e.g., patient not found).

## ANALYSIS

Comparisons between API and White elders were made within diagnosis groups using ordinary chi-square tests of independence for binary categorical variables, and t-tests for continuous variables. Utilization measures, which typically exhibit high levels of skewing, underwent a natural logarithm transformation prior to comparison in order to normalize their distributions.

A logistic regression was conducted to model the likelihood that patients within each diagnosis group would be discharged to self/community care. These models examine the effect of ethnicity on discharge status controlling for age, sex, living situation, insurance status, referral source, cognitive functioning, confusion, anxiety, and physical functioning.

## *RESULTS*

### *Patient Characteristics*

Several sociodemographic characteristics differed between API and White elders across the three conditions (i.e., diabetes, hypertension, and CVD). The average age of API elders in the sample was 77.5 years; White elders in the sample were 81.2 years of age on average ($t = 8.08$, $p < .001$). Among API elders, 40.5% were male, compared to 30.2% of White elders ($\chi^2 = 11.69$, $p < .001$). A larger proportion of API elders were dually eligible for Medicare and Medicaid ($\chi^2 = 146.53$, $p < .001$). API elders in the sample entered home health care with more ADL ($t = 4.16$, $p < .001$) and IADL dependencies ($t = 4.55$, $p < .001$) as well. However, White elders entered home health care with a higher level of anxiety ($t = 3.94$, $p < .001$), and were more likely to live alone ($\chi^2 = 46.35$, $p < .001$) compared to API elders. These comparisons are provided only to present an overview of this particular sample of patients and should be viewed with caution, since they do not take into account the relative proportion of API or White elders across the sample within each condition, and thus are susceptible to diagnosis-specific biases.

Table 2 shows the difference in socio-demographic profiles between API and White elders by diagnosis. Among diabetic elderly patients in the sample, APIs were significantly more likely to be either dually eligible for Medicare and Medicaid ($\chi^2 = 45.16$, $p < .001$), or to have Medicaid as their only source of health insurance ($\chi^2 = 4.44$, $p < .05$). However, White elders with diabetes were more likely to live alone ($\chi^2 = 12.32$, $p < .001$) at admission to home care.

TABLE 2. Profile of API and White Elders in Home Health Care by Diagnosis

| | Diabetes | | Hypertension | | CVD | |
|---|---|---|---|---|---|---|
| | API (n = 141) | White (n = 758) | API (n = 149) | White (n = 1,055) | API (n = 118) | White (n = 667) |
| Age (= years) | 78.03 (6.6) | 79.22 (7.6) | 79.36 (7.6) | 83.35 (7.6)[c] | 77.30 (6.9) | 81.29 (8.0)[c] |
| Gender (= male) | 34.40% | 32.53% | 33.05%[b] | 20.86% | 50.89% | 41.72% |
| Lives alone | 30.47% | 47.31%[c] | 37.50%[c] | 54.15% | 11.50% | 31.91%[c] |
| ADLs | 3.91 (2.7) | 3.66 (2.8) | 4.03 (2.6) | 3.62 (2.6) | 6.18 (2.1)[c] | 5.04 (2.7) |
| IADLs | 4.82 (1.3) | 4.59 (1.4) | 4.93 (1.1)[a] | 4.67 (1.2) | 5.54 (0.8)[c] | 5.16 (1.0) |
| Cognitive functioning | 0.50 (.8) | 0.51 (.9) | 0.53 (.8) | 0.51 (.9) | 0.74 (1.1) | 0.75 (1.2) |
| Confusion | 0.78 (1.1) | 0.68 (1.1) | 0.68 (1.0) | 0.67 (1.0) | 0.84 (1.2) | 0.80 (1.3) |
| Anxiety | 0.59 (.8) | 0.67 (.9) | 0.57(.8) | 0.76 (.9)[a] | 0.37 (.8) | 0.62 (.9)[b] |
| Dually eligible for Medicare and Medicaid | 49.22%[c] | 20.96% | 48.33%[c] | 18.40% | 41.59%[c] | 14.40% |
| Medicaid only | 16.41%[a] | 10.03% | 11.67% | 10.83% | 7.96%[b] | 2.78% |
| Medicare only | 28.91% | 59.13%[c] | 37.50% | 63.69%[c] | 41.59% | 67.76%[c] |
| Other insurance | 5.46% | 9.88% | 2.50% | 6.83% | 8.84% | 15.06% |
| Referred by hospital | 40.63% | 39.67% | 29.17%[b] | 42.80% | 52.21% | 48.77% |

Note: T-tests and chi-square were used for tests of significance. [a]$p < .05$; [b]$p < .01$; [c]$p < .001$. Values in parentheses are standard deviations.

Among hypertension patients, there were more male patients among API elders compared to Whites ($\chi^2 = 9.01$, $p < .01$). API elders also had more IADL dependencies ($t = 2.28$, $p < .05$) and were more likely to be dually eligible for Medicare and Medicaid ($\chi^2 = 56.08$, $p < .001$). But compared to API elders, the average age of White patients was higher ($t = 5.42$, $p < .001$), significantly more White elders lived alone ($\chi^2 = 11.85$, $p < .001$) and had a higher level of anxiety ($t = 2.43$, $p < .05$) at entrance to home care.

API elders with a primary diagnosis of CVD were more likely to have a greater number of ADL ($t = 5.03$, $p < .001$) and IADL ($t = 4.51$, $p < .001$) dependencies compared to White elders with CVD. Similar to diabetes patients, more CVD API elders were dually eligible for Medicare and Medicaid ($\chi^2 = 46.48$, $p < .001$), or have Medicaid as their only source of health insurance ($\chi^2 = 7.40$, $p < .01$) compared to White elders. However, White elders with CVD were older than API elders ($t = 5.48$, $p < .001$). White elderly CVD patients were also more likely to live alone ($\chi^2 = 19.40$, $p < .001$) and entered home health care with a higher level of anxiety ($t = 3.06$, $p < .01$) compared to API elders.

### *Service Use and Discharge Outcomes*

Utilization of home health skilled nursing, social work, and home health aide services by API and White elderly across the three primary diagnoses are presented in Table 3. For all three conditions, API elders received significantly more home health services than White elders ($t = 7.56$, $p < .001$). For patients with a primary diagnosis of CVD, API elders received a greater number of skilled nursing visits as well ($t = 2.16$, $p < .05$).

Patient outcomes, as measured by discharge to self/community care, are presented across diagnoses in Tables 4, 5 and 6. After controlling for physical functioning, insurance status, psychological functioning, and sociodemographic factors, discharge outcomes were not significantly different for API elderly compared to White elderly. Across all three diagnoses, having more ADL/IADL dependencies, being dually eligible for Medicare and Medicaid, having Medicaid only, and living alone, were associated with a decreased likelihood of being discharged to self/community care.

Overall, the findings show that for chronic conditions (i.e., diabetes and hypertension), API and White elders in the sample differed on a limited set of demographic characteristics, but shared similar clinical profiles. However, for acute conditions (i.e., CVD), API elderly were more likely to have entered home health care with more ADL/IADL dependencies. Despite being more likely to be living with others, API elders received similar or more formal care services than White elders.

## *DISCUSSION*

These findings highlight several differences among API elders and White elders to consider for home health care providers. Overall, we found API elders to be younger, with a higher proportion of men. These differences do not necessarily represent unique characteristics of APIs in home care, so much as it reflects the population in this region (U.S. Census Bureau, 2001). However, it is unclear why API elders tend to be younger and have a higher proportion of men than White elders in gen-

TABLE 3. Home Health Service Use by Diagnosis

| | Diabetes | | Hypertension | | CVD | |
|---|---|---|---|---|---|---|
| | API (n = 141) | White (n = 758) | API (n = 149) | White (n = 1,055) | API (n = 118) | White (n = 667) |
| Skilled nursing visits | 2.37 (1.0) | 2.28 (1.3) | 2.04 (1.1) | 1.93 (1.0) | 1.86 (1.0)[a] | 1.63 (1.0) |
| Social work visits | 0.37 (.7) | .26 (.6) | 0.30 (.55) | 0.27 (.57) | 0.27 (.5) | 0.24 (.5) |
| Home health aide hours | 3.29 (2.8)[c] | 1.91 (2.5) | 3.28 (2.8)[c] | 2.04 (2.4) | 2.87 (2.7)[c] | 1.97 (2.3) |

Note: All services were log transformed; t-tests were used for analysis of significance
[a]p < .05; [b]p < .01; [c]p < .001.
Values in parentheses are standard deviations.

TABLE 4. Logistic Regression of Discharge to Self/Community Care for Patients with a Primary Diagnosis of Diabetes

| Variables | Unstandardized Coeffiecent (SE) | Odds Ratio |
|---|---|---|
| Total ADL/IADL dependencies | −0.23 (.03) *** | 0.80 |
| Dually eligible for Medicare and Medicaid | −1.23 (.22) *** | 0.29 |
| Eligible for Medicaid only | −1.66 (.36) *** | 0.19 |
| Lives alone | −0.47 (.19) *** | 0.62 |
| Intercept | 1.80 (1.0) | |

Note: Model $\chi^2_{(11)} = 163.92$, $p < 0.001$
Only significant variables are included. Non-significant parameters in the equation include: Ethnicity = Asian, age, cognitive functioning, confusion, anxiety, sex, referral to home care from a hospital.
Reference group for dually eligible or Medicaid only is: Medicare only or other insurance.
Model fits the likelihood that patient was discharged to self/community care.
* p < .05; ** p <.01; *** p < .001.

eral. Further research needs to be conducted to better understand this issue.

We also found that API elders were more likely than White elders to be dually eligible for Medicare and Medicaid, an indicator that has been associated with a variety of risk factors for poor health. A recent Government Accounting Office report (2000) found that people who were dually eligible for Medicare and Medicaid were more likely to have a serious disease or chronic condition (e.g., stroke and diabetes), and suf-

TABLE 5. Logistic Regression of Discharge to Self/Community Care for Patients with a Primary Diagnosis of Hypertension

| Variables | Unstandardized Coeffiecent (SE) | Odds Ratio |
|---|---|---|
| Total ADL/IADL dependencies | −0.21 (.03) *** | 0.81 |
| Dually eligible for Medicare and Medicaid | −1.64 (.19) *** | 0.19 |
| Eligible for Medicaid only | −1.54 (.29) *** | 0.21 |
| Lives alone | −0.42 (.17) ** | 0.65 |
| Intercept | 2.95 (.93) *** | |

Note: Model $\chi^2_{(11)} = 193.21$, $p < 0.001$
Only significant variables are included. Non-significant parameters in the equation include: Ethnicity = Asian, age, confusion, anxiety, cognitive functioning, sex, and referral to home care from a hospital.
Reference group for dually eligible or Medicaid only is: Medicare only or other insurance.
Model fits the likelihood that patient was discharged to self/community care.
* $p < .05$; ** $p < .01$; *** $p < .001$.

TABLE 6. Logistic Regression of Discharge to Self/Community Care for Patients with a Primary Diagnosis of Cardiovascular Disease

| Variables | Unstandardized Coefficient (SE) | Odds Ratio |
|---|---|---|
| Total ADL/IADL dependencies | −0.17 (.03) *** | 0.84 |
| Dually eligible for Medicare and Medicaid | −1.13 (.23) *** | 0.20 |
| Lives alone | −0.49 (.21) * | 0.61 |
| Intercept | 3.56 (1.0) *** | |

Note: Model $\chi^{2(11)} = 100.65$, $p < 0.001$
Only significant variables are included. Non-significant parameters in the equation include: Ethnicity = Asian, age, confusion, cognitive functioning, anxiety, Medicaid only, sex, and referral to home care from a hospital.
Reference group for dually eligible or Medicaid only is: Medicare only or other insurance.
Model fits the likelihood that patient was discharged to self/community care.
* $p < .05$; ** $p < .01$; *** $p < .001$.

fer from more functional limitations. Furthermore, dual eligibles were found to have less access to a regular source of care or preventive care, more often using emergency department services for primary care. If API elderly face greater barriers to access of health and long-term care services at appropriate times (Chee & Kane, 1983; Die & Seelbach,

1988), they may be at a greater risk for experiencing an acute event, and may find themselves entering the health care system at a more advanced stage of illness. This might, in turn, require more intense utilization of services. Policy makers need to be aware of this potential chain of events, which could be costly to Medicare and Medicaid, as well as decrease the quality of life for older APIs. Clark and Hulbert (1998) estimated that while only 17% of Medicare beneficiaries were dually eligible in 1997, they accounted for about 28% of total Medicare expenditures for the same year. This suggests that it would be appropriate to develop targeted interventions to provide better access to care or preventive care for dually eligible API elders.

Consistent with the association between dual eligibility and risk of poor health, we found that API elders had more functional dependencies at admission to home care, and received a greater volume of home care services overall. These findings imply that API elders enter home care in poorer health and in greater need of care, which suggests that API elders may remain without care to a higher level of health severity. Several factors may play a role in this finding. API elders may have greater difficulty gaining access to care due to language and cultural barriers (Chee & Kane, 1983). In addition, API elders may be less aware of available services. Moon, Lubben, and Villa (1998) have found that knowledge of community-based services can explain differences in general health service utilization. Social workers can play an important role in addressing these issues in several ways: through outreach efforts in the community; by breaking barriers to access through education of elders and their families about available services and prevention techniques; by connecting API elders with needed services; and by advocating for API elders to receive appropriate care.

Our findings indicate that White elderly in the study sample were more likely to report greater anxiety across the three conditions. It is possible that this may be associated with their relative isolation, as they were more likely to live alone compared to API elderly. However, it is also possible that linguistic or cultural barriers to the interpretation and perception of anxiety may lead to underreporting of anxiety by API patients. As greater emphasis is placed on the role of psychological functioning on patient outcomes, it is important to critically examine how the subjective and highly culturally specific nature of many psychological constructs applies across diverse populations.

Although API elders were more likely to be dual eligible and thus at greater risk for poor health outcomes, we found that API elders were as likely to be discharged to self or community care as White elders. While this implies that API and White elders fare similarly in home health care, the aggregation of API elders into a single category in this study does not accurately portray the diverse socioeconomic and health status within this group (Tanjasiri, Wallace, & Shibata, 1995).

Finally, the study suggests that API elders need and utilize home care, even when they are not living alone. This offers some evidence contrary to the popular belief that API families in the United States follow the tradition of filial piety–shouldering the burden of care for their elders without formal support.

These findings provide a first look into how API elders utilize services and fare once they enter the home health care system. However, the interpretations of these findings should be done with the following limitations in mind. The API elders included in this study are from a single home health agency, within a large urban setting. They are also limited to elders with three specific medical conditions: diabetes, hypertension, and CVD. Although these three conditions are highly prevalent diagnoses for API elders in home care, they do not represent the wide range of conditions found among API elderly who use home health care. Furthermore, the study does not distinguish between the various API ethnic groups who received home health care. To better understand and address the needs of API elders in home health care, it is critical that future research continues to examine their service use patterns and outcomes across larger samples of API elders.

## REFERENCES


Administration on Aging. (1999). Profile of older Americans: 1999. <http://www.aoa.dhhs.gov/aoa/stats/profile/default.htm> (19 May, 2000).

Chang, J., & Moon, A. (1997). Korean American elderly's knowledge about and perceptions of elder abuse: A qualitative analysis of cultural factors. *Journal of Multicultural Social Work*, 11, 139-154.

Chee, P., & Kane, R. (1983). Cultural factors affecting nursing home care for minorities: A study of black American and Japanese-American groups. *Journal of American Geriatric Society*, 31, 109-111.

Clark, W.D. & Hulbert, M.M. (1998). Research issues: Dually eligible Medicare and Medicaid beneficiaries, challenges and opportunities. *Health Care Financing Review*, 20(2), 1-10.

Die, A.H., & Seelbach, W.C. (1988). Problems, sources of assistance, and knowledge of services among elderly Vietnamese immigrants. *The Gerontologist*, 28, 448-452.

Espino, D.V., & Burge, S.K. (1989). Comparisons of aged Mexican-Americans and non-Hispanic white nursing home residents. *Family Medicine*, 21(3), 191-194.

Gelfand, D.E. (1994). *Aging and ethnicity: Knowledge and Services*. New York: Springer Publications.

Greene, V.L., & Monahan, D. (1984). Comparative utilization of community-based long-term care services by Hispanic and Anglo elderly in a case management system. *Journal of Gerontology*, 39(6), 730-735.

Guttman, D., & Cuellar, J. (1982). Barriers to equitable services. *Generations*, 6, 31-33.

Holmes, D.J., & Holmes, M. (1983). Differences among black, Hispanic, and white people in knowledge about long-term care services. *Health Care Financing Review*, 5, 51-67.

Koh, J.Y., & Bell, W.G. (1987). Korean elders in the United States: Intergenerational relations and living arrangements. *The Gerontologist*, 27, 66-71.

Komisar, H. (1997). *Medicare Chart Book*, The Henry Kaiser Family Foundation.

LaVeist, T.A. (1995). Data sources for aging research on racial and ethnic groups. *The Gerontologist*, 35(3), 328-339.

Lin-Fu, J.S. (1988). Population characteristics and health care needs of Asian Pacific Islanders. *Public Health Reports*, 103(1), 18-27.

Liu, W.T., & Yu, E.S.H. (1985). Asian/Pacific American elderly: Mortality differentials, health status and use of health services. *Journal of Applied Gerontology*, 4, 35-64.

Mauser, E., & Miller, N.A. (1994). A profile of home health users in 1992. *Health Care Financing Review*, 16(1), 17-33.

Moon, A., Lubben, J.E., & Villa, V. (1998). Awareness and utilization of community long-term care services by elderly Korean and non-Hispanic white Americans. *The Gerontologist*, 38(3), 309-316.

Morrison, B.J. (1982). Sociocultural dimensions: Nursing homes and the minority aged. *Journal of Gerontological Social Work*, 5(1/2), 127-145.

Shaughnessy, P.W., Crisler, K.S., & Schlenker, R.E. (1998). Outcome-based quality improvement in home health care: The OASIS indicators. *Quality Managed Health Care*, 7(1), pp. 58-67.

Shaughnessy, P.W., Schlenker, R.E., Hittle, D.F.: Volume 2: Technical Report. A study of home health care quality and cost under capitated and fee-for-service payment systems. Denver, CO. Center for Health Policy Research, February, 1994.

Spence, S.A., & Atherton, C.R. (1991). The black elderly and the social service delivery system: A study of factors influencing the use of community based services. *Journal of Gerontological Social Work*, 16, 19-35.

Stuttlesworth, G.E., Rubin, A., & Duffy, M. (1982). Families versus institutions: Incongruent role expectations in the nursing home. *The Gerontologist*, 22(2), 200-208.

Tanjasiri, S.P., Wallace, S.P., & Shibata, K. (1995). Picture imperfect: Hidden problems among Asian Pacific Islander elderly. *The Gerontologist*, 35(6), 753-760.

United States Census Bureau. (2001). American fact finder. Data set: 1990 Summary Tape File 1 (STF1). <http://factfinder.census.gov/servlet> (7 February, 2001).

United States Department of Health and Human Services. (2001). *Healthy People 2010*. Washington, DC.

United Stated General Accounting Office. (2000). *Medicare and Medicaid: Implementing state demonstrations for dual eligibles has proven challenging.* GAO/HEHS-00-94: Washington DC.

Wallace, S.P., Anderson, R., & Levy-Storms, L. (November, 1993). *Access to long-term care by minority elderly: Implications of health care reform.* Paper presented at the Gerontological Association of America Annual Meetings, New Orleans, LA.

Wallace, S.P., Levy-Storms, L., & Ferguson, L.R. (1995). Access to paid in-home assistance among disabled elderly people: Do Latinos differ from non-Latino Whites? *American Journal of Public Health*, 85, 970-975.

Weissert, W.G., & Cready, C.M. (1988). Determinations of hospital-to-nursing home delays: A pilot study. *Health Services Research*, 23(5), 619-647.

Wolinsky, F.D., Coe, R.M., Miller, D.K., Prendergast, J.M., Creel, M.J., & Chavez, M.N. (1983). Health services utilization among the noninstiutionalized elderly. *Journal of Health and Social Behavior*, 24, 325-337.

Yu, E.S.H., & Liu, W.T. (1994). Methodological issues. In N.W. Zane, D.T. Takeuchi, K.N. Young (Eds.), *Confronting critical health issues of Asian and Pacific Islander Americans*. Thousand Oaks, CA: Sage Publications.

Yu, E.S.H., Chang, C.F., & Liu, W.T. (1984). Asian white racial differentials: Are there excess deaths? In M.M. Heckler (Ed.), *Report of the secretary's task force on black and minority mental health: Crosscutting issues in minority health.* Washington, DC: Department of Health and Human Services.

# APPENDIX

OASIS measure of cognitive functioning:
M0560: Cognitive Functioning

0–Alert/oriented, able to focus and shift attention, comprehends and recalls task directions independently
1–Requires prompting (cueing, repetition, reminders) only under stressful or unfamiliar conditions
2–Requires assistance and some direction in specific situations (e.g., on all tasks involving shifting of attention) or consistently requires low stimulus environment due to distractibility
3–Requires considerable assistance in routine situations. Is not alert and oriented or is unable to shift attention and recall directions more than half the time
4–Totally dependent due to disturbances such as constant disorientation, coma, persistent vegetative state, or delirium

OASIS measure of confusion:
M0570: When Confused (Reported or Observed)

0–Never
1–In new or complex situations only
2–On awakening or at night only
3–During the day and evening, but not constantly
4–Constantly

OASIS measure of anxiety:
M0580: When Anxious (Reported or Observed)

0–None of the time
1–Less often than daily
2–Daily, but not constantly
3–All of the time

# Frail Older Persons in Nutrition Supplement Programs: A Comparative Study of African American, Asian American, and Hispanic Participants

Namkee G. Choi, PhD

**SUMMARY.** Home-delivered and congregate meals, funded by Title III of the Older Americans Act (OAA), target low-income, frail, isolated elders and provide them with a minimum of one third of the daily Recommended Dietary Allowances (RDAs). Despite the benefits of these programs, Asian American and Hispanic elders are underrepresented among the participants. In order to inform researchers and practitioners of more effective outreach strategies for these minority elders, this study compared sociodemographic and need characteristics of African American, Asian American, and Hispanic participants in elderly nutrition programs in a large metropolitan area in the Pacific Northwest. Findings show that being Asian American and lacking English language proficiency decreased the likelihood of participation in home-delivered meal programs, even when nutrition and health sta-

---

Namkee G. Choi is Professor, Graduate School of Social Work, 400 University Center Building, Portland State University, P.O. Box 751, Portland, OR 97207-0751 (E-mail: choin@rri.pdx.edu).

The author would like to thank Joan Smith and Jordi Santaularia of the Loaves and Fishes Centers, Inc. for providing necessary data for this research.

[Haworth co-indexing entry note]: "Frail Older Persons in Nutrition Supplement Programs: A Comparative Study of African American, Asian American, and Hispanic Participants." Choi, Namkee G. Co-published simultaneously in *Journal of Gerontological Social Work* (The Haworth Social Work Practice Press, an imprint of The Haworth Press, Inc.) Vol. 36, No. 1/2, 2001, pp. 187-207; and: *Social Work Practice with the Asian American Elderly* (ed: Namkee G. Choi) The Haworth Social Work Practice Press, an imprint of The Haworth Press, Inc., 2001, pp. 187-207. Single or multiple copies of this article are available for a fee from The Haworth Document Delivery Service [1-800-HAWORTH, 9:00 a.m. - 5:00 p.m. (EST). E-mail address: getinfo@haworthpressinc.com].

tuses were controlled for. Culturally acceptable outreach strategies are discussed. 

**KEYWORDS.** Elderly nutrition programs, home-delivered meals, congregate dining, Asian Americans, African Americans, Hispanics

Home-delivered meals and congregate dining programs are essential, low-cost, long-term care services enabling frail elders to continue living independently in the community and to age in place. By providing a minimum of one third of the daily Recommended Dietary Allowances (RDAs) with a hot noonday meal, these programs help low-income, frail, and often isolated elders ameliorate their nutritional problems and contribute to preventing further deterioration in their physical and functional health. The periodic nutrition screening, assessment, education, and counseling for the participants in the meal programs, required by Title III-C1, Title III-C2, and Title VI of the Older Americans Act (OAA), the major federal funding source for the programs, also help them become aware of possible signs of nutritional problems and needs as they may relate to health concerns such as hypertension and diabetes. In addition, elderly participants' regular contact with volunteers who deliver daily meal(s), in the case of home-delivered meal programs, and the socialization with other older persons and staff in the congregate dining centers, often serve as their only conduits for human contact. Volunteers and congregate dining program staff carry out the roles of sentinel and gatekeeper, watching out for possible signs of trouble and the need for health and social services among the participants and reporting and/or linking them to pertinent health/social service agencies and program staff. The combined nutrition, health, and social support benefits of the elderly nutrition programs may help participating frail elders delay or avoid costly institutionalization, both contributing to their quality of life and saving taxpayers' money.

Despite these potential benefits, many eligible frail older persons are not served by the programs (Mui, Choi, & Monk, 1998; Ponza, Ohls, & Millen, 1996). Even though 123 million meals were served to 2.4 million people at congregate sites and more than 119 million meals were delivered to 989,000 home-bound elders in 1995 alone (Administration on Aging [AoA], 2000), these numbers represented only a portion of those who needed the services. The national evaluation study of the elderly nutrition programs, 1993-1995, shows that non-Hispanic African Americans and Hispanics each constituted 12% of congregate meal program participants and 18% and 5%, respectively, of home-delivered meal program participants under Title III (Ponza et al., 1996). Considering that both types of meal programs emphasize targeting low-income, frail, isolated elders, however, more minority elders need to be served, and continued outreach to minority elders is required. Because of their lack of sufficient financial resources and lack of transportation needed for food shopping, low-income elders and elders who live alone are at greater risk than other elders of having nutritional deficiencies (Horwath, 1991; Lee & Frongillo, 2001; Posner, Jette, Smith, & Miller, 1993). Since minority elders are two to three times more likely to be poor than white elders, they face greater risk of nutritional problems. A recent study of population-based estimates of eligibility for and actual participation in home-delivered meal programs in New York state found that Hispanics and "other" races were underrepresented among actual participants despite the finding that they faced greater nutritional risk than did whites, African Americans, and "unknown" races (Melnik, Blizniak, Lannon, Porter, & Wales, 1999).

The purposes of this study were (1) to examine sociodemographic, nutrition, and health status characteristics of African American, Asian American, and Hispanic participants in home-delivered and congregate meal programs in a large metropolitan area in the Pacific Northwest; and (2) to compare three types of participants–those who had received home-delivered meals but recently terminated; those who were currently receiving home-delivered meals; and those who were currently participating in congregate meals–within each racial/ethnic group as well as across the groups, in order especially to examine whether the relatively lower proportion of Asian Americans and Hispanics receiving home-delivered meals (as opposed to congregate meals) may be explained by cultural differences and language barriers rather than health-related factors. White persons aged 50 and older who were currently receiving home-delivered meals were also included as a reference group. Although an attempt was also made to examine reasons for termination by those who no longer participated in the home-delivered meal programs, a large amount of missing information meant that only a tentative finding could be reached about reasons for termination.

The geographic area under study is predominantly white in its racial composition. According to the 2000 Census, the proportions of African Americans, Asian Americans, and Hispanics among those 18 years or older in the area were almost identical, with 5.7% African Americans, 5.7% Hispanics, and 6.0% Asian Americans (U.S. Bureau of the Census, 2001). The African American population in the area under study has been stable over the years. However, in recent years, the area has experienced a large influx of Asian Americans and Hispanics, and the large increase in Asian American and Hispanic populations in the past decade may have increased the proportions of their elderly members relative to that of African American elders. In response to these growing Asian American and Hispanic communities, the staff members of a large congregate and home-delivered meal program in the area, in collaboration with many other health and social service programs for elders, have made considerable outreach efforts to serve elders in these ethnic communities. However, the results of the outreach efforts have not yet been too successful. The numbers of Asian American and Hispanic participants are significantly smaller than the number of African American participants.

Culturally sensitive outreach and service delivery efforts are especially needed for Asian American and Hispanic immigrant elders, who tend to stay within the boundaries of their ethnic enclaves due to language and other cultural barriers. The lack of links to formal support services for frail elders often results in overload of their informal support systems, and yet the informal support systems alone tend to be insufficient to meet the needs of these elders adequately.

Despite the significance of elderly nutrition programs, the volume of research done on them is scant compared to that done on other home- and community-based long-term care programs. Little research has been done on racial/ethnic minority elderly meal program participants, especially those other than African Americans. Because the region's growing Asian American and Hispanic populations mirror those throughout the country, the findings of this study on these two racial/ethnic groups have potential for application to elderly nutrition programs in other cities and regions. The comparison between racial/ethnic minority and white participants in the meal programs will also be useful in identifying similar and dissimilar characteristics and risk indicators, and thus, forming more effective, culturally appropriate outreach efforts and service delivery plans for eligible, nonparticipating racial/ethnic minority elders.

## UNDERUTILIZATION OF ELDERLY NUTRITION PROGRAMS

One reason elders underutilize meal programs stems from the fact that many have waiting lists. According to Ponza et al.'s (1996) national evaluation study of the elderly nutrition programs, 1993-1995, this was true of as many as 41% of the home-delivered meal programs, with a mean of 85 and a median of 35 elders on the lists. Ponza et al.'s study showed that the mean duration of time an elder waited on the delivery roster ranged from two to three months, and the median length was one month. Federal funding for services through Title III has always remained a minuscule proportion of the total federal outlays for old age benefits. The 2001 appropriation levels for Title III-C1 and Title III-C2 under the OAA Amendments of 2000 are merely $378 million and $152 million (AoA, 2001). Almost all local aging networks providing elderly nutrition programs supplement the federal funding with income from private fund raising and/or commercial marketing and sales ventures. Even with this additional income, absorption of all those on the waiting lists may not be fiscally possible for many meal programs.

In addition to the problem of waiting lists, a study by Burt (1993) found that a majority of eligible elders did not participate because they did not believe they needed the meals, and only a small proportion cited food preferences, discomfort with the application, a sense of stigma, and lack of program awareness as reasons for their nonparticipation.

Lack of awareness of the need for meal services among eligible nonparticipants is likely to stem from their lack of awareness of the significance of the link between nutritional status and health status. Maintaining optimal nutritional status is of vital significance to maintaining good health. Research has also proven that functional deficits in physiological systems, possibly an inevitable process of aging, can in fact be modified by diet (Roe, 1992). In reality, however, Burt (1993) estimated that 8% to 16% of American elders, or 2.5 million to 4.9 million, suffer food insecurity at least some of the time during any six-month period, with economics, race/ethnicity, and health as important underlying causes. (Food insecurity exists whenever "the availability of nutritionally adequate, safe foods or the ability to acquire personally acceptable foods in socially acceptable ways is limited or uncertain" [AoA, 1994; Campbell, 1991]).

Although Burt's study found that a small proportion of eligible nonparticipants in general cited food preferences, discomfort with the application, a sense of stigma, and lack of program awareness as reasons for their nonparticipation, the relative significance of these factors as inhibitors to participation is likely to be much higher among racial/ethnic minority elders than among white elders. Especially among Hispanic and Asian American elders, a large proportion of whom are immigrants, unique dietary patterns and traditional food beliefs, established long ago, will not change with old age and frailty (see Lynn, Kang, & Ludman, 1999; Yan, 1985). Because of language barriers, these elders are also likely to have limited access to necessary information on the meal programs and to feel uncomfortable about the application process. Unless the meal program is offered at an ethnic senior center or congregate dining site with ethnic staff, ethnic food, and other elders from the same ethnic group, these minority elders are likely to be reluctant to enroll in the program.

While many eligible elders do not participate because they never enrolled in the programs in the first place, many also terminate their participation and thus increase their risk of food insecurity and deterioration in health. Choi (1999) found that African American recipients of home-delivered meals in a New York county were more than twice as likely as white recipients to discontinue their participation for reasons of food preferences, dissatisfaction with meals, or poor appetite. Given that food habits among elders represent one of the most culturally embedded and enduring patterns (Read & Schlenker, 1993), frail racial/ethnic minority elders may find the foods offered by these programs not so palatable and become reluctant to enroll or more likely than white elders to discontinue following their initial enrollment.

## *CONCEPTUAL FRAMEWORK AND RESEARCH QUESTIONS*

The conceptual framework for this study is drawn from Andersen and Newman's health services utilization model (Andersen, 1995; Andersen & Newman, 1973) and a service model that Wallace (1990) proposed to facilitate organization of community-based long-term care. The Andersen-Newman model posits that the utilization of health-related services by individuals is governed by the interaction of predisposing, enabling, and need factors. Predisposing factors refer to an individual's demographic background (age, gender, and marital status) and social/structural and cultural backgrounds (education, occupation, race/ethnicity, social support networks, and social interactions) that may or may not predispose him/her to utilize the services to a greater extent than others. These factors are believed to reflect individuals' relative life-cycle position and culturally determined health beliefs–attitudes, values, and knowledge about health and health services–that have been established prior to their illness episodes. In addition, such psychological characteristics as cognitive impairment and autonomy are included as predisposing factors (Andersen, 1995).

Enabling factors refer to both community resources and personal means to access and obtain the services: availability of health personnel and facilities in areas where people live and work; family income; health insurance; a regular source of care; and travel and waiting times. The need factors refer to the most immediate reason the services are needed: health problems–both objective conditions and people's subjective view of their own general health and functional state. Because each person experiences symptoms of illness and pain differently and makes judgments whether or not to seek professional help based on that unique experience, the perceived need factor as well as the objective health conditions have been included as possible determinants of health service use (Andersen, 1995).

The Andersen-Newman model has been widely adopted in studies of both health and social service use among elders. Its comprehensive array of predictor variables provides a conceptual framework applicable to any type of service utilization. The model is suitable for the present study, given that the elderly nutrition programs have both health and social service components and that elders' participation or nonparticipation in the programs is likely to be influenced by their demographic characteristics, beliefs about health and nutrition, availability of social support systems that can or cannot prepare meals for elders and/or advocate for and link them to the meal programs, availability of and accessibility to meal programs, and elders' physical and functional health status.

As shown, the Andersen-Newman model includes race/ethnicity and cultural background as predisposing variables for health service utilization. As discussed in the preceding section, the influence of these variables cannot be overemphasized as determinants of participation or nonparticipation in meal programs. That is, because individuals' food habits and dietary patterns cannot be changed overnight, the acceptability of the kind of meals offered is likely to play a bigger role than the acceptability factors in the case of heath care service utilization. Wallace (1990) pointed out that even when technically adequate, certain services may not be acceptable to some elders, and therefore not be used. Hispanic and Asian American race/ethnicity, especially for recent immigrants, is likely to pose a barrier to utilizing the meal programs, unless ethnic meals are offered.

These were the main research questions in this study: (1) whether or not the racial/ethnic minority participants–African Americans, Asian Americans, and Hispanics–were significantly different from one another and from white participants with respect to their predisposing/demographic, enabling, and need characteristics; and (2) especially given that the proportion of home-delivered meal participants among Asian Americans and Hispanics was much lower than that among African Americans, whether or not cultural difference and language barriers may be factors inhibiting the former groups from utilizing home-delivered meals.

## *METHOD*

### *Sample and Source of Data*

The study subjects consisted of 545 African Americans, 173 Asian Americans, and 77 Hispanic Americans who had terminated home-delivered meal services in the preceding two years, current (as of December 2000) home-delivered meal participants, and current congregate meal participants, all aged 50 and older at the time of their enrollment/first assessment, in a large home-delivered and congregate meal program in a Pacific Northwestern metropolitan area. White persons aged 50 and older who were currently participating in home-delivered meal programs (n = 1,892) are also included as a reference group. (The meal program, through its central kitchen and 17 neighborhood centers, serve an average of 3,500 meals daily to frail elders aged 60 and older and to some disabled persons under age 60. Due to their small number n (n = 44), Native American participants were excluded from the analysis.)

As shown in Table 1, 220 African Americans, 100 Asian Americans, and 30 Hispanics were participating in the meal programs as of December 2000, and 325 African Americans, 73 Asian Americans, and 47 Hispanics had terminated their participation within the preceding two years. A relatively large proportion of current Asian American and Hispanic participants, 81% and 30%, respectively, as opposed to 13.2% of African American participants, were being served at congregate dining centers, which cater to those who are mobile and not home bound. Most Asian American participants in congregate meal programs were served at three dining centers located in ethnic neighborhoods, where both foods delivered from the meal program's central kitchen and ethnic meals prepared on site were provided.

Data used in this study were extracted from the meal program's computerized client data-management system. An intake assessment of nutritional and health statuses is done for every participant in the home-delivered meal program at the time of his/her enrollment, and the

TABLE 1. Type of Meal Programs Partcipating by Race/Ethnicity (%)

| (n) | White (1,892) | African American (545) | Asian American (173) | Hispanic (77) |
|---|---|---|---|---|
| Home-delivered (closed) | na | 59.6 | 42.2 | 61.0 |
| Home-delivered (open) | 100 | 35.0 | 11.0 | 27.3 |
| Congregate (open) | na | 5.4 | 46.8 | 11.7 |

Note: For whites, only those currently participating in home-delivered meal programs are included in the study.

information is constantly updated as dieticians conduct periodic reassessments. As for participants in congregate meal programs, however, an assessment is conducted only for those who come to the dining centers on a consistent basis–six months or longer. Those elders who utilized the services only sporadically and thus did not have their assessment done were excluded from the study because of the lack of data on their nutritional and health statuses.

### *Variables and Method of Analysis*

For this study, clients' characteristics at the time of their enrollment/first assessment were analyzed. For predisposing/socio demographic factors, the client's age, gender, race/ethnicity, and marital status were examined. Race/ethnicity was used as a proxy for cultural and health beliefs and for food preferences. Marital status may also be considered an enabling factor, considering that a spouse can provide emotional as well as instrumental support, including grocery shopping and meal preparation. For other enabling factors, family income status (income below the poverty line or above the poverty line); home ownership (owner occupant or renter/other); type of housing (residential home, apartment, or other–mobile home, transitional housing, or group facility); U.S. citizenship (citizen or noncitizen); and primary language spoken (English, Spanish, Chinese, Korean, etc.). An elder's ability to speak English is considered a significant factor enabling him/her to access information and seek linkage to necessary services.

For need factors, nutrition screening score (a maximum possible score of 21, from a 10-item questionnaire about food insecurity, with higher scores indicating higher nutritional risk); number of instrumental activities of daily living (IADLs) with difficulty; number of activities of daily living (ADLs) with difficulty; body mass index (BMI); and type of diet the elder was receiving (regular, soft, low sodium, diabetic, and low cholesterol). The difficulty with IADLs and ADLs, consisting of seven items each, was measured on a four-point scale, with scores ranging from 0 (no difficulty) to 3 (cannot do) for each item. The maximum possible score was 21 for IADLs and 21 for ADLs. In addition, the client data system contained a caseworker's detailed narratives about the elder's health conditions–type and status of chronic illnesses, falls, recent hospitalizations, mental health status, and so forth. Because of difficulty quantifying the narrative statements, excerpts from this qualitative portion of data are presented in the text as case examples.

For analysis of data, bivariate tables comparing possible racial/ethnic differences in these variables were constructed. Then, a logistic regression analysis of determinants of participation in home-delivered meals versus participation in congregate meals was done among racial/ethnic minorities alone, with African Americans comprising the reference group.

### *Limitations of the Data Set*

Given that this is a case-controlled study, in which only past or current participants were included, the implications of the study's findings have only limited generalizability. In the absence of an extant knowledge base on Asian Americans participating in elderly nutrition programs, however, this study offers valuable information.

## *FINDINGS*

### *Racial/Ethnic Differences in All Participants' Characteristics*

As shown in Table 2, whites were the oldest of all, followed by Asian Americans and African Americans, and then by Hispanics ($p < .05$). Although it appears that Asian Americans had a higher proportion of men than the other racial/ethnic groups, the differences were not statistically significant when only minority groups were compared. Asian Americans had the largest proportion of the married. In terms of economic status, nearly half of Asian Americans and Hispanics, as compared to a little more than a third of African Americans, had income below the poverty line, although the difference was not statistically significant. A statistically significant indicator of the lower income status of Hispanics than that of African Americans and Asian Americans was the former

TABLE 2. Sociodemographic Characteristics by Race/Ethnicity: Both Past and Current Participants

| | White | African American | Asian American | Hispanic |
|---|---|---|---|---|
| (n) | (1,892) | (545) | (173) | (77) |
| Age (yr) | | | | |
| Mean (SD) | 78.1 (9.5)[a] | 75.6 (9.7)[b] | 76.6 (8.4)[b] | 72.9 (10.2)[c] |
| Sex (%) | | | | |
| Men | 33.0 | 40.9 | 48.2 | 41.6 |
| Women | 67.0 | 59.1 | 51.8 | 58.4 |
| Marital status (%)* | | | | |
| Married | 25.9 | 22.7 | 47.3 | 21.9 |
| Widowed | 51.4 | 47.8 | 41.8 | 41.1 |
| Divorced/separated | 12.3 | 14.7 | 3.0 | 15.0 |
| Never married | 10.0 | 9.4 | 7.3 | 17.8 |
| Domestic partnered | 0.3 | 0.8 | 0 | 2.7 |
| Unknown | 0.1 | 4.6 | 0.6 | 1.4 |
| Income below poverty line (%) | 31.3 | 37.6 | 43.4 | 42.7 |
| Owner occupant (%)* | 55.7 | 30.8 | 29.2 | 20.9 |
| Type of housing (%)* | | | | |
| Residential home | 56.6 | 59.9 | 48.1 | 43.2 |
| Apartment | 37.8 | 37.3 | 48.1 | 54.5 |
| Other | 5.6 | 2.9 | 3.8 | 2.3 |
| Non-U.S. citizen (%)* | 0.3 | 0.2 | 14.5 | 9.1 |
| Primary language spoken (%)* | | | | |
| English | 99.1 | 99.8 | 38.2 | 57.9 |
| Spanish | | | | 42.1 |
| Chinese | | | 8.9 | |
| Korean | | | 17.6 | |
| Vietnamese | | | 22.9 | |
| Filipino | | | 10.0 | |
| Japanese | | | 1.2 | |
| Laotian | | | 1.2 | |
| Other | 0.9 | 0.2 | | |

[a,b,c]: Significantly different racial/ethnic groups based on the Scheffe test at $p < .05$.
* Significant racial difference among minority groups only at $p < .01$.

groups' comparatively lower proportions of owner occupants. As expected, 14.5% of Asian Americans and 9.1% of Hispanics reported that they were not U.S. citizens. Only 38.2% of Asian Americans and 57.9% of Hispanics spoke English. Within non-English-speaking Asian Americans, Vietnamese was the most popular language, followed by Korean, Filipino, and Chinese.

With respect to nutrition and health status (see Table 3), Asian Americans appear to have faced the lowest nutritional risk and had significantly fewer problems with IADLs and ADLs than the other groups. The mean BMI also shows that Asian Americans may be the fittest of all; however, the BMI distribution shows that as many as 16.3% of Asian American participants were underweight at the time of their enrollment, although the proportion of the obese (7%) was the lowest of all racial/ethnic groups. Nearly one-fourth of whites and more than one-third of African Americans and Hispanics were obese. The types of diet the participants were receiving also indicate their health status and special diet needs. A higher proportion of Asian Americans than the other groups received regular meals. At least one third of African American and Hispanic participants were getting diabetic meals.

### *Racial/Ethnic Differences Among Home-Delivered Meal Participants and Congregate Meal Participants*

Data in Table 4 show characteristics of past and current home-delivered meal participants and congregate meal participants separately. To reiterate, for whites, only current home-delivered meal participants were included in the study. Thus, the comparison among past home-delivered meal participants and congregate meal participants was done only among racial/ethnic minority groups. The data show differences, or lack thereof, between racial/ethnic groups as well as within each racial group by type of meals.

Among past home-delivered meal participants (referred to heretofore as closed cases), Asian Americans were significantly older than Hispanics. However, no significant age difference by race/ethnicity was found among current home-delivered meal and congregate meal participants. The comparison within each racial/ethnic group of the closed cases, current home-delivered meal participants, and congregate meal participants shows no significant age difference among them.

Among closed cases, the proportions of women among Asian Americans and Hispanics were significantly lower than that among African Americans. No significant gender difference by race/ethnicity was

TABLE 3. Nutrition and Health Status at Intake by Race/Ethnicity: Both Past and Current Participants

| | White | African American | Asian American | Hispanic |
|---|---|---|---|---|
| (n) | (1,892) | (543) | (173) | (77) |
| Nutrition screening | | | | |
| Score | | | | |
| Mean (*SD*) | 7.5 (3.8)[a] | 8.5 (4.1)[a] | 5.7 (4.1)[b] | 7.9 (4.1)[a] |
| No. IADLs with difficulty | | | | |
| Mean (*SD*) | 6.1 (4.9)[a] | 4.6 (5.5)[a] | 2.4 (4.8)[b] | 6.0 (6.3)[a] |
| No. ADLs with difficulty | | | | |
| Mean (*SD*) | 2.0 (2.8)[a] | 1.9 (3.6)[b] | 0.8 (2.0)[c] | 1.9 (3.8)[b] |
| Body Mass Index (BMI) | | | | |
| Mean (*SD*) | 25.9 (6.6)[a] | 27.8 (8.4)[b] | 22.4 (4.2)[c] | 28.9 (7.0)[b] |
| Underweight (%)* | 5.5 | 5.1 | 16.3 | 2.4 |
| Obese (%)* | 23.9 | 36.4 | 7.0 | 38.1 |
| Type of diet (%)* | | | | |
| Regular | 59.9 | 48.7 | 68.3 | 57.9 |
| Soft | 5.2 | 1.8 | 1.2 | 0 |
| Low sodium | 12.4 | 14.2 | 7.3 | 9.2 |
| Diabetic | 18.0 | 33.3 | 15.2 | 31.6 |
| Low cholesterol | 4.4 | 2.0 | 7.9 | 1.3 |

[a,b,c:] Significantly different racial/ethnic groups based on the Scheffe test at $p < .05$.
* Significant racial difference among minority groups only at $p < .01$.

Note: Statistics on BMI were based on only some of the participants: 1,485 whites; 390 African Americans; 44 Asian Americans; and 43 Hispanics.

found among open cases. Poverty rates among minority groups were not significantly different for either closed or open cases, although a lower proportion of whites than the others appeared to be poor. For Asian Americans, a significantly lower proportion of congregate meal participants than home-delivered meal participants were able to speak English.

With respect to nutrition screening score, no significant racial/ethnic difference was found among home-delivered meal participants, but Hispanic congregate meal participants had a lower score than their African American counterparts. On the other hand, Hispanic current home-delivered meal participants had a higher number of IADLs with difficulty than the other groups. The comparison within African Ameri-

TABLE 4. Comparison Between Home-Delivered and Congregate Meal Participants

| | White | African American | Asian American | Hispanic |
|---|---|---|---|---|
| Age (yr) | | | | |
| Home-delivered (closed) | na | 75.9 (9.9) | 78.0 (9.2)a | 72.7 (9.1)b |
| Home-delivered (open) | 78.1 (9.5) | 75.8 (8.9) | 77.0 (6.7) | 74.2 (12.1) |
| Congregate (open) | na | 72.2 (11.6) | 75.2 (7.7) | 71.1 (11.4) |
| Female (%) | | | | |
| Home-delivered (closed)* | na | 55.7 | 46.4 | 42.6 |
| Home-delivered (open) | 67.0 | 68.6 | 63.2 | 85.7 |
| Congregate (open) | na | 34.5 | 53.8 | 77.8 |
| Married (%) | | | | |
| Home-delivered (closed)* | na | 21.5 | 39.7 | 24.4 |
| Home-delivered (open) | 25.4 | 25.1 | 31.6 | 9.5 |
| Congregate (open)* | na | 4.0 | 58.1 | 33.3 |
| Income below poverty line (%) | | | | |
| Home-delivered (closed) | na | 38.5 | 44.9 | 37.8 |
| Home-delivered (open) | 31.3 | 36.0 | 44.4 | 52.4 |
| Congregate (open) | na | 37.9 | 41.8 | 44.4 |
| Speaking English (%) | | | | |
| Home-delivered (closed)* | na | 100 | 50.0 | 65.2 |
| Home-delivered (open)* | 99.1 | 99.5 | 42.1 | 47.6 |
| Congregate (open)* | na | 100 | 26.6 | 44.4 |
| Nutrition screening score | | | | |
| Home-delivered (closed) | na | 8.5 (4.3) | 7.4 (3.7) | 9.0 (3.8) |
| Home-delivered (open) | 7.5 (3.8) | 8.5 (3.8) | 7.1 (2.5) | 7.9 (3.5) |
| Congregate (open) | na | 7.6 (4.1)[a] | 3.8 (3.9) | 2.3 (2.5)[b] |
| No. IADLs with difficulty | | | | |
| Home-delivered (closed) | na | 3.5 (4.9) | 3.9 (5.3) | 4.7 (5.6) |
| Home-delivered (open) | 6.1 (4.9)[a] | 7.2 (5.8) | 5.6 (7.1)[a] | 11.3 (5.2)[b] |
| Congregate (open) | na | 0.3 (1.0) | 0.3 (1.7) | 0 |
| No. ADLs with difficulty | | | | |
| Home-delivered (closed) | na | 1.3 (2.5) | 1.0 (2.2) | 1.3 (2.8) |
| Home-delivered (open) | 2.0 (2.8) | 3.2 (4.8) | 1.9 (3.9) | 3.9 (5.6) |
| Congregate (open) | na | 0.3 (0.8) | 0.3 (0.5) | 0.3 (0.5) |
| Underweight (%) | | | | |
| Home-delivered (closed) | na | 6.7 | 15.4 | 3.7 |
| Congregate (open) | na | 0 | 0 | 0 |
| Home-delivered (open) | 5.5 | 3.1 | 20.0 | 0 |
| Obese (%) | | | | |
| Home-delivered (closed) | na | 31.8 | 3.8 | 40.7 |
| Home-delivered (open) | 23.9 | 43.2 | 13.3 | 35.7 |
| Congregate (open) | na | 20.0 | 0 | 0 |
| Receiving regular meal (%) | | | | |
| Home-delivered (closed)* | na | 49.7 | 65.7 | 56.5 |
| Home-delivered (open)* | 59.9 | 43.5 | 31.6 | 52.4 |
| Congregate (open) | na | 72.4 | 79.5 | 77.8 |
| Receiving diabetic meals (%) | | | | |
| Home-delivered (closed)* | na | 31.2 | 17.9 | 28.3 |
| Home-delivered (open)* | 18.0 | 39.8 | 42.1 | 42.9 |
| Congregate* | na | 13.8 | 6.4 | 22.2 |

| | White | African American | Asian American | Hispanic |
|---|---|---|---|---|
| Receiving low cholesterol diet (%) | | | | |
| Home-delivered (closed) | na | 2.5 | 9.0 | 0 |
| Home-delivered (open) | 4.4 | 1.6 | 15.8 | 4.8 |
| Congregate (open) | na | 0 | 5.1 | 0 |

na: Not available.
a,b,c: Significantly different racial/ethnic groups based on the Scheffe test at $p < .05$.
* Significant racial difference at $p < .01$.

Note: Statistics on BMI were based on part of the participants only: 1,485 whites; 390 African Americans; 44 Asian Americans; and 43 Hispanics; chi-square tests were not performed because of small sample sizes in some categories.

cans of the closed cases, current home-delivered meal participants, and congregate meal participants showed no significant difference in nutritional risk. However, Asian American and Hispanic congregate meal participants faced significantly lower nutritional risk than their home-delivered meal counterparts. As expected, for all races, current participants in home-delivered meal programs had the most problems and congregate meal participants had the fewest, with IADLs and ADLs.

Although no test for statistical significance was done on BMI because of many missing values, the data show that as many as 20% of Asian American current home-delivered meal participants for whom information was available were underweight. On the other extreme, a large proportion of African Americans and Hispanics appeared to be obese. With respect to the type of diet, the proportion of Asian Americans who received diabetic meals was significantly lower than that of the other racial/ethnic groups among closed cases, but it was not different from that of African Americans and Hispanics and was significantly higher than that of whites among current participants in home-delivered meals. The proportion of Asian Americans who received a low-cholesterol diet appears to be higher than that of any other racial/ethnic groups. Regardless of race/ethnicity, the type of diet also indicates possibly the worst health conditions of the current home-delivered meal participants of all past and current participants in meal programs.

### *Summary of Bivariate Findings and Case Examples*

The bivariate analyses showed that, as expected, current participants in home-delivered meal programs faced significantly higher nutritional and functional health risks than did past participants in home-delivered meal programs and current congregate meal participants, regardless of race/ethnicity. Among current participants in home-delivered meal programs, all minorities and whites were shown to have similarly bad nutritional and functional health statuses, although Hispanics appear to be a little worse off than the others in functional health status and Asian Americans, based on their higher need for special-diet meals, may have worse physical health conditions. The following excerpts from caseworkers' case notes are presented here as examples of the health and other social service needs of current home-delivered meal participants.

Case 1: 69-year-old African American male: Early-stage dementia; dizziness of undetermined origin; uses two canes for balance; fell down steps recently; CAT scan and spinal scan 9/99; significant hearing loss; depression due to multiple health problems; minor surgery 2 weeks ago.

Case 2: 68-year-old African American female: Obesity; osteoarthritis; very limited mobility: uses wheelchair or walker; heart murmur; had pneumonia 3 weeks ago; cellulitis in left leg; family helping but needing respite.

Case 3: 72-year-old Asian American male: Recent release from hospital with renal failure; needs to keep diabetes under control, and wife is unable to understand how to prepare diabetic meals. Son stated dad getting weak from kidney disease and diabetes, losing weight, 5 pounds in a week. Very limited understanding of English.

Case 4: 80-year-old Asian American female: Arthritis in back and hips. No appetite and difficulty swallowing. Very frail and speaks very little English. Daughter lives upstairs from her but works during the day, so she is alone during the day, not eating right.

Case 5: 70-year-old Hispanic male: Stroke; heart attack; says gets very dizzy and falls a lot; insulin-dependent diabetic; hearing loss–having trouble adjusting to hearing aid; legs tremble when sitting–unsure if this is a nervous condition. Speaks no English.

Case 6: 87-year-old Hispanic female: Poststroke; has pacemaker; depression over loss of daughter; does not get much support from grandson; lost 53 pounds in the last month for not eating. Speaks no English.

### *Determinants of Participation in Home-Delivered versus Congregate Meals*

As shown in Table 5, selected predisposing, enabling, and need factors were entered in a logistic regression model to determine predictors of participation (either currently or in the past) in home-delivered versus congregate meal programs among racial/ethnic minorities. Of the predisposing factors, race/ethnicity alone turned out to be significant.

TABLE 5. Determinants of Participation in Home-Delivered versus Congregate Meal Programs: Logistic Regression Coefficients

| Variable | **B (*SE*)** | **Odds Ratio** |
|---|---|---|
| Age | .022 (.015) | |
| Female | .008 (.274) | |
| (Male) | | |
| Marital status | | |
| Widowed | .164 (.356) | |
| All others | −.596 (.365) | |
| (Married) | | |
| Race/ethnicity | | |
| Asian American | −1.919 (.379)** | .147 |
| Hispanic | −.394 (.485) | |
| (African American) | | |
| Income below poverty line | .019 (.265) | |
| (Income above poverty line) | | |
| Renter | −2.448 (1.048)* | .086 |
| (Owner occupants) | | |
| Not speaking English | −.696 (.359)* | .499 |
| (Speaking English) | | |
| Nutrition screening score | .162 (.036)** | 1.176 |
| No. IADLs with difficulty | .290 (.065)** | 1.337 |
| −2 LL chi-square (df) | 396.25 (11) | |

**p < .01; *p < .05
Note: n = 769 (161 Asian Americans; 75 Hispanics; and 533 African Americans); due to missing values, 26 cases were excluded from the logistic regression analysis.

Being an Asian American, as opposed to being an African American, decreased the likelihood of participating in home-delivered meal programs by 85%. Of enabling factors, income status was not found to be significant, but being a renter decreased the likelihood of the individual's receiving home-delivered meals by 91% and not speaking English decreased the likelihood by 50%. It is possible that renters were more likely to live in senior housing or apartment complexes and thus were closer to senior centers/congregate dining centers, but Hispanics (and Asians) had lower rates of owner occupancy than African Americans. Both need factors–nutrition risk score and number of IADLs with difficulty–increased the likelihood of an individual's receiving home-delivered meals as opposed to participating in congregate meal programs. An increment of one point in the nutrition screening score increased the likelihood by 18%, and an increment of one point in the number of IADLs with difficulty increased the likelihood by 34%.

### *Reasons for Termination*

Elders are likely to terminate their meal services for both improved and deteriorating health. Improved health is likely to make them ineligible for the service, while deteriorating health is likely to necessitate a move to a care facility or arrangement of home care, and even result in death. In addition, elders may terminate the service because they no longer want the meals delivered due to dislike of the foods or dissatisfaction with the other components of the service. Information on reasons for termination among the closed cases in this study was obtained from only a small proportion of them. For African Americans, 6.8% of the closed cases were due to the participants' death, but death-related information was not available for the other groups. (The death rate among African Americans is also speculated to be much higher than 6.8% if information on all terminated cases were available.) Among Asian Americans and Hispanics, only three and one persons, respectively, were recorded to have declined the service, but it is speculated that many more cases might have been terminated because elders chose to decline the service.

## *DISCUSSION AND IMPLICATIONS*

The findings of this study relating to Asian American and Hispanic meal participants are especially informative because little research has been done on these two groups. Given their different food habits and preferences and the lack of English language proficiency among many recent immigrant elders, it is not surprising to find that far fewer Asian Americans and Hispanics than African Americans participated in elderly nutrition programs, especially in home-delivered meal programs. Economic status variables showed that Hispanic participants were more likely to be poor than African Americans and that Asian American participants were as poor as African Americans. Not surprisingly, however, participants from all three of these racial/ethnic minority groups had lower economic status than white participants.

In terms of nutrition and functional health status, Asian Americans as a whole appeared to be better off than any other racial/ethnic group, apparently because this group included the largest proportion of congregate meal participants, who were doing much better than home-delivered meal participants. When analyses were done separately for home-delivered meal participants and for congregate meal participants, Asian Americans were not better or worse off than whites or African Americans, although Asian Americans currently receiving home-delivered meals still appeared to have a better functional health status than their Hispanic counterparts. But given that a significantly higher proportion of Asian American home-delivered meal participants than those in any other racial/ethnic group were getting special diet foods, including diabetic and low-cholesterol meals, Asian Americans appeared to have more problems relating to physical illnesses/conditions. This finding points to the possibility that Asian American and Hispanic elders tend to wait too long before they enroll in the program and that they use the program as a last resort rather than as a preventive service.

The multivariate findings point to the significance of Asian race/ethnicity and lack of English proficiency (which is also the case for many Hispanic elders) as factors associated with the lower likelihood of using home-delivered meal services as opposed to congregate meal services, even when nutritional and health risk factors were controlled for. For lack of insufficient data on reasons for termination, a definitive statement cannot be made. However, these barriers to utilizing home-delivered meal services could also have contributed to high rates of voluntary termination or declining of services among Asian Americans and Hispanics.

Based on these findings, it can be safely speculated that there must be more Asian American and Hispanic frail elders who need daily nutritious meals. That is, even if the current participants were to represent the worst off of all in each racial/ethnic group, nonparticipants who are a little better off than the current participants are quite likely to be eligible for and benefit from the meal programs. Given their equally low income status and high initial nutritional risk score, many Asian American and Hispanic past participants could have benefited if they had continued in the program, especially if they declined the services voluntarily.

There are several implications of the findings of the study for outreach efforts and service delivery in Asian American and Hispanic communities: First, staff members of elderly nutrition programs must design an outreach strategy focusing on the preventive nature of the program and enrolling elders before their nutritional risk becomes too high. Considering limited English proficiency among immigrant elders, bilingual and bicultural outreach workers need to be hired to go out into the ethnic communities to inform elders and their families about the availability and benefits of the meal programs. Second, the provision of ethnic menus and/or more diverse choices in menus that would be more acceptable to these elders' palates and traditional food beliefs must be considered to entice more eligible nonparticipants who are at high nutritional risk and to prevent premature termination among participants. Third, considering their low income status and high nutritional risk, these minority elders are more likely to need frequent nutrition assessment and counseling and a second meal to supplement their noonday meal. Box dinners and/or packaged food that can be easily warmed up in a microwave oven must be provided. Fourth, congregate dining programs for ethnic minority elders need to be expanded and used as a stepping-stone for their later transition to home-delivered meals. Congregate dining programs located in ethnic enclaves can also be more efficient than home-delivered meal programs in preparing and serving ethnic meals to participants; thus they can attract more minority elders. Fifth, recruitment and training of volunteer drivers who are bilingual and bicultural need to be integrated into outreach and service delivery efforts. Volunteer drivers who speak participants' language and share their culture will increase the acceptability of the meal programs. Elderly nutrition programs also must establish close partnerships and referral links with health and social service agencies serving ethnic communities. Sixth, more research on racial/ethnic minority meal program participants and eligible nonparticipants is needed to build up a knowledge base about their nutritional and health status as well as factors contributing to and barriers to their participation and termination.

## REFERENCES

Administration on Aging (1994). *Food and nutrition for life: Malnutrition and older Americans*. Report by the Assistant Secretary for Aging, Administration on Aging, Department of Health and Human Services. Washington, DC: Author.

Administration on Aging (2000). *1995 state program report for Titles III and VII of the Older Americans Act.* [On-line]. Available: <http://www.aoa.gov/napis/95spr/ OVERview.html>.

Administration on Aging (2001). *Older Americans Act Amendments of 2000.* [On-line]. Available: <http://www.aoa.gov/Oaa/oaaapp.html>.

Andersen, R. M. (1995). Revisiting the behavioral model and access to medical care: Does it matter? *Journal of Health and Social Behavior*, 36, 1-10.

Andersen, R. M. & Newman, J. F. (1973). Societal and individual determinants of medical care utilization in the United States. *Milbank Memorial Fund Quarterly Journal*, 51, 95-124.

Burt, M. R. (1993). *Hunger among the elderly: Local and national comparisons*. Final report of a national study on the extent and nature of food insecurity among American seniors. Washington, DC: Urban Institute.

Campbell, C. C. (1991). Food insecurity: A nutritional outcome or a predictor variable? *Journal of Nutrition*, 121, 408-415.

Choi, N. G. (1999). Determinants of frail elders' lengths of stay in Meals on Wheels. *The Gerontologist. 39,* 397-404.

Horwath, C. C. (1991). Nutrition goals for older adults: A review. *The Gerontologist*, 31, 811-821.

Lee, J. S. & Frongillo, E. A. (2001). Factors associated with food insecurity among U.S. elderly persons: Importance of functional impairments. *Journal of Gerontology: Social Sciences, 56B, S94-S99.*

Lynn, L. L., Kang, K. J., & Ludman, E. K. (1999). Korean elderly: Diet, food beliefs, and acculturation. *Journal of Nutrition for the Elderly,* 19(2), 1-13,

Melnik, T. A., Blizniak, P., Lannon, P. B., Porter, M. F., & Wales, K. R. (1999). Home delivered meals program in New York State: Population-based estimates of eligibility, program targeting, and nutritional risk. *Journal of Nutrition for the Elderly*, 18(3), 33-44.

Mui, A. C., Choi, N. G., & Monk, A. (1998). *Long-term care and ethnicity*. Westport, CT: Auburn.

Ponza, M., Ohls, J. C., & Millen, B. E. (1996). *Serving elders at risk: The Older Americans Act nutrition programs national evaluation of the elderly nutrition program, 1993-1995*. Report prepared by Mathematica Policy Research, Inc., for the U.S. Department of Health and Human Services; Office of the Assistant Secretary for Aging. Washington, D.C.

Posner, B. M., Jette, A. M., Smith, K. W., & Miller, D. R. (1993). Nutrition and health risks in the elderly: The nutrition screening initiative. *American Journal of Public Health*, 83, 972-978.

Read, M. & Schlenker, E. D. (1993). Food selection patterns among the aged. In E. D. Schlenker (Ed.), *Nutrition in aging* (2nd ed., pp. 284-312). St. Louis, MO: Mosby.

Roe, D. A. (1992). Geriatric nutrition (3rd ed.). Englewood Cliffs, NJ: Prentice Hall.

U.S. Bureau of the Census (2001). *Census 2000: Basic facts, quick tables.* [On-line] Available: <http://www.census.gov/servelet/BasicFactsServlet>.

Wallace, S. P. (1990). The no-care zone: Availability, accessibility, and acceptability in community-based long-term care. *The Gerontologist*, 30, 254-261.

Yan, A. (1985). Dietary factors of frail elderly Chinese in community-based long-term care. *Journal of Nutrition for the Elderly*, 5(1), 37-46.

# Index

Numbers followed by "n" indicate notes.

BAKER COLLEGE LIBRARY
3 3504 00554 4988



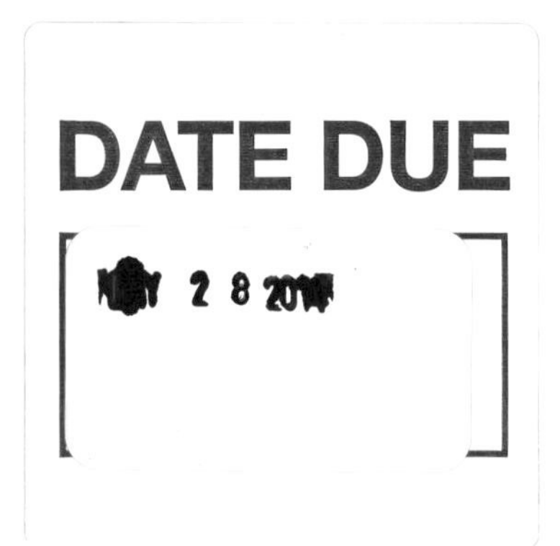
DATE DUE